AFTER BIG GAME IN CENTRAL AFRICA

M. ÉDOUARD FOÀ, F.R.G.S.

AFTER BIG GAME

IN

CENTRAL AFRICA

RECORDS OF A SPORTSMAN FROM
AUGUST 1894 TO NOVEMBER 1897, WHEN
CROSSING THE DARK CONTINENT FROM THE
MOUTH OF THE ZAMBESI TO THE FRENCH CONGO

BY

ÉDOUARD FOÀ, F.R.G.S.

GRANDE MÉDAILLE D'OR OF THE PARIS GEOGRAPHICAL SOCIETY

AUTHOR OF 'MES GRANDES CHASSES DANS L'AFRIQUE CENTRALE'
'DU CAP AU LAC NYASSA,' 'LE DAHOMEY,' ETC.

TRANSLATED FROM THE FRENCH, WITH AN INTRODUCTION
BY
FREDERIC LEES

With 71 Illustrations and a Sketch Map showing Route

ST. MARTIN'S PRESS
NEW YORK

To the Reader:

The editors and publishers of the Peter Capstick Adventure Library faced significant responsibilities in the faithful reprinting of Africa's great hunting books of long ago. Essentially, they saw the need for each text to reflect to the letter the original work, nothing have been added or expunged, if it was to give the reader an authentic view of another age and another world.

In deciding that historical veracity and honesty were the first considerations, they realized that it meant retaining many distasteful racial and ethnic terms to be found in these old classics. The firm of St. Martin's Press, Inc., therefore wishes to make it very clear that it disassociates itself and its employees from the abhorrent racial-ethnic attitudes of the past which may be found in these books.

History is the often unpleasant record of the way things actually were, not the way they should have been. Despite the fact that we have no sympathy with the prejudices of decades past, we feel it better—and indeed, our collective responsibility—not to change the unfortunate facts that were.

—Peter Hathaway Capstick

Library of Congress Cataloging-in-Publication Data

Foà, Édouard.
      After big game in central Africa / Édouard Foà.
            p.   cm.
      Translated from the French by Frederick Lees.
      Originally published in 1899.
      ISBN 0-312-03274-9
      1. Big game hunting—Africa, Central.   I. Title.
SK251.F634   1989
799.2'6'0967—dc20   89-34977
                                                                CIP

10 9 8 7 6 5 4 3

EDITOR'S NOTE TO
THE REPRINT EDITION

To most readers who share my fascination for and admiration of the great, early hunters of colonial Africa, Édouard Foà and his fine book, *After Big Game in Central Africa* have been a bit of a "sleeper". After all, unless you are a hardened collector to whom price is little object, the name of this adventurous and astonishing Frenchman has only come to light in a few forms of "facsimile" reprints, far beyond the price of the books in this Library. Foà shows that it was not just the Britons who were out in the *nyika* and who left entertaining, informative and downright intriguing tales for the generations who followed. Foà was there too.

That only this book—Foà's fourth—has been translated into English is a fair reason why he is rather peripheral in English hunting literature when one thinks of Stigand, Lyell, Letcher, Roosevelt, and the others who make up this collection of reprints. Were he not good, his book would not be featured here.... And he's good!

It is a matter of opinion, of course, but there is hardly anyone else in Nineteenth Century African exploration and hunting who packed as much adventure into such a short lifetime as did Foà, except, perhaps, for Cornwallis Harris in the 1830s. But even he spent nowhere near the seventeen years Édouard Foà did in Africa, and in territory almost equally wild.

EDITOR'S NOTE

As European hunters and explorers of Africa go, Foà can be considered nothing less than a prodigy. In fact, I can't think of a single person who covered more territory— with the possible exception of "Cape to Cairo" Grogan, who walked the length of Africa to win the hand of a lady. In a period of less than four years, Foà covered 7200 miles— from the delta of the Zambezi on the east coast of Portuguese East Africa to the mouth of the Congo on the west coast. The French Ministry of Public Instruction had entrusted him with major African explorations from the Cape northwards and, as indicated in this book, from east to west. And Foà covered most of the terrain on foot!

In his way were substantial considerations such as cannibals, a dozen terrible diseases, the threat of starvation, man-eating lions and leopards and every other species of dangerous game. With some 380 men to feed on his expedition and with only twenty-five of them armed, we can hardly imagine what he faced, knowing that he had none of the means of instant communication and help we take for granted today.

These daily risks notwithstanding, Foà accomplished a great deal in the way of scientific observations in the field on such issues as astronomy, climatology, natural history, ethnography, linguistics, anthropology and cartography, in addition to bringing back to Paris some 500 specimens, ranging from portions of elephants and other big game to birds, fish, insects, and shells. These remarkable achievements made Foà as well known in his French world as was Stanley in the English-speaking world. In fact, apart from being awarded the gold medal of the Paris Geographic Society—its highest honor—he was also made a Fellow of the British Royal Geographic Society, despite what may have been a touch of envy from other, non-French members. Other learned French societies honored

EDITOR'S NOTE

him and he received a decoration from the King of the Belgians for his Congo achievements. The real plum, however, was the award from the Académie française, founded in 1635 by Cardinal Richelieu and destined to become the watchdog of all aspects of French culture. This award was made for one of Foà books, published in 1897, and describing his African explorations from the Cape to Lake Nyassa.

Foà wrote six books in all, apart from his many learned scientific reports and lectures. His first book, *Le Dahomey* (called Benin since 1976) appeared in 1895 and concerns his extensive explorations there from 1886 to 1889 where he shot a huge number of crocodiles and revelled in wingshooting for teal. Foà was an avid hunter in Africa from his very first experiences in North Africa from 1880 onwards.

Foà's next book, referred to in footnotes in this book, also appeared in 1895 and translates loosely as *Big Game Hunting in Central Africa*. Two years later, he published a work called *Across Central Africa: From the Cape to Lake Nyassa* in which he tells of his experiences between the years 1891 and 1894. The book you are holding is a translation of his *Chasses Aux Grands Fauves* which appeared in 1899 and which became his best-known work, largely because of Frederick Lees' translation, the subsequent review in *The New York Times* and the reprinting of the translated version twice in the year of publication of the original French version. Foà had long since attracted a great deal of attention from the scientific world of his day and the appearance of a non-academic book of broad appeal enhanced his reputation.

In 1900, Foà's fifth book appeared, called *Across Africa: From the Zambezi to the Congo*, a book concentrating on his scientific observations and explorations. In 1908,

EDITOR'S NOTE

a posthumous, erudite tome of his was published and was called *Scientific Data From the African Journeys of Édouard Foà*, with a preface by E. Perrier. Foà had been dead seven years.

Obviously a French citizen and native speaker, Foà appears to be from northern Italian stock as his surname is found in the area of Venice. He was born in Marseilles in 1862 and travelled in Africa from the tender age of eighteen—a year younger than was Selous when he first came to Africa—until 1897, actually circumnavigating the continent in the process. The original French version of this book has a much more detailed map of Foà's travels in Africa, the translated edition merely having a sketch map of his epic journey from the mouth of the Zambesi to the Congo estuary. The more detailed map shows Foà's routes through North Africa, where he hunted, to West Africa and the Cape where he arrived in 1891, subsequently travelling north to areas not far from where I have lived and hunted and where he had his first experience of hunting on horseback with the Boers in the north-western Transvaal and the Crocodile River, before heading for the mighty Zambezi River and the rich hunting fields of central Africa.

I have been unable to root out Foà's education but, considering his age and accomplishments, my earlier description of him as a prodigy could not be much amiss. He did not become an African explorer and big game hunter/wildlife collector by accident. The fact that the French Government appointed him, in obvious cooperation with the Paris Museum, to make his journeys, and the appearance of all his books and the subsequent awards all point to an educated man of character and endurance.

A keen observer, Foà sketched, painted and photographed and had a natural aptitude for languages. These

EDITOR'S NOTE

qualities, together with his tremendous stamina, made him an ideal choice for African exploration. For example, he became proficient in the then almost unheard-of language of Chinhunguè, basic to north-western Mozambique and the lower reaches of Lake Nyassa. Hugely respected for his hunting skills, Foà was famous among the Nhunguè tribesmen as *mzoungoniakoumbarumè*, meaning "skilled white hunter".

How good was Foà? In my opinion, he was the equal of his British counterparts and, in fact, was superior to a number of them. His hunting experiences were as lively and, what is more important, he tells them well. He was very familiar with the British hunters of those times, his personal hero being F. C. Selous to whom he dedicated his second book, *Mes Grands Chasses Dans L'Afrique Centrale*. This was a huge honor between professionals. Foà also read and admired the works of Cumming, Drummond, and Baker, to mention a few of the earlier African adventurers.

Foà's first chapter on rifles and his experiences after having used many different types is downright fascinating. Remember, he had been hunting in Africa for many years before he drew his conclusions, as told here. He was severely against the use of telescopic sights on his sheet-steel reinforced rifles, but I suspect this was because they could not stand up to the punishment they received, mounted on heavy-bore arms. He also would never trust the idea of reloading cartridges in the field or at all for use against game. Too unreliable. His in-depth observations as to the concept of explosive bullets is a real taste of the times. He didn't like them but Sir Samuel Baker, his contemporary and revered British explorer and hunter, kept an ace up his bushjacket called "Baby". Using a bursting charge of fine gunpowder confined in a seltzer

EDITOR'S NOTE

bottle cartridge surrounded by swaged lead, it was a half-pound (2-bore) shoulder cannon that would blow elephants to perdition and part of the way back. *Nothing* ever walked away from either end of "Baby", the recoil was initially so stunning.

There being so many addicts of black powder arms today, it is most interesting to note that Foà didn't go along with the idea of hardening bullet metal with mercury or tin. I can't decide why he preferred pure lead bullets, although from breech-loaders, but he missed a lot of penetration he could have certainly used on big game with harder bullets.

But then, Foà was in an age of firearms transition. That he purely distrusted the hammerless double barrels which have been the apogee of the gunmaker's art since his day may show that the boxlock, carried over a three-year period in the bush, was not sufficiently reliable and that the guns with detachable sidelocks seemed to advertise that things could and well might go wrong. Foà did a lot of experimentation with lighter calibers in his later days but he preferred his big guns, usually .577s, 8- and 12-bores, mostly produced by the French firm of Galand.

Obviously, there is no Translator's Introduction in the original book in French, but it is worth noting that Foà's own Preface is not closely translated in this English version. The original book also has a different frontispiece. In fact, it is the picture with a dead elephant appearing opposite page twenty two of your copy.

By all means, don't skim over Foà's appendices as there is a great deal of delicious material in them, especially concerning anecdotes on guns and hunting. There are a couple of translated terms and opinions throughout the text on which I should like to comment. In his observations on elephants, Foà indicates that ivory from an elephant will not grow back if damaged. I think that what he meant and what the translator, Frederick Lees, did not follow, was that Foà was referring to the *nerve* of the tusk being destroyed. He would have to have noticed regrowth of earlier broken tusks of at least some of the elephants he killed. Today, we know that ivory is worn down and regrown constantly during an elephant's lifetime. It has even recently been suggested that elephants could be kept—as was also suggested in the matter of rhinos and their horns—for the commercial growth of their ivory, which could be removed in sections and left to grow back. Well, I wouldn't want to feed one for the time required for a crop!

Another of the gems of this book is Foà's table of the sizes, tusk weights, sex and such of the elephants he killed. That he shot only *three* of twenty one elephant that did *not* have native slugs in them must give some idea of the pressure elephants were under, even then. He even comments that, in his day, there were hardly any elephants in British East Africa! Well, I don't know how hard he looked but that's a bit difficult to understand when those were the very years during which ivory hunters such as the legendary Neumann were making a great killing of large tusks.

Of course, the Frenchman had many close brushes with elephants that nearly resulted in his becoming—I can't resist it—*pâté de Foà gras*. Should you want a real pang of nostalgia, read the schedules of game laws, licenses, and prices for the different countries in 1899!

A couple of other confusions I may be able to unravel for you would be some archaic names for beasties that don't match up with today's terminology. The first would be concerning the picture you see on page fourteen of

EDITOR'S NOTE

"bluebucks". These are actually Blue duikers (*Cephalophus monticola*) and are not be confused with the extinct Bluebuck of the South African Cape (*Hippotragus leucophaeus*) which filed a Chapter 11 back around the year 1800.

The "nswala" facing page thirty two is the Southern impalla, the name nswala being the term used in several allied native languages in the areas in which Foà hunted, especially near the south-eastern lake regions such as Lake Nyassa, better known today as Lake Malawi.

There are no "wolves" in sub-Saharan Africa but the Wild Dog or Cape Hunting Dog (*Lycaon pictus*) was universally called by this term before the Twentieth Century. The term "wolf" is also used in some old hunting books to refer to hyenas. And while linguists will nitpick as to the correctness of the brief multilingual vocabulary compiled by Foà for this book, let us not forget that the Dutch-based language spoken in South Africa at the time was not even recognized as an official language, separate from Dutch, and it had no standardized spelling rules. The same goes for the other languages, except for Arabic, which had only been committed to writing by missionaries. Foà picked up the essential words as he travelled and wrote them down as he believed they sounded. He did pioneering work concerning many indigenous languages.

On the last page of Lees' Introduction, he presumes overmuch that the reader has at least some command of French when he quotes the well-known French lion hunter, Jules Gerard. The comments of Gerard are a bit more revealing than an observation that lion hunting is a fever he cannot shake.

Freely translated, the passage reads: "It's impossible…it's like an attack of fever; then I just have to go back and hunt. If this fever hits me again, I'll just have to go

EDITOR'S NOTE

back to it. He who drinks, will drink again." Curious that this would appear in the last of Foà's books he would live to see. Édouard Foà had most certainly drunk, and his footprints were ineradicably deep in the mud of the African riverbanks. But his fever would cool and he would drink no more. In 1901, in the bright flame of his fame, he died, probably of an overdose of Africa and her diseases that travel so well. Far from his *real* home, he breathed his last in the charming town of Villers-sur-Mer on the Normandy coast, just west of Le Havre and fashionable Deauville.

He was 39 years old.

—PETER HATHAWAY CAPSTICK

PREFACE

DURING the accomplishment of the mission with which I was charged by the Minister of Public Instruction, I travelled in Central Africa continuously in wild countries, far from civilised regions, and often, even, from districts inhabited by natives. I was thus able to devote myself wholly to my ruling passion— the pursuit of big game;—and I had the good fortune to be able to collect for the Paris Museum specimens of large fauna, having on this occasion, as on previous occasions, shot many animals. Naturally, my occupation was not exempt from danger. So I thought that readers who gave a good reception to a work of mine published four years ago [1] would like to return with me on a journey through the African bush. On my latest journey I took care to photograph the animals I killed, as well as the wild haunts in which they lived, in order that illustrations

[1] *Mes Grandes Chasses dans l'Afrique Centrale.* Paris: Firmin Didot et C[ie]. In 8vo. 1895.

should assist the text even better than in my previous book, of which this may be considered a continuation.

The detailed narrative of my journey through Central Africa, from the Zambesi to the French Congo, with its incidents, its vicissitudes, its discoveries, and its results, will be found in another work. Here I propose only to relate matters of sport as they occur to me, without obliging myself to follow their chronological order. I shall guard myself against the desire to make the reader be present at the death of my 500 victims, which would be very monotonous to him; for, after all, though circumstances may vary, the result of a hunt after wild animals is always the same. There will be found in this volume, therefore, only the principal episodes of my most recent years in hunting, with the addition of some notes on the habits of African fauna.

In excuse for the excessive use of the personal pronoun, the reader will do well to recollect that I relate here only what I have done myself or seen with my own eyes. Faithfully as I have endeavoured to depict nature, and the circumstances of my encounters with the wild inmates of the woods, I have fallen, in spite of myself, far below reality. There will always be lacking in my narratives that which sight alone could add to them — the imposing and fierce appearance of magnificent animals defending their lives with that savage instinct, that tenacity, with which nature has endowed them; the faces of hunters, black or white, with the gamut of innumerable human feelings which are alternately seen upon them, feelings ranging from fear to triumph after passing through anxiety, hesitation, calm, and anger. Finally, nothing can describe that dazzling African sun, that clear air, that atmosphere peculiar to the country, those delightful or imposing landscapes, that clear sky, or, on the contrary, the menacing and terrifying appearance of the elements at the time of storm in the equatorial region. There will ever be between these encounters and the account I have given of them the difference which there is between the word and the deed, the description and the thing described. The reader must use his imagination to replace in the proper environment the vicissitudes which I have described with all sincerity, but, doubtless, in a very imperfect manner.

More used to handling a rifle than a pen, I shall be pardoned my faults of style.

In order not to repeat what I have said on the subject of wild animals and their habits, I refer the reader to my previous work, already mentioned. May he live over again with me the happiest days of my life as a hunter, and experience a little the feelings through which I myself have passed !

PARIS, *February* 1899.

CONTENTS

CHAPTER I

ARMS AND OUTFIT

Large-bore arms : Express and Metford—Their ammunition—Various projectiles, their respective values and uses—Explosive bullet useless—The
expansive bullet—Varieties of sights and locks—Rockets—Traps—
Luminous sights, Bengal lights, various accessories — Telescope and
night field - glass—Water - bottles — Dress and hunting outfit — Photographic apparatus—The departure

CHAPTER II

ARRIVAL IN AFRICA·—HUNTING PREPARATIONS——MY ASSISTANTS—
MY METHODS

At Chiromo—Winter season—Arrival of my men—Their portraits, their
aptitudes, and their devotion—Work in the woods—Duties of each
person—Systematic methods of hunting—Studies preliminary to night-
watches

CHAPTER III

TRIALS WITH THE SMALL-BORE RIFLE——CHANGE OF DISTRICT——
COMMENCEMENT OF SPORT

Shooting in the neighbourhood of Chiromo — Eland, hippopotamus, and
crocodile—Encampment on the Upper Kapoche—Wild nature—The fula
—Buffalo-hunting—The man-eater—His death

CHAPTER IV

CHAPTER V

CHAPTER VI

CHAPTER VII

CHAPTER VIII

CHAPTER IX

CHAPTER X

CHAPTER XI

GIRAFFE-HUNTING—HIPPOPOTAMI ON LAND AND IN THE
WATER—ELEPHANTS

CHAPTER XII

SOME ANIMALS OF THE CONGO

ILLUSTRATIONS

PRINTED SEPARATELY FROM THE TEXT

PRINTED IN THE TEXT

Illustrations

INTRODUCTION

JUDGING from experience, I think that there is but little doubt as to the manner in which the majority of people in Great Britain look upon foreign sportsmen and their achievements. It would seem to be only natural that it should be with a certain misgiving. Englishmen have taken such a high position in the domain of sport, and are so much identified with everything sportsmanlike in conduct, that we can well excuse those who, hearing that a foreign sportsman has returned from a successful expedition, doubt his ability to excel or even to equal our countrymen, and promptly ask for an explanation of the methods by which he attained so remarkable a result. This question of methods is, indeed, of paramount importance in all cases. It would, therefore, have been with some diffidence that I should have introduced these records of three years' sport in Central Africa to English readers had I not been personally acquainted with their author and his methods, which are so completely above suspicion that I can recommend his pages with as much confidence as though they were written by one of our own countrymen, whose authority to write on so important and wide a subject as that of big-game shooting we should not dare to question.

After Big Game in Central Africa is a book which appeals to a much wider audience than that of sportsmen alone. Though it will be found to contain a great deal of matter of incalculable value to those who go to Africa in search of wild animals (practical information about rifles, methods of beating districts for game, and seasons,—in short, everything which the hunter will do well to know), the general reader will find quite as much to interest him in the many adventures which this French sportsman had with animals, in his glowing descriptions of the ever-changing African scenery, in his account of three years' pleasures and discouragements while crossing Central Africa. A technical work for the sportsman and a faithful account of incidents, grave and gay, in the everyday life of a professional hunter—such was the object which the author sought to attain in writing his book.

For the better understanding of M. Edouard Foà's pages, it will be as well to give here a few details of that arduous journey which he made in 1894-97 across the Dark Continent, during which he collected materials for this narrative—a journey, by the way, for which he was well equipped in every respect, for there is no part of Africa over which he has not travelled, rifle in hand, during the past fourteen years. In 1880 he travelled through Tunis, Algeria, and Morocco; from 1886 to 1890 he wandered from the Ivory Coast to the Niger, thence to the French Congo, making a stay in Dahomey; and in 1891, entrusted with his first mission by the Minister of Public Instruction, he left the Cape for the Zambesi, and, after crossing the Orange Free State, the Transvaal and the Gaça countries, passed through unknown or little-known regions, which he described from a sportsman's point of view in a work—no less interesting than this—entitled *Mes Grandes Chasses dans l'Afrique Centrale.* These were difficult journeys; but not so difficult or important as his recent travel. Though crossing the African Continent may not nowadays be considered an extraordinary undertaking, in comparison with certain more difficult feats of exploration which have been accomplished in recent years, it is one of which any traveller may be proud. What made the journey so noteworthy was that M. Foà was able, not only to shoot an enormous quantity of big game (to carry out, in fact, his main object), but also to study in a most thorough manner the natural history of the countries through which he passed from various points of view, and to make important geographical discoveries. Moreover, the journey was remarkable from this point of view alone: with the exception of the descent of the Congo, it was accomplished entirely on foot:

about 4000 miles were traversed in that way. In many respects, M. Foà's journey well merits comparison with that which Dr. Sven Hedin made about the same time across Asia.

The Foà expedition consisted of 380 men, twenty-five of whom were well armed. Leaving the River Chinde at the mouth of the Zambesi, in August 1894, in company with two old African travellers, M. E. de Borély and M. Camille Bertrand,—the first of whom went as far as Lake Nyassa, the second as far as Lake Tanganyika—it followed the course of the Zambesi for several months. A stay of more than one year was made in the partly unexplored country north and north-east of the Zambesi in search of big game. Mountainous in parts and flat in others, densely covered with vegetation here, waste and marshy there, these regions were crossed and recrossed many times by the hunter. Pushing still farther north, he explored, when passing through the Makanga, Maravia, and Angoni countries in the direction of Lake Bangweolo, various tributaries of the Zambesi, principally the Aroangwa. This great stream had already been visited several times before ; but most of its length and its source were indicated on maps as unexplored. M. Foà crossed it several times in various districts, and visited its source. Later he explored the shores of Lake Nyassa in a gunboat, *The Pioneer*, which was lent to him by Mr. M. Alfred Sharpe, the Governor of British

Central Africa. During the trip, which lasted for nine days, the explorer made astronomical observations which will have the effect of modifying the map of the great lake.

The explorer left Lake Nyassa to ascend the high plateau which separates the lake from Lake Tanganyika at Karonga. The exploration of unknown regions and the deciding of some important geographical questions took up several months at this period of the journey. The explorer entered upon an entirely new route in the Ubemba country, and mapped hydrographically the Chozi and Chambezi. It has been thought that some of the sources of the Congo were in the neighbourhood of these two rivers; but I believe that M. Foà is the first to show that this really is so by mapping the network of small streams which flow into the Chozi and Chambezi in the Ubemba country.

Tanganyika was then explored. in a similar manner. Embarking at Urungu, M. Foà devoted three weeks or more to visiting its shores in an arab dhow. He drew up a detailed map of the lake in five parts, and studied the question of its origin. The shells which he brought back with him for the Paris Museum support the theory of the naturalist Günther that it is a former arm of the sea isolated by the rising of surrounding land—*i.e.*, it is a "relicten-see." On Tanganyika and in the immediate neighbourhood he saw the good work which is being done by the Pères Blancs, the mission of Cardinal Lavigerie, in putting down the slave trade; and, on touching at Ujiji, noted what slow progress was being made by the Germans in their large East African colony. About this time occurred one of the most interesting episodes of the expedition.

M. Foà tried to reach the Kassai, the great tributary of the Congo, by crossing almost unknown countries. He entered the Urua country, and in crossing the Mitumba mountains encountered great difficulties. Many times the natives threw down their loads and refused to go a step farther. At last, however, the journey of seventy-five miles over most difficult ground was accomplished and the River Luizi was reached — only to find that progress was barred by the whole district being up in arms. As there was nothing for it but to turn back, the expedition did so, and descended towards the valley of the Lukuga river.

M. Foà then set out to reach the Congo by crossing the Manyema under the guidance of a troop of Wanyamwezi, a warlike people who live on the opposite side of Lake Tanganyika. Full of danger and most laborious this journey was, as much on account of the mountains — similar to those of the Urua country—which had to be crossed, as owing to the fact that the country was in a state of rebellion. The course of the Luama (or Lugumba) was explored, and that well repaid any difficulties which the

expedition had to overcome. The tribes of the
Manyema are cannibals. They are constantly at
war with one another ; and, though they were not
hostile to the travellers, a sharp look-out had to
be kept, lest there should be treachery. In fact,
during part of the journey the expedition had
to be protected by a convoy of troops placed at its
disposal by Baron Dhanis of the Congo Free State.
The country through which it passed had rebelled
against the Belgian Government, and many were
the hair-breadth escapes which it had,—one night in
particular, when it passed within alarming proximity
to the rebel camp, fortunately without being seen.
The crossing of the equatorial forest, of which Sir
H. M. Stanley has given such a vivid account, took
up twenty of the forty-one days which were occupied
in travelling from Tanganyika to the Congo. Like
Stanley and others, M. Foà met with the pygmies.
He took measurements of many of them, studied
their industries and customs, and will probably throw
very interesting light on these people when he
publishes the detailed account of his journey.

The rest of the crossing of Central Africa was a
question of time only. The explorer and his men
descended the Congo in a pirogue to New Antwerp,
and took the steamer to Stanley Pool. At first
M. Foà thought of reaching the coast by way of the
French Congo, *viâ* Franceville and the Ogowe river ;
but, the rainy season setting in, he returned to the

left bank of the Congo, and, when near Tampa, took train on the recently constructed Congo Free State railway, which brought him to Matadi.

The main scientific results of this three - years journey, in addition to those which I have already mentioned incidentally, may be roughly enumerated as follows: 800 astronomical observations with sextant, theodolite, chronometer; three years' observation of magnetic declinations, meteorology, and temperature; six thousand miles of mapping; the collecting of many natural-history specimens, including large and small mammals, birds, fishes, insects, shells, etc., for French museums; the taking of ethnological notes on 150 different tribes; and the preparing of forty vocabularies.

Such is a brief account of M. Foà's journey, the scientific results of which were considered of such importance that the Paris Geographical Society presented him with its *grande médaille d'or*. The Brussels and the Antwerp Geographical Societies awarded him medals, and the King of the Belgians gave him a decoration.

My *résumé*, though inadequate (owing to limitation of space), will suffice to give the reader an idea of the difficulties which had to be overcome almost at every turn, and will make him wonder that any time at all was found for sport. M. Foà killed nearly five hundred head of big game. As I have already said, sport was his main object in crossing Africa; and

never once did he lose sight of it during the whole
of the journey.

M. Germain Bapst, in his *Mémoires d'un Siècle*,
tells us that Marshal Canrobert once met Jules
Gerard, shortly after that French hunter had been
made an officer, and asked him if he intended to
give up killing lions. "C'est impossible," said the
celebrated lion-killer : "ça me prend comme la fièvre;
alors il faut absolument que j'aille à l'affût. Si cette
fièvre me reprend, je serai obligé de recommencer.
Qui a bu boira." M. Foà is no exception
to this rule. Once a man is seized with a passion
for hunting, it never leaves him. As will many
times be seen in reading *After Big Game in Central
Africa*, no one could well show more devotion to
his pursuit than M. Foà has shown. Ably assisted
by those native hunters of whom he speaks so highly,
—Tambarika, the skilled tracker of game, Tchigallo,
the cool-headed, Rodzani, the tenacious, and Msiambiri,
the ever-cheerful—he went about his work with a
systematic thoroughness which could only result in
success.

FREDERIC LEES.

Paris, 1899.

After Big Game in Central Africa

CHAPTER I

ARMS AND OUTFIT

Large-bore arms : Express and Metford—Their ammunition—Various projectiles, their respective values and uses—Explosive bullet useless—The
expansive bullet—Varieties of sights and locks—Rockets—Traps—
Luminous sights, Bengal lights, various accessories—Telescope and
night field-glass—Water-bottles—Dress and hunting outfit—Photographic apparatus—The departure.

BEFORE entering upon my subject I must tell the
reader of the arms and equipment which I took for
this expedition, with a view to shooting animals which
inhabit Central Africa, including the elephant, rhinoceros, hippopotamus, lion, leopard, panther, giraffe,
buffalo, antelopes of several species, wart-hog, and wild
boar, hyena, and certain smaller carnivorous animals.

I am still of the same opinion on the subject of
large-bore weapons,[1] and if you possess neither 12-
bore nor 8-bore rifles I do not advise you to buy them
unless you are certain of visiting a country where
elephants abound, and those countries are becoming,
alas, more and more difficult to find. Amid certain
circumstances, however, these weapons may be useful. As I was to travel through parts of Central

[1] See *Mes Grandes Chasses*, pp. 331, 332.

1

Africa where I counted upon finding elephants, I took one of two 8 - bore double - barrelled rifled guns which I possessed and 200 cartridges. My principal weapons were two express double-barrelled rifles of 577-bore. One of them had been made specially for me by M. Galand, the well - known gunsmith, who had already armed me several times, and according to my own indications. I had asked for an *exceedingly small* reduction of the bore at the top part of the barrel; a small increase in the thickness of the barrels, without respect to weight; shortening of the barrels; a large pea-sight; a treble lock, top-lever, and a solidity equal to the severest test. This rifle, which I call my express No. 1, is so well made that after three and a half years' shooting, tribulations, jolts, and handling, after having fired 600 or 700 cartridges it only required cleaning upon my return. As to its penetration, that will be seen in reading the chapters which follow, and more especially the tenth chapter. Express No. 1 weighs 11 lbs. 1 oz. No. 2 is the weapon already known to my readers. It also was made in the workshops of M. Galand, and with it I killed more than 300 animals during my hunting expeditions from 1891 to 1893. The barrels are a little longer, the two sights are diamond ones, and its weight is a little less, 10½ lbs. only. I took with me on trial, and not without a little mistrust, a double-barrelled English rifle of 303-bore—that is, a little smaller than the Lebel. This weapon, which had the appearance of an express rifle very small for its bore, was one of the first examples of the Metford Express which had appeared on the London market; it was an adaptation of the Lee-Metford army weapon which fires six shots and has a single barrel. To adapt it to sporting purposes, it was supplied with two barrels; but the repeating mechanism was done away with, as in ordinary rifles. The first two weapons of the kind had burst in the face of their owner. The third, that which I took with me, had been strengthened so as to resist the action of English army smokeless

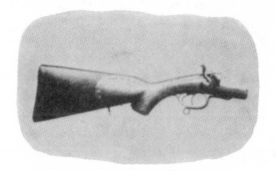

STEEL-PLATED STOCK.

powders, cordite, and rifleite, which put the barrels to severe tests, so that it weighed, notwithstanding its small bore, almost as much as an express— 10 lbs. 1 oz. This weapon, which I shall call my 303, has proved that it was admirably built, since I have fired with it nearly 1000 cartridges without the slightest accident. A telescope adjusted on the barrel is intended to magnify and consequently to bring the quarry nearer; but I was never able to use this instrument, and I recommend you, if one is suggested to you, not to make this useless expenditure.

All these rifles had the stock plated—that is, protected by a steel plate, which is a precaution against the ease with which it can be broken should it receive a violent blow or should an animal walk over it.

In the matter of unrifled weapons I took only a 12-bore Winchester fowling-piece, capable of firing six shots—a very good gun for rough service, having the advantage of possessing interchangeable pieces, and quite sufficient for killing a few guinea-fowls or firing buck-shot. To defend oneself against natives, especially at night, buck-shot are infinitely better than bullets. I had also a small 32-bore double-barrelled fowling-piece for small birds, intended for collections, and which it was necessary not to spoil; finally, two large Galand revolvers and a small *tue-tue*, in case of emergencies, for it must not be forgotten that I proposed upon setting out to cross regions where Stanley, Peters, Wissman, and many others had experienced extreme difficulties with the natives.

Here, then, is a list of the arms which I took with me :—

1. 1 double-barrelled 8-bore rifle.
2. 2 express 577-bore rifles.
3. 1 express 303-bore rifle (Metford).
4. 1 smooth 12-bore Winchester six-shot repeater.

As to the ammunition taken I give here the detailed enumeration :—

8-bore—100 small cartridges, with round $2\frac{1}{2}$ ounce bullets (5 drachms of powder), for buffaloes or to dispatch large pachydermata.

8-bore—100 large cartridges with conical 4 ounce 1 drachm
bullets (8 drachms of powder), for elephants and rhinoceroses.

Express 577—1600 express bullet cartridges (6 drachms of
powder), with copper tube, weighing 1 ounce 2 drachms.
    800 cartridges with solid bullets, ordinary lead, of
1 ounce 5 drachms.

Express 303 (Metford)—500 cartridges, with solid bullets of
great penetration for defence or shots at the head (hippopotami, elephants, rhinoceroses), weighing 7 drachms.

$$2400 \begin{cases} \text{Cartridges with Jeffery bullet (8 drachms).} \\ \quad,, \quad \text{with hollow bullet (7 drachms).} \\ \quad,, \quad \text{with soft-nosed solid bullet (7 drachms).} \\ \quad,, \quad \text{with soft-nosed express bullet (7 drachms).} \end{cases}$$

Let me say a word or two to explain these various
kinds of bullets. The solid bullets are like those
of the Lebel rifle, completely
covered with nickel. The Jeff-
ery bullets are truncated at the
point, and present longitudinal

SOLID 303.

holes which enable them to spread out; they
are what have recently been called Dum-Dum.
The hollow differ from them in not being split;
on the other hand there is a hollow space from the
point to the middle, and this is filled with wax. The
soft-nosed solid have a nickel envelope only three-
quarters of the way up, fixed in such a manner that at
the point the lead is bare. The soft-nosed express are
made in the same way, but their apex is hollow and
filled either with wax or with a copper tube. Of the
last four kinds, taken with me so that I might
try them, and submitted to many and conclusive
tests, I have retained only two—the hollow and the
soft-nosed express, both of which have cavities filled

with wax.   For small animals, and antelopes ranging to the eland *exclusively*, they are excellent.   From the eland upwards, the 577 express is necessary.

All my ammunition supplied by Eley and Kynoch was packed in soldered zinc boxes, ten cartridges in a box.

I use new cartridges only; I never refill my old cases.   Refilling is exceedingly dirty work; the powder which one may procure fouls the barrels, the bullets are badly moulded, and the percussion - caps often miss fire.   In the case of a partridge it is a matter of no importance; but when your life depends, perhaps, on a cartridge, can one run such risks ? Out of the 5000 cartridges which I took with me, I do not think one missed fire.   I may say, therefore, that they were irreproachable.   As one can obtain them nowadays wholesale at very reasonable prices, and as they keep indefinitely in the boxes of which I have spoken,

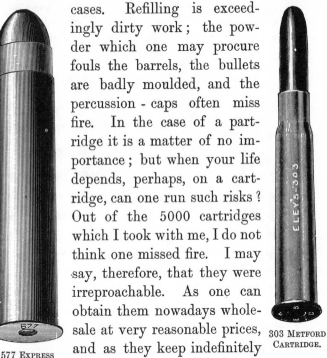

577 Express
Cartridge.

303 Metford
Cartridge.

what advantage is to be gained by refilling empty cases ?   Besides, the question of refilling only applies to the express rifle and to the 8-bore, the 303 having a kind of ammunition which can only be made by means of special machines.

As every one asked me upon my return home if I had used explosive bullets, I will express my opinion about them once and for all. Whether they be "Devismes" or "Pertuiset" or "Jacob Shells," I find them full of inconveniences. Either the explosive bullet is a breakable projectile charged with some explosive substance,—picrate of potash, gun-cotton, fulminating mercury, powder, etc.,—in which case one is obliged at the last moment to place a percussion-cap on a nipple, exactly as in the case of a cap-gun; or it is a bullet charged with a detonator which is protected by a cap when not in actual use. Five times out of ten it does not explode, doubtless because, in your emotion caused by the presence of danger, you have forgotten to take off the protector; or else, if it bursts, it does so on a level with the skin, almost outside in the case of thick-skinned animals, and it no longer has the necessary penetrative force; while in the case of animals with tender skins it does damage which, as one can attain the desired result with ordinary bullets, is useless. And then you expose yourself to the danger of letting these projectiles fall, or of forgetting them in a cartridge case, with the result that you and your men run a risk every moment. In short, the explosive bullet, which I doubt if anybody has ever used with success, may be classed nowadays in museums of balistics, side by side with mortar-pieces and flint-locks. Possessing modern arms and projectiles they are no longer necessary, and are always dangerous.

On the other hand, the expansive bullet is much

used and very practical.   Its destructive power is due
not to the action of an explosive charge, but to its
method of construction.   About three-quarters of the
way up the bullet is hollow, and in this hollow is
placed a copper tube which is simply intended to plug
it, and thus to prevent the resistance which the air
would offer it during its flight if the hollow were open ;
it acts the same part as the wax in the 303 bullets.
The impact causes the bullet to expand.   Often it
breaks into pieces; or else takes a mushroom shape, the

577 Express   Hollow 303   8-Bore Solid   577 Express
Bullet.   Bullet.   Bullet.   Solid Bullet.

head, in its tremendous velocity, dragging and catching with its edges the flesh and viscera ; and it often
happens in the case of delicate animals that upon
leaving the body it makes a hole as big as the crown
of a hat.   The express 577 bullet, the hollow or the
soft-nosed express of my 303, which are of that type,
may be used successfully for all animals with a soft
skin or of average corpulency, which, in the African
fauna, are the lion, leopard, cat, wild-boar, and all
antelopes, with the exception of the eland.

The eland, buffalo, rhinoceros, giraffe, and elephant are, on the contrary, more massive animals; and the expansive bullet being insufficient because of the thickness of the flesh and bone, the solid bullet is used. Some sportsmen recommend that a third part of tin or a fifth part of mercury be added to the lead to increase its hardness. What is the good? For my part, I have always left the lead in its natural state; it crushes the better for it, and penetrates admirably the hide of elephants or rhinoceroses, in spite of the statement that it is impossible to cut those animals' skins. The solid bullet of ordinary lead shot from a modern rifle, as, for example, the express, passes right through. The statement that the hide is impenetrable is a legend to be relegated to a museum of curiosities with the explosive bullet, with the belief in the protected and impenetrable scales of the crocodile, with the phosphorescent eye of the lion, an eye which glistens in the obscurity like a bicycle lamp. It is also to the human imagination that we owe the idea that the lion can jump over a wall with a calf in its mouth; it is to the imagination that we owe the theory of certain sportsmen on the method of proceeding to see his sight, and to take aim on a dark night when on horseback with sufficient precision to shoot animals like the rhinoceros right in the eye. The eye of the rhinoceros is, as we know, very small.

As to diamond sights, telescopic sights, or others more or less extraordinary which imaginative gun-smiths invent at every moment, the only object which they reach is, most certainly, the pocket of the sportsman. Nothing equals the small pyramid, surmounted or not by a ball. It is good to have it in platinum, in silver, or in ivory, because it stands out better; the material of which it is made is a mere matter of taste and habit. Diamonds are not worth much; I have tried them, as all other modern inventions in gunnery, and have returned to the silver sight upon which at night can be placed a large pea in white or phosphorescent enamel.

In regard to the lock system for a rifle for ordinary use, nothing is equal to the English T or a treble lock top-lever of the best quality. The hammerless does not seem to me to be sufficiently sure enough yet for countries where there are no gunsmiths.

Pistol grips are indispensable for rifles, first because they adapt themselves better to the hand, and then because they allow of the stock being grasped in a particular way. As was seen above, I plate my stocks with steel. So much for the armament.

My hunting equipment was very simple,—a cartridge belt for each kind of ammunition,[1] one or two cartridge-pouches to carry reserve ammunition and a few small objects, water-bottles of a special pattern, some rockets to smoke out hyenas, traps for large animals, a set of luminous sights, a Trouvé projector, some phosphorus, white Bengal lights, some knives and axes, a folding telescope, and a night field-glass.

---

[1] I repeat that the solid bullet and the expansive bullet are sufficient for all kinds of shooting; with cartridges of both kinds and a good Express a hunter is in a position to kill all the animals of the two hemispheres.

My dress is already known, since it is the same as on previous journeys : during the daytime it consists of a thin cotton shirt without sleeves, generally dark chestnut brown, short breeches of the same colour, a dark helmet, socks, and shoes.[1] My hunting-boots are made of canvas with indiarubber soles, so as to make no noise ; when on tramp I use shoes made of brown, supple leather with thick soles. Round my waist I wear a leather belt, to which the cartridge-case is attached, and carrying a small pocket for my watch and a sheath for my knife. That completes the nomenclature of my outfit. My neck, arms, and legs are bare. During the cool season in the evening, or on the high plateaus, I wear a warm vest, which may be used also on night watches ; but upon those occasions I prefer generally a small cape made of swanskin, and provided with a hood—a piece of clothing which, if thrown over the shoulders, has the advantage of leaving the arms free.

I had always with me in one of the cartridge-cases a note-book and a pencil, a pocket medicine-chest, bandages, and Dr. Calmette's anti-venomous serum for accidents, a tape measure for measuring animals, complete outfit for cleaning guns, a thorn extractor, a spare sight, one or two rockets, a tinder box, tobacco, and a pipe, a small flask containing some cordial or other, melissa water, brandy, etc.,—the whole of which did not exceed the volume of a cigar box.

The other pouch was for reserve ammunition ; it

---

[1] I am unfavourable to the use of wool in any form in tropical climates.

contained a little of each kind in proportion to needs
and unforeseen eventualities.

The water-bottles, each of which held three quarts
and a half, were made of zinc, covered with a thick
felt covering; and to prevent this envelope being torn
by contact with thorns, it also was protected by a
network of ordinary string. These vessels, strongly
suspended at each end of a short stick, were thus
carried on the shoulder, and necessitated a special
man, the water-carrier, who is indispensable in these
regions. This method of attaching the water-bottles
was employed with the object of preventing the heat of
the body from warming the liquid, which would have
been the case had they been carried on a belt passed
over the shoulder. By taking care to wet the felt
covering each time water was met with, the evapora-
tion kept the contents of the bottle in a very satisfactory state of freshness. These seven quarts of
water were often very useful on account of the great
distances which we covered sometimes without coming across a river, and in case of accident (sunstroke
or other causes) we had the wherewithal to meet
first necessities. More than once we were able to cook
a sweet potato or brew tea with the contents of these
precious reservoirs.

I had at the camp also some small wood barrels for
the carrying of water, and some canvas water-bottles
which I make myself; but those could be used only
on the spot, and not when on the march, like the
water-bottles which I have just described. These
latter are my own invention, like many other useful

objects with the idea of which experience inspired me, and for which I have not taken out any patent.[1]

I shall speak of the use of rockets, traps, Bengal lights, phosphorus, etc., at the proper time and place. As to the telescope which I carried, it was a very powerful one, and had at the same time the advantage of closing into a very small space; it rendered me great services in flat districts and elsewhere, and more than once enabled me to discover in the distance a village or animals. The night field-glass must, to be good, be of short focus and wide-angled, the large lens having at least eight times the diameter of the small ones. How useful this instrument has been to me will be seen later.

Such, generally speaking, were the things which formed my hunter's baggage. Naturally I do not here speak of the considerable matériel which accompanied the expedition, necessitating, at the outset of our journey, more than 300 carriers: an inventory of it would occupy more that 200 pages. Suffice to say that it was sufficient to meet all the necessities of life of three Europeans for more than three years. In this chapter there is only question of that which we shall find in daily use in the hunting episodes which I propose narrating.

As will be seen in the course of this work, I made use continually of the photographic camera; but, photography entering rather into the domain of the scientific results of the journey, I refer readers who

[1] For the model of a provision basket, see *Du Cap au lac Nyassa*, p. 364.

wish to profit by the little experience which I possess in that art to my narrative of the expedition properly so called; here I give them only the results in the form of illustrations. The two cameras which I used continuously were an 18 - by - 24 Dalmeyer bellows camera with a Ross lens, and a 9-by-12 hand-camera of the Kodak kind, both using cut celluloid films of the thickness of Bristol board.

This being said, and the reader having inspected with me my arsenal, *en route* for Marseilles, let us take there the *Ava*, the steamboat of the Messageries Maritimes, and let us leave for Central Africa, *via* Chinde, Zambesi.

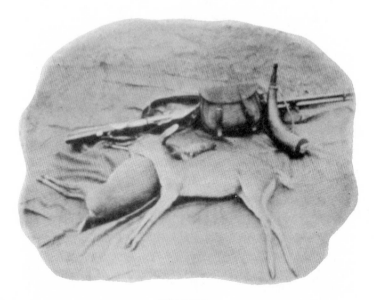

BLUEBUCKS.

WINTER CAMP AT CHIROMO.

CHAPTER II

ARRIVAL IN AFRICA—HUNTING PREPARATIONS—MY ASSISTANTS—MY METHODS

At Chiromo—Winter season—Arrival of my men—Their portraits, their aptitudes, and their devotion—Work in the woods—Duties of each person—Systematic methods of hunting—Studies preliminary to night watches.

THE journey which I was about to attempt commenced in the region where the previous one ended,— namely, at Lake Nyassa. In August 1894 MM. De Borely and Bertrand, two old African explorers, and myself reached the Zambesi and those banks which were already familiar to me. This time we had with us an enormous quantity of matériel, and a large number of servants and boats. Past lessons had borne fruit, and this time experience presided so well on the occasion of our preparations that, extraordinary as it may seem, we had neither forgotten anything which was indispensable, nor taken anything which was superfluous. Nothing forms the mind better than suffering and privation. I have returned to Europe from each journey which I have undertaken with a very accurate list of the things which I had forgotten.

M. C. BERTRAND.   M. E. DE BORELY.

After the 1894-97 expedition the list was a blank. That is saying much for the care with which all purchases and preparations had been made, and with which all precautions had been taken. De Borely and Bertrand, who were not sportsmen, were charged with the administration of the expedition. The former had under his charge the diary and the accounts; the latter looked after the provisions, the contents and the arrangement of the packages, food for the Europeans, and shared with me the care to be devoted to natural history specimens and the preparation of collections. De Borely was separated from us for a long time, because he commanded a depôt camp which served as our headquarters, around which Bertrand and I have ranged for nearly a year.

The season was fairly advanced when we reached Chiromo, on the river Shire, a northern tributary of the Zambesi; it was mid-September, and hardly worth while undertaking anything seriously that year, the good season ending in November to give place to a period of abundant rain, the season when the grass is high and swamps are numerous.

It was necessary, therefore, to prepare to winter, as they say in certain parts of Africa,—that is, to pass under shelter the rainy season, which is really the summer.

Chiromo seemed to us to be a convenient spot on which to pitch our camp. Three months afterwards we had to abandon it, having been first of all visited by locusts which ruin the country, then by a fire which nearly ruined ourselves, and finally by a flood which almost cost us our lives. So the expedition moved towards the west, again visiting the countries of the Magandjas, between the Zambesi and the Shire, Makanga, Undi, and western Maravi, which had been the theatre of our previous exploits. During our stay at Chiromo I set to work immediately to reorganise my staff of hunters. I had sent emissaries into the districts where Msiambiri, Rodzani, Tchigallo, and Tambarika lived, so as to give them notice of my return, and to inform them

that I counted upon them still. I have often spoken
of these fine fellows in *Mes Grandes Chasses,* but I
can never say enough of the services which they have
rendered me. Their lives have been so intimately
connected with my own life, they have shown me so
many marks of attachment, that I cannot forget them
at the opening of this narrative, in which their share
of glory and of danger equals mine, and in which
we shall be together always, working with a common
object. In the course of these seven years of sport
not an animal has been killed without my hunters
having contributed to the result singly or con-
jointly; there is not a joy or a triumph in which
they have not had their part, not a difficulty which
they have not undergone with their master. True,
they did not kill with the rifle; but, after having
taught me how to track game, they assisted me in
my researches. And, in my marked position of inferiority, if one compares the means at my disposal
with those of sportsmen of Central Africa—Gordon-
Cumming, Drummond, Selous, and many others, who
hunt with bushmen, spare horses and dogs, often in
countries where the difficulties are not great,—it is
thanks to the sagacity of my native hunters, thanks
to their astonishing instinct for the life of the
woods — an instinct with which they partly have
endowed me—that, without other assistants than
they, I have killed almost as many animals as
the Nimrods of former times. They have left their
countries, their families, their wives, and their
children, to follow me when I have changed my

district, and two of them accomplished with me the crossing of the African continent. All of them would have accompanied me to the end of the journey had not the considerable expense of repatriating them forced me to keep only two, and to separate myself from the others when they were still able, without excessive danger, to return home.

At the time of my return, the date of which they were ignorant, my former assistants were somewhat scattered. One had gone to Blantyre, in Nyassa-land, in search of work; another lived at Tete, on the Zambesi; a third was acting as a cook on board one of the gun-boats on the low part of the river.

The first who reached Chiromo was Tchigallo, with a deputation of his countrymen, who brought me presents; another day, upon awakening, it was Tambarika; finally came Msiambiri and Rodzani. I cannot express the pleasure which I felt at again seeing these fine fellows. On the other hand, they also had a very satisfied expression, and confessed that since my departure they had "wept for the woods," as they say in their language. Powder being forbidden, they had been unable to shoot, and, in order to obtain a little calico, wherewith to clothe themselves, they had had to take to various occupations pending my return, because every one in the country had always counted, according to them, on the return of Tchandiu. Tchandiu was the name, it appears, which had been given to me in their country after my departure. It means "the purveyor of food."

Tchandiu[1] they said with an air of regret and with a sigh. This sobriquet clung to me, supplanting that of Niakumbarume (the hunter), which I possessed before.

The only one of my men upon whom I had not made a call was Maonda. As he had become very lazy recently, and did not agree with his companions, I had decided to do without his services.

Tambarika had brought with him one of his countrymen, the son of an elephant-hunter; a very young man he was, possessed with an extraordinary passion for hunting, and promising to become a worthy member of my quintet. Later he justified these previsions, and has been an excellent assistant. His name is Kambombe, and he carried out with Msiambiri the duties of hunter and valet, receiving, like him, an additional salary.

Msiambiri's real name is Matingambiri—he was called Msiambiri by abbreviation. Born at Kariza-Mimba, on the Upper Zambesi, the son of a celebrated elephant-hunter, he had passed the whole of his life in the woods. When I knew him first he was at Tete, employed as an elephant-hunter by a Portuguese mulatto named Msungo Appa. I took him into my service at first as a hunter, and then as a servant. Possessing an agreeable physiognomy with saw-like teeth, like those of the Sengas, his compatriots, he was tall and spare, sinewy, never prone to stoutness.

---

[1] *Ndiu* means confusedly meat, fish, vegetables, or any ragoût, which they eat with *ncima* or baked flour, the bread of the blacks of that region.

His sight and sense of smell were extraordinary, but he was only a second-class tracker of animals. Continually gay, ever having a joke on his lips, he amused every one in camp. A man with more good qualities than defects, very reasonable and conscientious in his duties—such was Msiambiri.

Rodzani, who was a native of the banks of the middle Zambesi, had been an elephant-hunter also ; his eye was only second-class, but his hearing was extraordinary. His countenance was open, and upon it I could read his impressions ; his appetite was insatiable ; his body was rather small and thick-set. A good tracker but slow, very tenacious and very patient Rodzani sometimes lacked determination, but was devoted at bottom and rather cheerful in character.

Tambarika was a pure Magandja, son of a powerful chief, and more difficult in temperament. His early years had been fairly happy. Later, his father having been defeated, he resigned himself to look for work. He had passed his youth and almost his life in the woods, consequently possessing a well - established reputation as a remarkable bowman : hence his name, which signifies "he who shoots straight." Later, when he was taught to use firearms, he became a remarkably good shot for a black, and was passionately fond of this form of hunting. He was a very intelligent man, a veritable professor of natural history : there was not a tree, plant, or insect of which he did not know the name. As a tracker of animals he was extraordinary, having an eye of extreme sharpness and an ear of inconceivable delicacy; he was the one among us all who followed a track the quickest. Thin and dry, of middle height, possessed of an immense mouth, rather gloomy of countenance, he was fairly cheerful. Difficult to manage at first, he ended by becoming very obedient.

One who did not turn a hair, as the expression goes, and laughed rarely, was Tchigallo, the calmest of the band. However, he got on well with his companions, and, as a rule, made little noise. He was tall and strong; his face was rather agreeable; as a tracker he was fairly good. He had had a good experience of the woods; but I do not know whether he liked hunting, as he never appeared happier than when near his fire at the camp.

Kambombe had a very agreeable face and marvellous teeth. A youth when I engaged him, he changed during the three years he remained in my service, and when he left me he had become a tall, thick-set fellow. As fond of hunting as Tambarika, which is not saying little, he became a good tracker. As a servant he showed much good disposition in carrying out his duties; but he was taciturn, and rarely laughed.

Such were the men I had with me. All of them possessed to a high degree that instinct of the life of the woods, which is only acquired when one has grown up in their midst, that sharpness of the senses which was extolled formerly among the Red-skins, that gift of observation which nothing escapes—no more the bee which enters a little hole at

Tchigallo   E. Foà   Kambombe   Tambarika   Rodzani
  Msiambiri

M. FOÀ AND HIS NATIVE FOLLOWERS.

the top of a large tree than the hair pulled by a thorn from the mane of a lion, no more the almost imperceptible black point which marks in the midst of the grass the point of the horn of an antelope lying down eighty yards away than a spot of blood on a leaf though no bigger than a pin-head; a bird passing through the air, microscopic traces on the ground — everything was seen, nothing passed unobserved.

I will add that my men acquired the habit of being together and with me, so that there was constant collaboration between us. On my side, I profited by the three years' lessons which I took, and I brought all the attention, care, and intelligence of which I was capable, to bear on them. Without pretending to equal the natives, I was a fairly good tracker, and when in the woods my eyes and ears were open sufficiently to enable me to find out things when quite alone, as happened to me often. Moreover, my staff had much confidence in me. Without being a crack shot, I am accustomed to danger and possess great calmness; being cool, I take aim always with great care.

A week was taken up at Chiromo in shooting at a target, in order to make myself acquainted with my new weapons, and to habituate my men in the handling of the guns which they were to carry. Their duty consisted in loading, taking out the empty cartridge, and passing me the rifle with rapidity. Although they were to be intelligent gun-bearers rather than shooters, I put them through a few field exercises near to the target—from ten to forty yards distant—so as to familiarise them with the weapons, and to avoid certain errors which they had committed formerly, such as firing without bringing the gun to the shoulder, or trying to open a rifle unprovided with self-rebounding locks without first of all putting the hammers at half-cock, etc.—precautions which may seem unimportant, but were to bear fruit in the heat of the fight. All of them, however, were very careful in the handling of weapons, and had a veritable veneration for these engines of destruction.

Each gun had its appointed bearer: Msiambiri carried the Express No. 1, Tambarika the Express No. 2, Kambombe the 303, Rodzani the 12-bore Winchester, and Tchigallo the 8-bore. In addition, each bearer had ammunition proper for his gun, as well as a few small objects such as telescope, pouches, etc. Msiambiri was charged specially with the cleaning of the guns, which were carefully greased every evening without exception, and everywhere we happened to be.

Quite apart from hunting, each of my men had other special duties. Msiambiri and Kambombe acted, as I have said, as my servants; Rodzani was captain of the camp (that is, he was to look after the men, to cut up and to apportion out the meat, etc.); Tambarika managed what I call the research brigade (his mission was to survey the hunting zones, prepare the hiding-places, visit the pools, report traces of animals—in a word, to do in advance everything which was necessary to permit us to work with certainty, or at least with a knowledge of the ground). Tchigallo was a taxidermist, and assisted Bertrand and me in preserving our specimens.

I had not attained so perfect an organisation without difficulty. Time and patience had been necessary to make each of my men understand what I required of him. I had taken two years to do it, and when I returned to Africa they were, with the exception of the preliminary exercises necessary to make them acquainted with the new weapons which I brought, absolutely trained. Thus was I able to apply in my hunting a systematic method, an example of which I will give.

Arriving in an unknown district, and wishing to inform myself accurately about the animals which frequent it, I take one or two days in surveying it. With the aid of my assistants I am not long in surmising where the water is, the number of pools there are, and the kind of animals which drink there. If this preliminary examination is not satisfactory I go elsewhere; if, on the contrary, there are some of the animals for which I am seeking, and which are the elephant, the rhinoceros, and the lion chiefly, I have soon counted them. True, this does not apply to the elephant, which is a travelling animal; but in a week I know, without having seen them, all my lions and rhinoceroses, where they pass, drink, and feed. The only thing remaining to be done is to await them or to meet them : a question of patience, perseverance, and luck. That is the only methodical way of well beating a country without dogs and information. And, that this method of going to work should be thoroughly successful, the task must be taken to heart as in the case of an ardent, patient hunter, to whom time and difficulty are nothing provided he attains his ends; I may say, even, that it is necessary, like myself, to be almost of the profession of hunter, and to neglect nothing which may contribute to success. I have tried native dogs,

CROCODILE SKULL ($2^F 3'$).

but it will be seen in the course of my narrative that I have not succeeded with them. That is owing, I believe, to the fact that the breed is not the same as that of South Africa. Besides, had I found good sporting dogs, the tsetse-fly, I think, would have been fatal to them.

Having gained the experience that the night-watch, dangerous though it is, was the only way to possess certain animals, I have not hesitated to sacrifice my sleep, and each year I have passed nearly forty nights in places by no means agreeable, and in positions often more than uncomfortable, in order to assure success. Do not think that each time my patience was rewarded! No. How many nights have I not passed fruitlessly, finding the hours interminable? During forty night-watches, I have fired each year perhaps eight shots. But truly they have well paid me for my difficulties.

The reader is now fairly well acquainted with my weapons and the value of my assistants, as well as with my perseverance : it is time to make known to him also our quarry.

A VIEW ON THE KAPOCHE.

CHAPTER III

TRIALS WITH THE SMALL-BORE RIFLE—CHANGE OF DISTRICT—COMMENCEMENT OF SPORT

Shooting in the neighbourhood of Chiromo — Eland, hippopotamus, and crocodile—Encampment on the Upper Kapoche—Wild nature—The fula—Buffalo-hunting—The man-eater—His death.

THERE was hardly any big game in the immediate neighbourhood of our Chiromo camp. Opposite, on the left bank of the river, there was indeed a plain where unfortunate buffaloes, persisting in stopping there, were slaughtered, sportsmen of the locality firing upon them while smoking their pipes in hammocks carried by shrieking men in white shirts and red caps. The local administration ended by forbidding this butchery; but there were still pseudo sportsmen who killed in a morning seven or eight buffaloes without troubling themselves even to take away the bodies which they left to the vultures. At the present time this plain is transformed into a reserved hunting-ground, and in ten years elephants will return to it as formerly.[1]

To find game, it was necessary to get away from Chiromo towards the west, in the direction of the Anglo-Portuguese boundary, where there were a few buffaloes and antelopes. In that direction I went, therefore, to try my 303, sleeping at Nant'ana, a village situated nearly seven miles away. On the following morning a herd of hartebeests enabled me to make at its expense a few very conclusive experiments. The small-bore rifle appeared to me to be extraordinarily powerful; its precision was perfect; recoil next to nothing. Almost at each shot I killed my animal. Now, the Lichtenstein bubalis, the height of which is that of a small horse, is very swift; it is one of the species of antelopes difficult to kill, so much so that it has been baptized by the Boers *harte-beest,*— that is, "hard animal." Experience taught me later the inconveniences or advantages of certain projectiles of the 303; but I was then delighted with my new weapon. It was a complete success. The absence of smoke, which was a never-ending source of astonishment to the natives, had a great advantage : owing to the reverberation of the shot, the animal never

[1] See *Mes Grandes Chasses,* p. 318.

knew exactly where the hunter was if only he remained motionless.

I killed successively in a few days bubalis, zebras, nswalas, and an eland.[1] The latter was killed under circumstances which showed the value of my new rifle in regard to range and precision.

It was in the neighbourhood of Nant'ana, where elands are rather rare. One morning I saw one of them on a grassy plain more than four hundred yards away.

It saw us immediately, and began to look fixedly at the spot where we had suddenly crouched down in the grass as soon as we perceived ourselves discovered. I resolved to do everything possible to try my new rifle on this magnificent animal. The eland is the largest of antelopes, reaching the corpulence of one of our oxen and the height of a guardsman's horse. It was necessary to approach him; but that was no easy matter. Examining the surroundings, I found that there was a small clump of trees on our right, and about two hundred yards behind him. I waited until his suspicions were set at rest, and he was eating; then I began to describe, by walking on all fours, the large circuit which I had to make. It took me a long time to reach the prolongation of the line formed by the animal and the clump of trees. Once shielded from his eyes, thanks to this natural screen, I reached the foot of the clump; but once there, it was impossible to go any

[1] For a description of these animals, see *Mes Grandes Chasses*, pp. 107, 25, 101, 299.

ELAND SHOT IN A THORNY DISTRICT.

farther. The grass was too short, and a step farther would have meant my trouble for nothing. On the other hand, the animal had moved slightly, and, scenting danger, still looked in the direction he had seen us at first. I was nearly 200 yards away; but there was no longer any time to hesitate. I raised myself slowly in a line with the trunk of one of the trees, took careful aim, and pulled the trigger.

Receiving my shot, the eland kicked, turned to the right, and fled at a headlong gallop. I was certain of having hit him; but, seeing him get away so swiftly, I thought him only slightly wounded. Still following him with my eyes, I saw him slacken his pace from a gallop to a trot; then suddenly he rolled over in the grass, kicked for a moment with his four feet, and disappeared. When we ran up a few minutes afterwards we found him dead. The bullet, passing through the heart, had shattered and very much damaged it.

Although satisfied with the precision of my rifle, I did not regard this trial as conclusive, because all animals which are wounded to the heart are irrevocably doomed, whatever may be the projectile or weapon. Later, experience taught me that the eland is too big for this kind of projectile, and that the Express 577 is the weapon with which to kill it without too much trouble or loss of time. When the animal is very corpulescent, and the quantity of flesh is considerable, a projectile which gives a violent shock is necessary to kill it, which is not the case with the small-bore bullets.

Some time afterwards I organised a small expedition into Portuguese territory around Chiperoni mountain, five or six days' journey to the north-east of our camp. In that district there was almost impenetrable grass, an undergrowth of a denseness not at all common at that time of the year. We found there numerous traces of game,—amongst others those of wildebeests, which I saw for the first time north of the Zambesi. Elephants also had frequented the district; but their marks were fairly old. A few rhinoceroses also lived there, and one day we even found ourselves quite near one of them; we heard it breathing and breaking roots of trees, but the vegetation was of such density, the grass was so high and so thick, that we were unable to see it after several hours' pursuit. We returned from our journey absolutely unsuccessful as far as big animals were concerned.

The surroundings of our camp were not at all satisfactory. I presumed that the first rain would bring game to the north-west of the Chiromo, and only a fortnight separated us from the time when the heavens would open their windows for a period of four months. In the meantime I began hunting hippopotami on the banks of the Shire. Up to then I had only kept the teeth of my largest specimens, and I needed for my collection a fine, entire head. But I did not find this time the trophy for which I was in search, although there was a great choice at that period, a number of hippopotami having collected a little below the confluence of the Shire and the Rui. Either those which I killed were too young,

A NSWALA.

or the teeth in the case of the old ones were worn out.

During these few days on the banks of the river my companions often amused themselves by shooting at crocodiles, several of which they killed. One morning when we were at lunch, one of these reptiles, measuring a good length, which had been killed the moment before, was dragged ashore, and they came to tell us that a man was in its stomach. Upon verification it was found that its intestines contained at least part of a human body. An arm with the hand attached, a foot with the ankle, and a few ribs were withdrawn—each part being clean cut from the body and hardly damaged, though the flesh was swollen and the skin was discoloured under the action of gastric juices shielded from the light. I ordered these remains to be buried, but nobody would touch them : so I had everything—crocodile and contents—thrown back into the river. The human remains floated, and the sailors of a gun-boat which arrived below stream reported to their officer that they had seen the arm of a white man descending the current of the river. This news caused great agitation in the district. On the following day another crocodile, containing the head and the shoulders of the man, a part of whose body we had found on the previous day, was killed. This discovery caused me in future to open the crocodiles which I shot, a thing I had never thought of doing before ; and thus I found several times rather strange things, including half a goat-skin rolled into a ball, and a red loin-cloth. At Lake

Nyassa, two years later, there was taken from the stomach of a gigantic crocodile over six yards long, an assortment of twenty-four copper bracelets and a large ball of frizzy hair, which the horrid beast had been unable to digest after having devoured the native lady to whom these objects belonged.[1]

The reader must think that here at last are *les horreurs qui commencent*, as a well-known song expresses it. Alas! I regret it, but that is all that I have to say about Chiromo, and the rest of our stay in those regions is so devoid of interest from the point of view of sport, that we shall pass without further transition to February of the following year, 1895, 270 miles from the Shire, into the midst of a savage country abounding in big game.

Like spectators at the theatre, the reader is now transported without fatigue to quite a different scene.[2] Instead of Chiromo, scorched by the sun, its trees leafless and twisted by dryness, we are here in the midst of abundant foliation, in the midst of an enchanting scene. Rain has not ceased falling for three months; the fresh grass is already two feet high; the trees are loaded, some with leaves and others with wild fruits; the birds sing gaily; the sky is clear between the showers—in a word, it is summer. This is the best season for elephants and buffaloes; the worst for lions, that at which they are to be feared

---

[1] For the habits, description, and hunting of the crocodile, see *Mes Grandes Chasses*, pp. 70, 75, 234, 235. Contrary to what I believed formerly, what I have seen in the great lakes has shown me that the maximum length may extend to twenty-three feet.

[2] The expedition was then on the Upper Kapoche (eastern Maravi).

A ZEBRA (Burchell's).

the most. It is also the time when you splash about everywhere, when nothing is dry, when you pass your life getting wet and drying yourself, and when, in the evening, to crown the day, you sleep in wet blankets, to the noise of the patting of the showers. Tents, however uncomfortable they may be, are considered delicious shelters. And to do your cooking it is necessary to gather the wood for the fire in advance, and to dry it before being able to use it.

Our camp is situated on a small hillock between two small rivers flowing over fine sand, and it is barricaded with abatis of branches and thorns, which act as a wall. It is composed of four tents and ten thatched shelters. De Borely being three days' journey away with the greater part of the expedition, I have with me Bertrand and twenty men only. There is not a village within a radius of thirteen miles, not a path in the immediate surroundings. The stillness of nature reigns over all things.

One morning, it might be seven o'clock, the men are conversing in hushed voices around their camp fires. The sun is shining, following the rain which prevents us setting out each day at dawn to survey the neighbourhood. Without noise we set out on march, dividing ourselves into two bodies. For two days past we have scented elephants : the day before yesterday we found a track made that very morning, yesterday one of the previous evening. The district is covered with a certain tree, the fula, the fruit of which has the appearance of a wild almond covered with a sweet and scented pulp, and of which elephants are very fond. But being unable to shake the fulas, which are gigantic trees, they have to wait patiently until their fruit falls to the ground. They have already visited the district, have made a circuit of the fulas, and as there was no fruit on the ground, have said to themselves in all probability, "We will come back in a week's time."[1] That is what we await. Tambarika sets out towards the north with five or six men; we leave in a southerly direction in search of tracks, but we return to the camp about three o'clock in the afternoon without having found anything anywhere. As we are in need of meat at the camp, and as we have seen buffalo tracks not far away, we decide to risk a rifle shot; if elephants come (and they come generally in the evening or at night) they will not be disturbed. It is always necessary to avoid making a noise in an elephant country; a noise is often quite sufficient to put them to flight.

Off we are, then, in pursuit of buffaloes, which we perceive in half an hour's time peaceably browsing on a hillock. We wind round the eminence, and, drawing near within a hundred yards, are soon able to see the whole herd, consisting of fifteen animals, of which three only are large males. One of the males, especially, is enormous. He is walking about slowly, and upon his back are a number of insectivorous birds,

---

[1] Another fruit which elephants eat is the *Matondo*, the fruit of the *Mtondo* tree. This fruit somewhat resembles outwardly a lemon; it is full of a sweet pulp, and contains two nuts. It is found in December and in January.

which flutter their wings and make a great noise.[1] It is strange that these birds have not already denounced us, for, ordinarily, they warn the animal of danger by flying away with shrill cries. As the big buffalo which I covet is badly placed and too far away, I decide to content myself with the one which appears to me the easiest to hit, and, accordingly, lodge a bullet in his shoulder in the hope of killing him on the spot. But the whole herd takes to flight. We follow the track of the wounded animal—proceeding with caution, as the ground is covered with a very dense vegetation—and soon perceive our animal lying down on the track and on the point of expiring. So as not to make unnecessary noise, we put it out of its misery with a piece of wood. The horns of this buffalo were magnificent. What a pity that I had to forego his elder, whose horns were finer still !

At half-past six o'clock the meat had been brought to the camp in quarters, and we commence to make biltong.[2] About eleven o'clock in the evening the lions give us a magnificent concert, but shortly afterwards they move away. Everybody is asleep, when some one cries : " Litumbuï, litumbuï ! " the name of large carnivorous ants,[3] which invade our camp in serried rows, attracted by the pieces of meat and the blood spilt on the ground. Each one gets up, relights the fires, and repulses the invasion with burning

[1] For insectivorous birds, see *Mes Grandes Chasses*, p. 163.

[2] See *Mes Grandes Chasses*, p. 125.

[3] *Ibid.* p. 315. They have been called black erroneously ; they are, rather, brown.

brands. As I do not wish to disturb myself, I heap up burning embers around the four iron supports of my camp bed, and go to sleep again quietly. Once more the *litumbuï* return to the charge, and then, again being repulsed with loss, give up the struggle.

The following day passes without incident; the research brigade returns accompanied by two natives who wish to speak to me on behalf of the chief of a village in the neighbourhood. It appears that there is a lion which has eaten an old woman of their village two days before, and that last night he again came prowling in the neighbourhood. As they know I have promised a prize, when accurate information is given to me on the presence of animals of which I am in search, they come to inform me. We set off immediately, and at night-fall arrive at the village after a continued march of four hours. The place is what the natives call "pafupi!"—"quite near." The night is as black as pitch, and I do not see what can be done in such darkness. The best thing, therefore, is to wait until daylight, advising the people not to leave their huts that night. To-morrow we may be able to follow a fresh track; it is too late now to organise a night watch; besides, ten minutes distant is another village, where they dance to the sound of tom-toms until ten o'clock in the evening, and I conclude that the man - eater would be somewhat embarrassed by the noise. Having taken care to bring my bed with me and something to eat, I lie down quietly, without, however, undressing myself.

At half-past four o'clock in the morning I hear

cries, a clamour of voices, which come from the
village where the people were dancing. At the
moment I rush outside, gun in hand, followed by
my men ; a woman in tears throws herself at my feet,
wringing her hands and crying that the lion has taken
her son. In the obscurity, through which flashes the
light of the straw torches carried to and fro by the
natives, we run to the village. Upon making in-
quiries we find that the lion carried off the poor boy
at the very moment when, half-opening the door of
a hut, he was passing outside the upper part of his
body to get some firewood which had remained on the
threshold. Natives are all the same : an accident to
one of them is never a lesson to the others. How
many times have I not seen blacks bathing at the
very spot where a comrade had been carried off by a
crocodile a few days before ! It will be understood
that after the cries uttered by the villagers the lion
had not remained in their midst; besides, it is impossible to find any track by the light of the torches.
There is nothing to do but to wait. We sit down
with the natives near a large fire, deafened by the
cries and lamentations of the women. Daylight is
not long in appearing.

I ask the natives not to come in any number ; ten
men only will accompany me, keeping the most profound silence. As soon as it is light enough to follow
a track, we go near the hut where the child was carried
off. The trampling of people's feet have effaced all
marks; but, on the little verandah which sur-
rounds the hut, one can see the impression of the

claws of one of the feet of the animal, and in an instant we find the track behind the hut, which proves that he passed round it. By the side of the track are marks left by one of the feet of the child, whom he must have seized by the top of the body. The animal followed one of the village streets leading to the river, passing with his load before more than twenty huts, the people in which must only have been awakened by cries after his passage. We thus reach the edge of the stream where the animal stopped, depositing his victim by his side as indicated by a little pool of blood; then he crossed the river, which contains a foot of water, descending the stream for four or five yards, and entered the reeds which border it. Before following him I send Tambarika to see if there are any traces of his exit at the far edge of that thick undergrowth. A well-known whistle tells us that there are: so we take the footpath, to arrive more quickly. After passing through some grass, where a fresh red pool indicates another stoppage, we enter a little plain, still on the track of the nocturnal male-factor; a wood comes after that, and in it we find clots of blood and the belt of pearls which the little fellow wore round his loins, then his loincloth torn off by a bush. A large pool of blood shows the spot where the animal began to tear its victim to pieces; but that was already more than an hour ago. At last, at the opposite edge of the wood, we enter the tall grass, when a growl makes us stop dead. We all listen. The enemy is there! Is he going to charge? . . . Nothing more is heard . . . I cock my rifle carefully, keeping within arm's reach my six charges of buckshot. I consider whether everything is ready; and I enter the grass my finger on the trigger, eyes directed well in front, ears on the stretch, without making the slightest noise with my feet. . . . We hear a rustling in the grass ten yards ahead; we see the tops move, but nothing more. We continue to advance slowly. Ah! there is a tree to my right! A sign to Kambombe, who climbs like a monkey, and in a trice he is at the fork on the look-out. . . . "There is the child," he says in a stifled voice, "but no lion. . . ." Then, turning his head to the right: "There he is! . . . quick, this way!" And, guided by his gesture, I run to my right; then, a thought striking me, I beckon to the villagers who follow us to approach, and with a movement of my arm tell them to wind round the grass to the left. I send Rodzani to ask them to make a noise so as to drive the lion towards me. I myself take up a position in a glade, standing motionless, all my faculties brought to bear on that square of brush which I count upon seeing the lion leave.

Kambombe gives me information in a low voice from his tree: "He's off . . . no, he comes this way. . . . He stops and looks in the direction of the men. . . . He raises his mane. . . . Ah! he comes in your direction . . . at walking pace. . . . He is going to pass the ant-hill . . . Ah! if you were here! . . . How well I see him. . . . He looks behind him. . . . There he is! there he is! . . . Get back a little; get back!"

.   .   .   .

One can understand with what anxiety I hear these words. Following his advice I retire two steps. My men are behind me with their weapons ready. "Only fire in case of necessity," I tell them. . . . "Don't hurry yourself," murmurs Tambarika.

The rustling grass bends forward, then opens on either side, and the lion walks out eight yards away from me, looking behind him, engrossed by the noise of the voices. Upon turning his head he sees me standing motionless, shows his teeth and snarls without deviating from his path. At the same time his tail rises, he flattens his ears, and I see he is going to charge at the very moment when, having followed him with my rifle and aiming at the nape of his neck, I pull the trigger. . . . His four feet give way under him, and he falls stone-dead without a movement.

I had counted upon the precision of my 303. It was with a hollow bullet that I had made this magnificent shot. I have often used it since with the same success. The animal must be hit at the point where the neck finishes and the skull begins, well in the middle of the thickest part of the neck, and it will fall dead. When one fires as near as under the circumstances above related, it must be remembered that all these rifles shoot high, and the Metford higher than any other; one must aim, therefore, well below the point one wishes to hit. Beyond 120 yards the bullet no longer rises.

My victim was a very old animal, of average size, and of extreme thinness. The following are

LION PREPARING TO CHARGE.

its measurements, made immediately after death:
total length, 9 feet 1 inch; height of withers, 2
feet 11 inches; fore-leg, 1 foot 5 inches in circumference.

The child which the lion had carried off might
be fourteen years of age. He had been seized and
killed almost at the same moment. Felines never
carry off a prey which struggles, unless they are
taken by surprise. But our lion had had ample
time in which to kill its victim. The mother had
heard a cry, and had guessed the terrible truth;
but her fright was so great that she had not had
strength to cry out immediately. When she went
outside it was too late, and when she aroused the
neighbourhood the child must have been already half-
way on the journey towards the river.

We carried back to the village the bodies of the
two actors in this nocturnal tragedy. That of the
child bore deep bites, which had terribly mutilated
the neck and right shoulder, and one of his thighs
was damaged to the bone. As to the lion, when it
was carried by eight men into the village with its
feet attached to a pole, the whole population wished
to throw itself upon it with guns, arrows, and assagais.
It is customary in such a case to mutilate the body
of the animal with gunshots and knives until its skin
resembles a riddle. As this method of preparing my
hunting trophies did not at all suit me, I interposed,
and explained to the natives that I had killed the
lion for them, that I demanded its skin intact with
claws and head, and that afterwards I would leave

the remains to them. I added, without waiting for their reply, that I was going to skin the animal, and that the first man who touched it would feel my stick. The whole of the population sat down in a circle waiting patiently until Tchigallo, assisted by Rodzani and Msiambiri, had finished removing the skin. Then they rushed upon the body, riddled it with projectiles, pierced it with assagais, and dragged

"RECORD" LION SKULL (1ᶠ 5′).

the footless, headless carcase, which vaguely resembled an ox prepared for the butchery, into all the neighbouring villages. Later, in the midst of the lamentations of the women, funeral dances and uproar, the remains of the lion were burnt on an enormous wood fire. Half-way on our journey back to the camp we still heard the cries and the tom-toms. At nightfall the gleam of the bonfire lighting up the horizon told us that the expiation was finished.

At the camp in the evening when looking at the sky sown with stars, so serene and calm, I was still thinking of the poor negress over there, her mother's heart so wrung, and I asked myself how many such unknown sorrows there are each day in the universe.

DEAD PANTHER.

CHAPTER IV

ELEPHANTS AND LIONS—THE RAINY SEASON—
ELEPHANT-HUNTING

Habits of the elephant—Famished lions—Leopard killed—Matériel and
    dress for elephant-hunting during rainy season—Pursuit and death of
    two elephants—Arrival of reinforcements—Cutting up an elephant—
    Tons of meat—Recipe for preparing elephant's foot—Shape, measure-
    ments, and weight of the tusks—Continual rain—Return to the first
    camp — Hartebeest-hunting — Departure, and construction of a new
    entrenched camp.

I EXPECTED that during our absence from camp
the elephants would have made an excursion in the
district, but very fortunately they had not yet
returned. In these countries, where the elephants
are hunted on all sides, they describe large circuits
without stopping ever more than a few hours in one
spot, generally returning to the place where they
have not been disturbed at the conclusion of a period
which varies from a week to a fortnight. When you
have found a district which they frequent, and where

their favourite plants grow, there is, therefore, great
likelihood of meeting them ; the only thing to do is
to wait patiently, without making any noise, and
walking about needlessly as little as possible, because
human tracks smell for several days and elephants
can tell very well whether they are fresh or old.
Hence our method of only going in a straight line
each day, intersecting the country lengthways, so as
to see if tracks of elephants crossed it in one direction
or in the other.

Upon our return to camp I learned that a leopard
had prowled around it and that it had even carried
off a piece of meat. The lions had contented themselves with prowling in the neighbourhood part of the
night, notwithstanding the rain which fell violently.

The rainy season is the most terrible time for
these large carnaria ; it is their period of hunger and
poverty. The presence everywhere of water has
scattered the animals upon which they feed—antelopes, wild-boars, and buffaloes,—and in spite of all
their efforts they do not eat every day : nay, they
fast often for a week, nature having endowed them
with the power of going without food for a long time.
But there is a limit to everything, and it is when
they are driven wild by hunger that they approach
the villages, eat dogs and fowls, and, lacking these,
attack the inhabitants. Only, it is rare for young
and vigorous animals to come to that. The old ones
especially are man-eaters, because they no longer
have strength to pursue and to kill a powerful
animal. Otherwise, if all famished lions attacked

man, we should have run the greatest dangers; we heard ten of them around the camp each evening, and nothing would have been easier for them than to await us in open daylight when without suspicion we were looking for elephant tracks in the high grass. Our bearers, also, would have been much exposed when they went out armed with nothing more than a matchet or an axe, to gather wood or to draw water, or even simply to walk about outside. On the other hand, I am persuaded that our passing to and fro in their locality has often disturbed our dangerous neighbours, and that they have withdrawn in another direction without our having seen them. Only nightfall, darkness, hunger, and the smell of meat attracted them around the camp, and I do not know to what extent a man would have been safe in leaving it at that time. Inside, provided the fires were kept up, we were very safe behind our thick wall of branches, outside which were piled two yards of thorns of all sizes,—and heaven alone knows what a choice and profusion of thorns the African bush offers. Lions instinctively fear thorns, which, once they have penetrated their soft paws, cause inflammation and gatherings, preventing them from attending to their business.

It will seem strange that, with so many lions around me, I have not tried to kill any of them; but during the rainy season that is a very difficult thing. During the day you never see them, or perhaps only once a year, and at night it is almost always raining. Getting wet is nothing, but the pattering of the rain on the leaves prevents you hearing anything; and the work, too, is somewhat dangerous, since you are not only deafened but blinded. And then the lion is very distrustful: nineteen times out of twenty he will refuse the bait, or if he decides to take it he will do it so quickly that your goat or piece of meat is gone before you have had time to bring your rifle to your shoulder. Note that he sees you very well when you do not know of his presence, and that he sometimes watches you for an hour unknown to you. Experience and many unsuccessful endeavours have told me that, quite apart from the danger run, you lose your time without any chance of succeeding by waiting for lions at a night-watch during the rainy season.

I have tried, with the assistance of the electric projector, to shoot over the camp fence; but the lion saw everything I did, and kept out of the ray. I have also set, across a path followed by lions, loaded guns to be discharged when they touched a taut string. By this means I have several times wounded lions, but I have never killed one. On the contrary, it will be seen by and by how I have proceeded during the dry season and the success with which my endeavours have been crowned several times.

Our leopard, then, emboldened by hunger and much less distrustful than his big brothers, returned in the evening and sprang on to a tree so as to get a better view of us. Only, he made the mistake of doing this straight in front of me, and as I had my Winchester within arm's reach, he received immediately, at a distance of six yards, a charge of buckshot. He fell like a lump of lead outside the camp, exactly against the fence. We heard him groan once or twice; then there was not a sound. The next day we were unable to find either the leopard or his tracks : only a pool of blood, and there is no doubt to my mind that the lions carried him off and devoured him. We followed their tracks for a time to clear our minds on the point, but following lions' tracks in the tall grass at that time of the year is like following the path of a bird through the air.

One more day passes without result ; the rain has not ceased falling, and we are very wretched in camp. We can only yawn or read old copies of newspapers ; and the men, huddled around their fires, smoke or converse in low voices. We have made our customary survey and have seen nothing. At nine o'clock at night a well-known noise strikes upon our ears—the trumpeting of an elephant, which is repeated once more shortly afterwards, the rest of the night being quiet, save, of course, for comings and goings of our nocturnal visitors—lions, hyenas, etc.

Before daybreak the loads for elephant-hunting are prepared. These consist of two light packages containing sorgho flour and biltong for three days, a stew-pot, salt, and night loin-cloths for eight men, a saucepan for myself, tea, sugar, a tin of milk, and some rice, a hammock, a blanket, and a hand-camera. With this little supplementary baggage we are ready to follow the elephants very far ; we can pass two or three nights out of doors.

When it rains during my hunting expeditions or marches in the bush, I undress myself completely, putting my trousers and shirt into a small waterproof bag and wearing a loin-cloth like the blacks. I retain only my helmet and shoes. Not that I can say I have a very elegant appearance in this dress, but I have found it is the most practicable during the rainy season. Immediately the rain stops the skin dries, and you have not the inconvenience of keeping on your wet clothes, which brings on fever and rheumatism. Should the weather clear up, I put my dry things on again and continue on my way. It is by walking about naked in the rain that the blacks do not suffer from it : the best waterproof ever invented is, without doubt, the human skin. As to grass and thorns, it is especially the arms and legs which feel them, and I am accustomed to that. I should like very much to be able to walk, like the blacks, with naked feet, which would have been a great advantage for a hunter ; but unfortunately that was impossible. Insensibility of the sole of the foot only comes from walking barefoot, like the natives, from your tenderest years. Formerly I tried it, but had to give it up.

I do not say that one can walk about with a helmet and a pair of shoes for your only dress on the fashionable promenades of colonial towns ; but it is different in the African bush, especially at a time of the year when in these very colonial towns honest colonists keep themselves well under shelter and postpone open-air excursions and expeditions in general until the fine season. The heavy rainy season in the midst of the jungle is very toilsome, and one must truly have a passion for hunting to support the difficulties which result. With Bertrand we have always preserved our good spirits; and I owe to that courageous companion, who lived this painful existence only through friendship for me (being no hunter himself), a good part of the happy life which I have had during the years of which these hunting expeditions have made up a large portion.

I return now to the morning of our departure. As soon as it is daylight I and my men leave the camp, accompanied by the additional bearers, who are to follow us at a distance. We go in the direction in which the elephants had made themselves heard on the previous evening, and about an hour afterwards the fresh track of five elephants is discovered. We follow them, and this brings us into the neighbourhood of the spot the buffaloes were a few days before. According to every appearance there are only females in the herd, and they are travelling without hurrying themselves but in Indian file, which shows that they are not eating. Probably they will stop a little later, unless they fed at night, in which case they may lead us a long way. About eight o'clock the rain stops, the sun appears, soon drying the grass, and the heat begins. I have said already that we are in the height of summer; the sun is at its zenith at this time of the year, and when its rays beat down we feel their heat very much —a very fortunate circumstance, because elephants feel the heat more than we do, and if it continues, they will probably slacken their pace, perhaps stop altogether. About noon—we are very far from the camp— they do, in fact, get under the shade from time to time to gather fulas. We are less than a mile behind them. At that moment the wind changes and makes us fear that all our trouble may be lost: so we turn immediately towards the right, in order not to be smelt. Very fortunately we have not been; we escape with nothing worse than a fright. At this time of the year elephants travel more slowly and for shorter distances; but on the other hand, the wind changes frequently,[1] and sometimes at the very moment you see your quarry.

About one o'clock in the afternoon the heat begins to be intense, but the sky to the north is black and we shall have rain soon. We must make haste. Soon we see the elephants in front of us: they are going at a walking pace among the trees; we can distinguish their large gray cruppers and, every now and then, their ears. Again the wind changes, but that does not trouble us. We make haste. When only thirty yards behind, I scrutinise the animals; my men, bearing to the right and the left, doing the same. We see that they are all females and all with tusks. One of them, which appears to be the biggest and the oldest, is a little in the rear. At that

---

[1] In these regions from August to November, the wind is very steady, blowing from the south-east; but during the rest of the year it changes often and blows during a day from the four points of the compass alternately.

moment she stops and rubs her back against the trunk of a fula. I go towards her, hiding myself behind a trunk, for the grass is only a foot high, and, with a final glance, sum up the situation. A little farther away than my old female, and in a line with her, is another elephant; and on my left a third, which has its hindquarters towards me, has stopped. My plan is to shoot first at the one which rubs herself, then at one of the two others, according to circumstances.

I cock my Express No. 1, draw within about ten yards of the first elephant, and lodge two shots in her heart. The animal on my left swings round and stops. I fire two shots with my No. 2 at it also, while the No. 1 is being reloaded ; and then run forward with the latter weapon, still firing upon one of the other elephants, which, however, I must have hit too much in front.

After a moment's hesitation the whole herd sets off running. The first animal at which I fired, without seeming to have noticed it, is ahead ; the other, after a deviation to the right, has rejoined the herd. We set off again in pursuit. I am certain of the first animal and almost sure of the second ; as to the third, I believe I have wounded it slightly on the shoulder.

After a few minutes' pursuit we find blood on the track, at first in small quantities and then more and more abundant : so we begin to look about us, knowing that if these animals are wounded in the lungs the shot has told. They are standing upright.

The country being fairly open, we can see well about us; but nothing is to be seen. Suddenly, we catch a glimpse of a gray mass behind a bush, and find that it is the first female elephant, stone dead. The two bullets really reached her heart. Let us continue. our search. Descending into a small valley, we see there, standing upright and facing the left near a clump of trees, an elephant—doubtless the second animal. At the same moment the storm breaks and the rain falls violently. My victim, which I see only through a curtain of rain-drops, visibly suffers, her flank swelling out abnormally and then subsiding; she is shot in the lungs. We pass round her in such a way that she shall not see us approach; but she seems more taken up with her sufferings than with us, and at the moment I am going to fire, she falls down on the grass, still breathing. I draw near and give her the *coup de grâce* behind the ear. Around her is a large pool of blood, which the rain carries in a red stream towards the bottom of the little valley.

It is a quarter past two o'clock, and we are almost fifteen miles from the camp. I send some men with a message to Bertrand to bring everybody here to-morrow during the day. By taking the shortest cut he will be able to reach us about eleven o'clock. When you kill large animals, instead of carrying their bodies to the camp, which would need too many bearers, you bring the camp to them. At the present time of the year, when water is found everywhere, there is nothing inconvenient in that; but during the dry season it is often very difficult.

In the meantime we rest a little, afterwards looking out for an encampment for the night. I choose a place at the bottom of the vale under the trees and near a stream, about fifty yards from the last elephant which fell. We make an enclosure of thorns there, and when the work is finished I go to measure and photograph my elephants.[1]

My men ask to be allowed to take a little meat; but I object, because touching the animals would mean that during the night all the carnivora of the neighbourhood would be attracted, while, the blood having been washed away, there is a great likelihood that the bodies will not be smelt. My men see my reasoning : so we content ourselves with biltong, and pass a quiet night, of which we are much in need.

Bertrand arrives at the expected hour on the following day, with the whole camp, and the work of cutting up the animals begins ; half the men, assisted by hunters, servants, and cooks, are employed therein, while the other half enlarges the camp for the evening.

As the elephant is lying on its side and the knives with difficulty cut the skin of the body, the ear is detached at the spot where it is tenderest. This being done, the skin of the neck and belly are taken off gradually with knives until the latter is uncovered. Then they commence to disarticulate the fore and hind limbs farthest away from the ground, eight men

---

[1] At the end of this work will be found a comparative table of measurements of some elephants.

CUTTING UP AN ELEPHANT.

harnessing themselves on to the gigantic legs, which they drag a few yards on to the grass. The skin of the belly is then cut longitudinally, and removed from the bottom of the ribs to the spinal column. The ribs are broken with the hands by opening them with force.[1] When the intestines are uncovered they are removed from the abdominal cavity—a task which is by no means easy, owing to their weight and size. The sight is a strange one. You would think you were looking at children struggling with an enormous, milky-white eider-down. As the liver, heart, and lungs are already removed, the body of the animal forms an immense cavity, generally full of blood; and, to be more at their ease, ten of the men get inside, where, covered with blood and bathed up to the knees in it, they continue their work. The head is detached; then, the blood having been preciously gathered in skins, all help in turning over the body, the same method as that described above being carried out with the side which is now uppermost. Once all the parts are detached the natives proceed to make biltong.

By working from eleven until eight o'clock, all that one can do that day is to carry the two elephants to the camp and to pile the meat there as well as may be, into a veritable mountain. In the evening the hyenas give us concerts with their mournful howling, and so well clean the place where the animals have

---

[1] The elephant has tender and spongy bones. There is an old native saying that "The hatchet does not sing when the elephant dies."

been cut up that one can recognise it only by the trampled grass. There is not a shadow of a lion, probably owing to the fact that this district is less frequented by game than that whence we have come. As to hyenas, their scent is so keen that they know of the presence of any animal *debris* several miles away, and arrive straight on the place, uttering at intervals their disagreeable cry.

As there is a village three hours' distance away, I send to the chief to inform him that I desire a few bearers. Fifty men soon answer to the call. They are accompanied by a few women, who come to sell us, in return for meat, produce of the country for which I have asked : sweet potatoes, a kind of spinach, green maize, fowls, eggs, bananas, etc. I send some venison to De Borely at headquarters under the guidance of one of my men; and, as the sun only appears every now and then, I smoke the elephant meat during the day and night, so that we shall be able the next day to get back to our starting-point with the remainder of the additional bearers.

On the average, forty men are required to carry a female elephant thus cut up, flesh and bones included ; fifty-two for a male. When the bones have been taken out and the flesh is dried, the numbers are reduced to about one-half—that is, twenty-five men for a male, twenty for a female. One can estimate the approximate minimum weight of the living animal at two tons for a male, and rather over one ton and a half for a female. Of all animals the elephant is the one whose flesh is the lightest after being dried, doubtless because more water enters into its composition; in fact, it loses more than half its weight in drying, while that of the buffalo and zebra diminishes hardly a third.

As to its quality, it is too hard and stringy for a European. The heart is tender and very nutritious. The trunk requires fifteen and the foot thirty hours' cooking; but these are succulent cates. Nothing can be found to equal them among European dishes. At the risk of hurting the feelings of our Parisian " vatels," I affirm that a piece of elephant's foot well prepared by the wife of an elephant - hunter is matchless. Bertrand and I have eaten for four or five days in succession this *mwendo wa nzou*. We have therefore, as you can see, a few compensations in Central Africa. Here is the recipe which I dedicate to housewives :—

How to Prepare Elephant's Foot

Take an elephant's foot, preferably young and very fresh; remove the white flesh which covers the bone, and cut it into strips the thickness of your finger, reminding one of sticks of *pâte de guimauve*. Place these appetising strips in the sun for two days to dry, and collect the pure fat which exudes from them in the form of clear oil. To make the dish known as *mwendo wa nzou*, take one of these strips, cut it into small pieces, put it into a saucepan containing a little water, place it on a gentle fire, and renew the water several times. When a jelly has formed add to it the oil in which you have browned a few onions, a little thyme, etc., or an equivalent aromatic plant, one or two very strong chillies, and let it cook gently for twenty hours, still adding water when necessary. Serve hot — with manioc flour or grated biscuit separately.

N.B.—This dish keeps several days, and only requires re-warming.

The tusks which I obtained from the large female weighed about seventeen pounds each, and the others ten pounds and a half, which is an average weight. Female elephants' tusks are generally slender and tapering, while those of males are proportionately short and thick.

I now resume my narrative at the time we leave our elephant encampment. We set out very early in the morning, leaving to the hyenas only the well-cleaned bones of our gigantic pachydermata, and while Bertrand with the column of bearers takes a short cut, I make a large detour, so as not to have the wind at my back if by chance we meet game. The weather is cloudy, and fine rain which obscures the air and forms a thin fog, preventing us from seeing far, is falling. We cannot have been very far from the camp when a tawny mass passes slowly between the bushes. Our first thought is that it is a lion; but, notwithstanding the drizzle, a moment's examination makes us certain about the animal—a belated hyena. The remainder of the day is passed under shelter. The research brigade beats the surroundings without

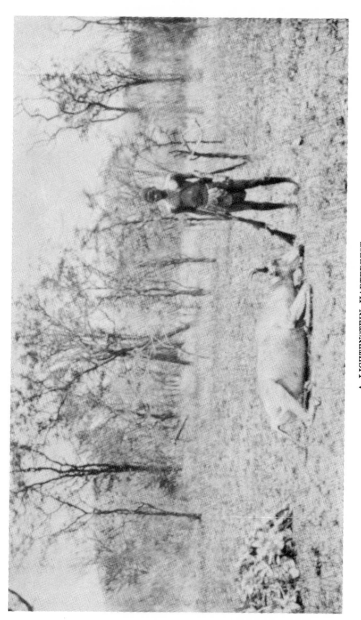

A LICHTENSTEIN HARTEBEEST.

finding a fresh track. We decide on the following day to go farther afield, and while the baggage is being packed I go out to try to kill an antelope, because Bertrand and I do not like too much elephant flesh. I find some hartebeest, and kill one of them amid rather curious circumstances. Having been wounded, it runs a long distance, and stops exactly behind a big tree. As I cannot move round it without again frightening the animal, I try to shoot

AN ANT-HILL.

it through the tree with a solid 303 bullet. The projectile passes through the trunk, which is a foot and a half in diameter, and breaks the withers of the bubalis, which falls dead. It was the same experiment which, for the first time, I saw tried in Dahomey with the Lebel rifle. The Dahomians hid themselves behind palm-trees, and the same projectile passed through tree and man.

We carry the bubalis whole to the camp, where it is soon cut up and placed on the loads. We sleep in the evening at the village where I killed the lion, and the next day we camp at the foot of the hills which one can see around, five minutes' distance from the River Kapoche, in the upper basin of which we have been for some time.

We make an entrenched camp like the one we have just left, carefully concealing it, because there are not only animals in this district, but also the Mpeseni plunderers, the famous Mafsitis.[1] One must be on one's guard against any attack on their part. I name this camp, around which we move for some time, *Niarugwe,*—that is to say, "Panther Camp," —on account of the visits which that animal paid us.

---

[1] See *Mes Grandes Chasses*, pp. 135, 137, and 152.

MALE RHINOCEROS (see p. 71).

CHAPTER V

IN THE MIDST OF THE JUNGLE—PURSUIT OF BIG ANIMALS

The Kapoche district—An excellent country for sport—The expedition in winter quarters—Niarugwe Camp—Temporary fortification—Favourable season for large pachydermata—The ant-eater—Superstitions about this animal—Rhinoceros-hunting—Inconveniences of dense vegetation —A faithful spouse—A panther in the middle of the camp—After elephants—Three elephants killed—Pursuit of buffaloes—Meeting with lions—Seeking for a wounded buffalo in the tall grass, and the danger of this undertaking—Night-watch for the panther and its death—A morning with lions—Missed !—In the dense jungle with a dying lion— The last hunt—Meeting with Mafsitis.

AT the present day all these regions have changed very much, owing to European advance; but at the time to which my narrative relates—that is, the year 1895—there were few parts of Africa which offered the hunter such resources as the Upper Kapoche, the north of Undi, and the neighbouring country. Between the Upper Tchiritse and the Kapoche, both of which are extreme tributaries of the Luyia, are still found the Luyia itself and the Loangwe. These four deltas were as deserted as the earth was before the creation of man, and one could march for a week there in any direction without meeting a village ; formerly there had been a few villages, but the Mafsitis had destroyed them.

The land was well watered by the four rivers which I have named, and by their many tributaries ; there were to be found shady places and swamps,—dear to elephants,—as well as gigantic thickets, pieces of forest-land, and grassy plains suitable for these animals. Flat in certain parts, mountainous in others, alternately wooded and open, level and undulated, the ground was fitted for all species, and was inhabited by them. Large pachydermata, hardly ever being disturbed, became less nomadic ; in brief, it was an excellent country for sport, provided that one knew how to make the best of it. There were, on the other hand, many difficulties for us,—density of vegetation, height of grass, and difficulty in moving through those almost impenetrable thickets, or those swamps which, though easy enough for an elephant or a rhinoceros, were difficult and fatiguing for man. Besides, the position in which the hunter placed himself became extremely perilous in case of danger. I must add that rain continued to fall heavily, and that the first day of our arrival at Niarugwe Camp we were unable to leave our tents.

The main body of the expedition under the command of De Borely wintered during this time to the north of Makanga. The bearers had been sent away for the time being, our comrade remaining with a few men and servants. Though you may persuade four or five hunters to tramp in the rain eight or ten hours a day, it is quite another matter with 400 bearers with loads on their heads—the column stops constantly and the packages are spoiled by the wet. The best thing, then, is to await the end of the rainy season, which falls generally at the beginning of May. I utilise the time by hunting. Will the reader now inspect our quarters, similar to all our camps ?

Our entrenchment is completely hidden from the outside, and any one passing near the forest would never suspect that forty men were living there, as comfortably as circumstances permitted. In the middle is an open, uncovered space of twenty yards ; at one end is my tent, Bertrand's tent and that for the baggage, specimens, and biltong ; all around, and inside the stockade of abatis and thorns, are the thatched huts of the men, their fires, firewood, the buccans, etc. Outside the camp is a spot in a clearing which is levelled and swept, where animals may be cut up, so as not to dirty the inside. There the skins are stretched and dried in the sun. When the sun does shine, many biltong-racks, upon which strips of meat are placed to dry, are also put outside ; these are carried inside the stockade at night, to be replaced in the morning. This is done with the object of not encumbering during the day the place which we occupy, and to keep the flies, which are attracted by the meat, at a distance. There is not the least danger in leaving the meat outside during the day, vultures rarely daring to touch it when men are in camp and carnivora being hidden in their lairs.

More than once it has happened that upon noiselessly returning to camp during the excessive heat of the day I have found the sentries, of whom there were always two or three, fast asleep, with twenty racks loaded with meat at their side. But at Niarugwe Camp we had not only the animals to fear : we had to beware also of Mafsitis: so we always left on guard at least six men armed with Martini rifles. In case of alarm, they had only to close the stockade " door." As bullets could leave the enclosure, but clubs and assagais could not enter, nothing was to be feared inside. The " door," of which I have just spoken, is very simple and a perfect protection. The camp enclosure is broken by an opening, at each side of which two posts are driven into the ground. A thick branch of a tree, provided with thorns, as long and as thick as the little finger, is then cut. It is dragged to the entrance, and the trunk is pulled violently from the inside between the two posts and fastened in such a way that the thorns are piled up at the entry, making it the most impregnable part of the fortification.

Two hundred yards from the edge of our part of the forest flows the Kapoche, where we obtain drinking water. The river is much swollen at this time of the year. Reeds and aquatic plants which line its banks attract innumerable mosquitoes : the reason why we keep some distance away.

Though this time of the year is fitted for the pursuit of the elephant, the rhinoceros, and the buffalo, other animals are never seen, hidden as they are by the density of the vegetation and warned of your approach by the noise of your progress through the grass. Thus, I have the greatest difficulty in finding an antelope or a wild-boar. On the other hand, during the dry season, when everything is burnt up, you can find as many as you like, provided, of course, you take the trouble to look for them. The first bit of sport we had in the Kapoche district is worthy of mention.

One dull, rainy morning, we see on an open space an animal which most of us have never seen before. We cannot distinguish it very clearly, and as it turns its back we make all kinds of conjectures. I see two large rabbit-like and flexible ears, a round back, and a fleshy tail. Can it be a kangaroo ? Not wishing to move, and run the risk of frightening it away, I aim at its back in the direction of the heart. It falls dead on its side. Tambarika, while his comrades and I are examining in astonishment this curious animal, recognises it immediately to be an ant-eater. A white skin with long, scanty, blackish-brown fur, a tapering snout similar to that of a pig with a hole at the end but no mouth, a tongue a yard long like a whip-thong, ears like those of a rabbit, enormous nails on its paws, a powerful short thick tail almost hairless, and the corpulescence of an adult pig—such is the not very flattering portrait of the ant-eater. It was received at the camp with all kinds of exclamations, the oldest declaring that this animal brought misfortune, and that it was customary upon meeting it to return home and not continue a journey. I feel quite certain upon hearing this that whatever happens will be put down to this unfortunate ant-eater. In fact, all our fruitless attempts to overtake elephants, ailments, everything, even the bad weather, will be attributed to it during our stay in this place.

That does not prevent my men from eating and declaring it excellent, in which I share their opinion. It is, indeed, difficult to find more delicate flesh. The ant-eater is an animal essentially nocturnal : consequently, it is rarely seen, and its habits being very little known accounts for the superstitions. Few natives among those who frequent the woods have ever seen it. Do not think that all blacks are accustomed to the bush.   The majority in these countries are farmers ; they know merely the names of the rare animals which they have met in following the paths leading from their village to neighbouring villages ; hunters among the population are the exception. A large number of my bearers did not know even the native names for all the antelopes which I sent to the camp. Every peasant in France is acquainted with the habits of hares and partridges. In Africa, where the large fauna keep in the thickets far from human beings, it is necessary not only to have weapons, but also to track and to possess special knowledge, to capture and to know animals. There is hardly one hunter in each village; thus, out of the thirty bearers I have in camp, only four are capable of following a track. However, hunters or not, all love the life which we live here.

The end of March comes without noteworthy incident, but April is fairly eventful. We spend the morning of the 6th in following two rhinoceros which have made many peregrinations in the tall grass during the night. Pursuit of them is very tiring, as we cannot see four yards before us; and we never know at what moment we are to meet these savage animals.

We arrive very near our goal without having been charged, in spite of the almost continual shifting of the wind; but it does not follow that we shall finish our day thus, for, in the very middle of a dense thicket, we hear, a few yards off, a snorting and then a snifting which we know well. In the midst of broken branches, overturned shrubs, and trampled grass, appears a huge mass which charges in our direction with the speed of a locomotive. We have only time to jump on one side. The animal passes, but so quickly that I cannot take aim, being hindered from doing so by a tree. It disappears in the grass. But in a few seconds we hear it returning on its steps, again seeking for that vitiated air, that smell of the enemy which has provoked its anger. It snorts and searches, turns and turns again like a gigantic pointer, with this difference that the rôles are reversed—we are the game which it is looking for. . . . This cursed vegetation is so thick that there is nothing to do but to wait; it is impossible to fire. I see the top of the grass wave and the shrubs lean over; I can guess, therefore, the position of the animal, but it remains invisible. However, its anger increases, and it continues to snort, making a noise somewhat similar to the grunting of a pig, only louder and deeper. It draws near. . . . From which way is the wind blowing? It is impossible to say, for the earth is wet and there is no dust.[1] . . . Time is pressing . . . Ah! it charges us a second time! . . . This time I see my animal a moment before it is upon us; although going at a gallop, it is not travelling over the ground so quickly as it was. We have jumped aside and everyone is hidden. . . . Stationed behind a tree I see it advance splendidly, and I decide to stop its passage. Doubtless smelling our fresh tracks, it slackens its pace when in front of us, and I take advantage of this to fire two shots, which make it swing round in a direction opposite to ours. Before disappearing through the smoke it receives still another express bullet in its cruppers.

But the battle is not over. At the same moment warning of another charge is given quite near to us; it is rhinoceros No. 2, which we have forgotten. Doubtless this is the female. He or she passes at a gallop five or six yards away, but not in our direction,

---

[1] When there is dust, a handful is taken up and thrown in the air; by which means one can tell the direction in which the wind is blowing.

blowing furiously. Look out for a fresh attack! It is terrible to be in the midst of vegetation so thick that it prevents you being warned of danger except through hearing. I send Rodzani up a tree to inspect the surroundings. He sees the last-named rhinoceros already at a great distance, and states that it is the male which is making off, and that it must be the female we have shot. But we are not long in finding he is wrong, because blood—that precious indication for the hunter — makes the pursuit of the first rhinoceros, which I believe I have wounded seriously, easy for us. After going one hundred yards he must have lain down, but got on his feet again after a final effort, to fall once more a little farther away. He has fallen on his stomach, his four legs giving way under him. Rhinoceros often fall in this way, probably because they do not die on the spot, but continue to walk until their legs refuse to carry them.

It is really the male which we have killed. Here are his measurements : withers, 5 feet 2 inches; length from the tip of the nose to the tip of the tail, 11 feet 1 inch ; diameter of the forefoot, 8 inches ; horns: front, 2 feet 3 inches; back, 1 foot 5½ inches. The measurements of the female, which was not long in dying, are as follows : withers, 5 feet 4 inches ; total length, 11 feet 2 inches ; diameter of foot, 8½ inches ; horns : front, 1 foot 8½ inches ; back, 1 foot 3 inches. It will be noticed that the female is larger than the male, a peculiarity which often happens.

Let us return to the male rhinoceros. After measuring and photographing the body I leave two men with it, and make ready to return to camp so as to send others. As I am going that way I cross the plain on to which the female rhinoceros charged after the firing of my two first shots. Fresh marks on the ground show us that it is the female which passed that way, and suddenly a snorting tells us that she has been waiting for an hour for the return of her companion. As at one side of us there is an open space seven or eight yards in extent, where the rocky ground has not allowed grass to grow, I run to take up a position there, so as to have, if possible, more room in front of me than during the preceding encounter. I take my 8-bore to please my men, who have just been reproaching me for not having used it, and place myself in the midst of the grass, motionless, on the side opposite to that on which I have heard the characteristic snorting of the unfortunate female. Here there are no trees in which one can shelter.

The animal is disquieted, but she has not smelt us. I hear her walking, and then, immediately afterwards, I see her coming towards us, but like an animal which goes about its own business. She is coming out to the right, will cross the open space, and in all probability will enter the grass again on our left. On she comes at a walk, and when seven or eight yards in front of me I fire. My men were persuaded that she would fall down dead on the spot. Msiambiri had even bet Rodzani a pot of moa (the beer of the country) that with the big rifle the rhinoceros would so fall. He loses, for upon receiving my bullet the animal throws herself upon us at full speed, making us scatter at once in the grass; but she quickly falls down and dies almost at our feet. There is a warm discussion on the conditions of the bet, Msiambiri, who is always having his little joke, now pretending that he bet merely that the animal would not go so far as the other. Don't let us waste time in discussing: let us again take measurements and return to camp! The meat is not got in before half-past ten o'clock in the evening.

It is here that the panther[1] enters on the scene again. About half-past eleven o'clock, when everybody is asleep, she jumps on to the stockade and misses her footing; falling on to a thatched shelter, upon which she slips and to which she tries to cling, she topples over with the roof into the midst of the camp. This noise awakens everybody with a start, and seeing the animal in the light of the camp-fires my men think they are attacked, and utter various cries. But the apparition was only like that of a lightning flash; the panther springs on to the thatch and retraces her steps before we know what the matter is. I go to bed again. The reception she received probably frightened her sufficiently to prevent her returning at least this evening.

Towards morning she is heard roaring. Judging from her footprints on the moist earth, which make one almost think that twenty-five panthers have been there, she must have prowled the whole night in the neighbourhood. She is going to be our companion

[1] Panther, according to Cuvier; leopard, according to Linnæus. It is the same animal. See *Mes Grandes Chasses*, pp. 94, 95, and 96.

for a great part of our stay here, until the day, in fact, I have prepared to play upon her a trick of my own.

The 7th passes without incident; on the 8th we follow the track of two male elephants, but they are too far ahead of us, and our trouble is for nothing. On the 9th we meet with the tracks of eight elephants, including two large males, and we overtake them after only two hours' march. I kill a big male. As to the other male and a female, I wound but lose them both after a day's pursuit. However, as the male seemed to me to be doomed, I send four men in search of it. They return without result, after passing the night out of doors.[1] The camp is transported near the dead elephant, passes two nights there, and then returns with the smoked meat. On the 13th I kill an old female which has twice charged Rodzani. I fire five bullets into the region of the heart, and she does not appear to be any the worse, but goes off quietly, hardly bleeding. We follow her at a distance, expecting every moment to see her fall. As she is going right towards the camp, it is so much labour saved. At last, at the end of more than half an hour, she decides to fall and die. She bled internally, and, her abdomen full of blood, travelled more than four miles!

On the 17th we meet with a herd of buffaloes, behind which I see three magnificent lions, which disappear before I am able to fire at them. We follow the lions for a time, but soon give them up to

---

[1] I found this elephant dead on the 26th, and extracted three of my bullets from it. I took its tusks, weighing about 35 lbs.

OUR CAMP IS BROUGHT TO THE DEAD ELEPHANT.

go in pursuit of the buffaloes. I overtake them and shoot two at hazard—that is, without having had time to select them for the beauty of their horns. The vegetation is so thick that one cannot see buffaloes: only portions of them can be seen vaguely here and there through the grass almost everywhere. I wound a third, and as he leaves the herd we go in pursuit of him. To follow a wounded buffalo in this compact brushwood is dangerous work, and we need all our coolness and presence of mind. Kambombe and the water-carrier[1] keep a look-out from the tops of trees. As to ourselves, we make more use of their eyes than our own. We follow the blood-stained path, and at each step we question with a look those who see on our behalf what is happening around and in front.

In the case of a rhinoceros or an elephant one is put on one's guard; one snorts violently, the other rends the air with its loud trumpeting or grunts with pain. The buffalo begins by remaining motionless and silent, so motionless that you would mistake it for an overturned tree or any other similar object. He holds his breath and keeps his ears well open in order to perceive your arrival. Should he hear you he does not stir. It is only when you are within range that he throws himself upon you, and it is generally too late for you to avoid him. Such, at least, is his demeanour in the bush. On open, or fairly open ground, he is forced to begin his

---

[1] The one who usually carries the water-bottles. During the rainy season he carries food, etc.

charge farther away, and you have time, if you are cool, to stop him in his course ; only, to fire with some chance of success, he must be very near and must have his head lowered to strike you with his horns.

Thus, you risk more by being charged by a buffalo than by a rhinoceros. The latter is, doubtless, a more dangerous adversary than the former ; but, buffaloes being more numerous, it is natural that accidents are more frequent with them. The charge of the lion and that of the elephant are, without denial, also extremely redoubtable ; once or twice you escape, but some fine day you do not, and there is a speedy end to your career.

Now let us return to our buffalo. Our scouts on the tree-tops have signalled him as being situated with his head to the left, and we endeavour to get round him without making a noise. But he hears us and slowly turns round,—so our scouts inform us, —then once more remains motionless, facing in our direction. I leave a man on the spot towards which he is looking with instructions not to move, but every now and then to break a small branch to make the animal believe that we advance from that direction, while noiselessly we return with the others to the track to which he now turns his back. This strata- gem succeeds ; while he is listening to the man who breaks the branches I put a bullet through his head.

This buffalo had the finest pair of horns I have ever seen, but unfortunately the tip of one of them was broken. They measured not less than 3 feet 6 inches between the curves. The height of the

A BUFFALO IN A "MITSAGNA" FOREST.

withers of the three buffaloes, which were formidable
animals, were 5 feet, 5 feet 3 inches, and 5 feet 2
inches. I have two taken to the camp, leaving the
third where it is, in the hope of attracting lions
during the night, my intention being to put meat
there for them one or two days if they return, so as
to give them confidence, and to be able afterwards
to lie in watch, as it is full moon.

During this time the panther has not abandoned
us; every night it prowls around the camp with
remarkable persistence, trying to enter at one side
or the other, roaring continually, and obliging us
to have night watchmen, for hunger makes these
animals exceedingly bold. Lions visit us at the
beginning of the night, but, when they find they
have no advantage in remaining, they go in search
of food elsewhere and leave us in peace. Hyenas
also come to wish us " good-evening." The panther
alone is tenacious. So I judge the time has come
to play her the little trick of which I have spoken.
As she springs into all the trees near the stockade to
.see what we are doing, I have a piece of meat placed
for her every day in the fork of an eriodendron
which is in the full light of the fires. I could poison
the bait with strychnine, of which I have an ample
supply, but I wish to kill her by nobler means. At
first the animal is suspicious and does not take the
meat, or only in the morning. Little by little
she grows bolder and carries it away when we
are still awake and in conversation ; she ends by
getting it down at night-fall. When at last I con-

sider the fruit ripe and ready for plucking, I content myself no longer with simply placing the meat on the tree; I have it securely attached, or rather nailed by the skin. I fix up my electric projector, and with the ray of its light I experiment on the tree situated barely ten yards from the centre of the camp, and whilst we converse as usual I wait comfortably seated smoking my pipe. Suddenly, without knowing how it happened, I see the panther on the branch, and direct the projector on to her, flooding her with light. She occupies herself with tearing the meat without troubling herself about our presence otherwise than by looking in our direction from time to time. I put a bullet in her neck and she falls like a lump of lead. By means of the projector we see her on the ground, and being assured that she is really dead, we bring her to the camp where Tchigallo cuts her up immediately.[1] It is appropriate, it seems to me, to quote this moral of La Fontaine :—

"Patience et longueur de temps font plus que force ni que rage."

And especially is this so in the hunter's profession.

The panther's death[2] happens on the eve of that of the three buffaloes: so we are able to sleep quietly on the following night. I am troubled, however, by the idea that the hyenas will probably profit by the god-send of buffalo meat, and that they will gorge themselves at my expense; perhaps,

[1] Carnivora must be skinned immediately, because decomposition sets in in a few hours.

[2] It was one of the finest panthers I have killed. Its skin measured 7 feet 5 inches.

on the other hand, if lions come they will not dare to touch the animal, for fear of a trap. At all events, at daybreak we advance over the damp ground without making the least noise, proceeding to the spot where I have left the body, about twenty minutes' distance from the camp. The weather is gloomy, the sky black, a very fine rain is falling, and a cold, damp north wind beats our faces. We arrive through the tall grass leeward of the spot, and without drawing too near get on to a hillock to look around. . . . We left the buffalo on the previous day in the middle of a bare spot. It is no longer there! . . . It is really there we left it; there is not the least doubt of that. . . . While we are looking, the idea of lions occurs to all of us—only lions are capable of having dragged it away. That is a matter to be found out: so we advance at the edge of the tall grass, and, thanks to the wind, which whistles continuously, we have not given warning of our presence. Tambarika, who is the most supple of all of us, is ahead; the others walk three or four yards in the rear. . . . We stoop down. . . . There is the buffalo, half hidden in the grass, surrounded by savage forms. . . . Are they lions or hyenas? All bend forward and look . . . They are lions: there is no doubt about it, for there are two or three hyenas standing at a distance, their large ears erect and their eyes fixed on the buffalo, waiting until the lions have gone, to approach in turn. The dirty yellow colour of the hyenas is so similar to that of the earth, that until we are within twenty yards no one has seen them. As to the lions, they are very busy, and it is possible for us to draw near to them in this tall grass without making ourselves heard and without disturbing them. We consult hurriedly in low voices, and this is what we decide to do. Tchigallo and Rodzani will wind round the grass behind the lions, and will walk straight towards them, talking as they proceed, without taking the slightest precaution. Hearing them advance, the lions will leave the carcase, and will come towards us. I fear one thing only, that I shall not see them clearly enough at that moment, for the weather is very dull and the rain is increasing. Nevertheless, we must make haste; if the wind changes and one of these animals scents us, they will disappear in the grass. Tambarika and Msiambiri, as usual, hold themselves ready with loaded rifles in case the lions charge. I, myself, trust to circumstances as to what I am going to do. Should the lions come upon us without seeing us, confusing us because of our immobility with the surrounding trees, we must not let them get too near. It is understood that I shall give orders when the time comes, but I advise my men not to fire in the direction of their comrades. The weapons are ready, I have prepared my 303, and we follow with our eyes our companions who are going to act as beaters. There is no need to state that it is this moment of expectation in the presence of danger which is terrible : there is no imminent peril, because the lions when they see us will be more frightened than we are. The shot which I am about to fire will decide our fate! Who knows if it will mean the death of one of us ?

Tchigallo and Rodzani are behind the lions, which are consequently between them and us. At a sign from me they enter the grass without precaution, exchanging a few words. . . . At the same moment three lions bound into the open space and turn round in the direction of the noise. . . . During the two or three seconds which elapse I examine them rapidly. Nearest to us there is a young lion or a female lion; in front is a female lion; and in the middle is a lion with his dark mane erect and his teeth showing. All three are growling, as all lions do when disturbed. . . . After glancing in the direction of the intruders, they swing round and come towards us, not straight but in such a manner that we are on the left. . . . "Don't move," I murmur to my men. . . . I let the lioness pass, and aiming at the lion's neck, pull the trigger. . . . Owing to the absence of smoke, I see that he does not fall: so, without taking my weapon from my shoulder, I fire a second bullet at his shoulder-blade, jumping aside with the other loaded rifle. The lion roars with pain, and disappears with his family in the grass. . . .

I am not at all pleased. First of all, I have missed his neck, because he was trotting; then, I do not know exactly where I have hit him at the second shot. In any case his roaring tells me that he is wounded. Seeing him spring forward with tail erect, I expected a charge. (I have already said that the absence of smoke, and the reverberation of the shot, prevent animals from finding out the position of the sportsman, and in this case the most natural movement the beast would make would be to throw himself forward.) My men immediately explore the surroundings by climbing trees; but, seeing nothing, we follow the track, where there is at first only a little, then a good deal, of blood. I hesitate very much in entering this dense vegetation. Suddenly, twenty-five yards farther on, Kambombe cries to us from the top of a tree : " There he is ! . . . He is dying. Draw near quietly. . . . He is looking that way "—indicating our direction. I confess that I would rather be elsewhere than in the tall grass in gloomy weather by the side of a dying lion. I know that powerful roaring, having heard it once before near Tete, and it was only by a miracle that I escaped out of that ugly business.[1] So it is with infinite precautions, eyes wide open and ears on the stretch, that I advance. . . . At one time the grass is no higher than a man, and I witness a few yards away a scene I shall never forget. The lion is sitting with his back to me, his head lowered. Losing his balance, he raises himself up painfully, and again falls with a harsh cry of anger, rage, or suffering, which swells out his large flanks when he is renewing his efforts. . . . I do not contemplate him long; what I describe here is a rapid vision which I have while carefully aiming at his neck. . . . I press the trigger, and without taking my rifle from my shoulder continue to aim, keeping the second shot in case of a charge. . . . But the first put him out of his misery.[2]

---

[1] See *Mes Grandes Chasses*, pp. 300, 301, 302, and 303.

[2] The accompanying photograph, " Looking for a wounded lion in the bush," was taken by M. de Borely amid similar circumstances a

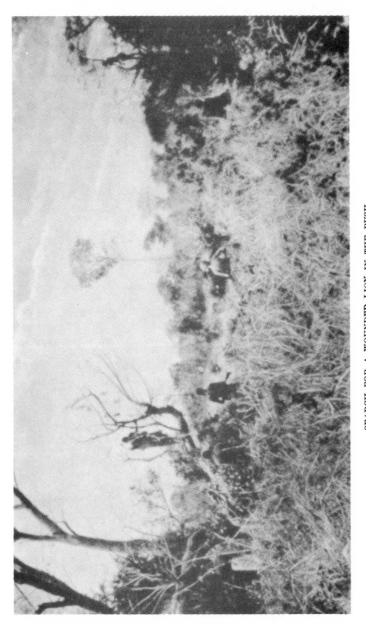

SEARCH FOR A WOUNDED LION IN THE BUSH.

I am persuaded that, if we had unfortunately arrived without precaution from the other side, and the animal had seen us, it would have made a supreme effort, and would have charged us, which would have been the death of the first of us it met. One must be exceedingly prudent in the tall grass with a wounded lion, and when there is no tree to serve as an outlook it is better to give up the chase and lose the animal, since you know neither what you are doing nor where you are going. Pursuit is already very perilous over semi-open ground, for you cannot imagine how easily a crouching lion can hide itself when it likes,—the smallest bush is sufficient, and when you see it, it is too late. There is, of course, the last resort of taking a snap shot, which one often does instinctively and without bringing the rifle to the shoulder under the emotion of the moment; but that is not taking aim, it is a matter of chance, and in these meetings with lions you must never rely on chance.

When you have dogs it is different, because first of all they warn you of the presence of the animal, and then, by circling round it, they occupy its attention sufficiently to allow you to draw near and to fire. Farther on it will be seen that I have never had these auxiliaries : otherwise in certain regions

year later. I reconstituted the scene on the very spot where I had killed a wounded lion a few minutes before.

This lion, without being of extraordinary build, was a very fine one. Its measurements were : withers, 2 feet 8 inches ; length, 9 feet 6 inches ; and skull, 1 foot 2 inches by 8 inches. It was in the full force of its maturity. Its mane contained hairs which were darker than the majority.

abounding in lions which I have visited, I should have obtained incredible results.

The lion above mentioned and one or two buffaloes were the last animals which I took to Niarugwe Camp.

Two or three days before leaving it we meet a band of 100 Mafsitis, natives of Mpeseni, probably on one of their pillaging expeditions. Seeing us all well armed and very indifferent, they place their shields, clubs, and assagais on the ground; then, advancing towards me in a compact group, clap their hands altogether three times, the manner in which natives salute their chiefs. I sit down at the foot of a tree with all these robbers, whose heads are dressed with feathers, in a circle round me. We talk for a moment or two about the rain and the fine weather, and then separate, wishing reciprocally never to meet again.

FEMALE RHINOCEROS. (See p. 73.)

PREPARING TO CUT UP A RHINOCEROS.

CHAPTER VI

A " BATTUE " WITH NATIVES—UNEXPLORED COUNTRY —GIANTS ON THE DECLINE

A lion hunt—The muzzle-loader in the hands of natives—A shower of bullets—The wounded—Precautions to be taken with firearms—Period for meeting with lions—The expedition moves—In the rhinoceros country—Pursuit of the rhinoceros—Worn-out horns—Beauty and laws of nature.

AT the moment we are preparing to leave Makanga with the whole expedition, the king of the country, to whom I have already said farewell, sends to inform me that a lion is committing many depredations in neighbouring villages, and that if I wish to try to kill it he will give me immediately all the men necessary for a " battue." As it will, after all, only mean being late a day or two, and will give me an opportunity of adding a fresh trophy to my collection

I let the expedition start, telling my comrades not to hurry, and to wait for me at a certain spot on a fixed date if I have not overtaken them.

I proceed to the village of Kamsikiri, on the Ponfi, where the lion has been reported to me, arriving there in the evening. The chief tells me that he has received orders and that there are many men ready to set out with me in the morning. The lion, which has already on his conscience the deaths of two women, a man, and some dogs, continues the series of his exploits that very night. The night is as black as pitch, and he profits by it to break open the low roof of a hut, and after having killed the five goats inside, eats one of them on the spot, being unable to carry it off. He does all this without the least noise. All the goats are bitten either on the neck or on the withers, but nowhere else, from which it is evident that the lion has been only playing with them. His lair is situated a short distance from the village, and the natives have made two "battues" without seeing him in the dense beds of reeds where he hides.

In the morning I observe that out of eighty men seventy-two have cap-guns. My first impulse is not to accompany them, because I know that kind of "battue"; it was not the first at which I had assisted, and I was determined that the former occasion was to be the last. I have asked the men to leave their weapons at the village; but they have answered, naturally, that they need them in case of danger, a reason which seems very just at first but is worth

nothing when one reflects on the use to which the
blacks are capable of putting their weapons. Their
first movement upon meeting a lion at bay, face to
face, is to throw down their guns or to take to
their heels, or, if they fire, to fire in haste, without
putting their guns to the shoulder, and thus missing to a certainty. They have not even an idea
of using the butt, so that a gun in their hands
is as much good as a reed-pipe. For the very
reason of their inferiority through lack of preparation, it is certain that these people have much merit
in attacking, half-naked — one might say, weapon-
less—a redoubtable animal; but an assagai is ten
times better for them, because it is their natural
weapon, and they are all accustomed to use it. Their
instinct to defend themselves would accomplish the
rest, and the lion would be riddled by well-directed
assagais. That is what happens in regions where
powder is rare; but at Makanga, where there is not
a man who has not a gun in view of war, they would
not miss such an excellent opportunity to make use
of it, and it is hardly probable that amid such
circumstances they would leave their rifles at home
to take their assagais.

As I just said, my first impulse is to refuse to
accompany this badly disciplined band, but it would
not be very easy to make them understand my
real reasons. Besides, I shall succeed perhaps in
organising the " battue." With this object I explain to my men by demonstration on the spot
that I desire them to form themselves into the

shape of a horse-shoe, at the toe of which I shall place myself; and that, should the lion be found to be in the middle, they must join the two branches of the horse-shoe to close the opening, and turn away from me so as to allow the animal an exit in the middle of which I shall alone be stationed. I advise them, also, only to fire in case of legitimate defence, and above all when nobody is in front of them.

This being well understood, we proceed to the place where the animal is supposed to be : in fact, we recognise tracks there. Then the men silently spread themselves out as has been arranged, around the bed of reeds. Ten tom-toms which the chief has thought well to add, which prudently keep behind the beaters, along whose line they are scattered, beat with re-doubled blows.

The first ten minutes pass without event; but the men on the left soon cry out, and we understand that the animal has been seen. As it is said to be going forward—that is, in the same direction as our-selves—I stop them for a moment, and, leaving my post, run rapidly outside the line of men to the opening of the horse-shoe in order to see the animal, if it continues to advance. I make the beaters close up. My men, scattered among the natives, make them carry out my orders; Tambarika alone accompanies me. Up to the present all is well. At a certain spot the reeds are overhung by lianas and large trees, with the result that everybody is in the midst of dense vegetation : we are in semi-darkness, and it is at this very moment that the lion tries to break the line to the right. Immediately gun-shots come from that side; then it is reported that the lion comes from the left, and the men on the left fire. Soon the uproar becomes indescribable. The cloud of smoke which has collected prevents one seeing; cries and reports prevent one hearing; and the roaring of the lion increases the general disorder. The *mêlée* is complete : one might think oneself on a battlefield.

At this moment my sense of humour gets the better of me, and I am seized with a fit of laughter to think of all those idiots who hear nothing and do not know even what they are doing. But I soon finish laughing. Bullets come whistling above my head, by my side, everywhere; and a piece of iron passing with a dry noise near my ear strikes the trunk of a tree, behind which I take shelter immediately with Tambarika. During the space of ten minutes the seventy-two muzzle-loaders are fired, loaded, and again discharged. Two more bullets strike my shelter; others pass by with a prolonged *bzz.* . . . At last the cries cease, the smoke clears away, and I understand that the hunt is abandoned. My men come to tell me what happened. The lion tried to find an opening at several points of the line time after time, and the shots drove him back. But he took advantage of a breach in the human barrier and escaped by the place we entered, without, apparently, having been wounded. Not so the natives, eleven of whom are wounded, two of them seriously. This is an extraordinarily moderate number, considering that eighty men formed a circle of 50 yards, towards the centre of which they fired, fortunately rather high, from all points of the circumference during a quarter of an hour. My men are uninjured, or hardly injured at all, having thrown themselves on their stomachs as soon as the fusillade began. However, Tchigallo has had his hair singed by a shot which was fired point blank a few inches from his head, and Rodzani has sustained a graze on his leg.

As to the lion, he runs still, and we have not seen a drop of blood on the track. Had he come up to me I should have no more seen him than I saw my neighbours : the smoke would have prevented me.

Such are the advantages—many, as you see—of a "battue" with natives armed with guns. I do not mind risking my skin in a good cause; but to be killed foolishly by a stray bullet, to fall a victim to the rifle of a native who makes a mistake, would be too ridiculous.

I have handled firearms continually, day and night, without accident ever happening to me, a fact which is owing to great precautions on my part and to similar habits which I have taught those who accompany me. I do not allow them to carry on their shoulders a rifle with hammers at full-cock, which would endanger the lives of those who follow, and I require that a loaded rifle should be carried always on the shoulder in the normal position—that is, with the butt in front. I cannot censure too much the habit which natives have, and some Europeans tolerate, of carrying a rifle with its butt behind, under the pretext that the weapon is better balanced. Leaving out of consideration the fact that perspiration from the hand rusts the barrels, if, unfortunately, the hammers are at full-cock a branch is quite sufficient when on the march to discharge the weapon. And then let those who are in front beware! Have we not enough enemies in Africa already, fever, sickness, anæmia, and animals, without having to fear a violent and unexpected death through the clumsiness of a servant?

Let us return to our lion. He was, doubtless, too singed for there to be a chance of again surrounding him. Muzzle-loaders would have had to be left at the village and the assagai would have had to be the only weapon allowed to ensure success. But that was impossible. I gave up the undertaking and left them to get out of their difficulties alone. Since this adventure I have laid down the following conditions each time that I have had to track a man-eater: no guns, but clubs, assagais, and arrows, and drums as many as they like. I have said already that natives never attack the lion which lives normally: when they meet it they give way to it: it is usual, on the other hand, to destroy at all cost lions which attack the inhabitants.[1] I left that work for them to do and overtook my expedition three days later.

This period was particularly fertile in adventures with lions. In fact, during April I met with several

[1] See *Mes Grandes Chasses*, pp. 207, 208.

as related in the preceding chapter, and at the end of the same month a lion wounded one of our men and destroyed much baggage, clothing, and utensils. It was at the opening of May that we had the fine "battue" I have just related, which almost assumed the proportions of a massacre. Finally, during May I experienced, on a certain night, a series of vicissitudes which I shall relate farther on. On the other hand, sometimes you may remain four or five months in regions where lions abound without even meeting one although you beat the bush the whole day and hear them at night. It is a matter of chance.

The expedition continues its studies and exploration to the west of the Kapoche, a region which is almost destitute of water during the dry season, and, consequently, little frequented by fauna. Our stay there is of short duration. We then go to the southwest, across a very mountainous region where game is rare, and we move to the west of Undi (of sad memory), about five days' march from Mbazi Mountain.[1] I meet there with the tracks of many rhinoceros, and pitch my camp for a few days to try my luck. The only other animals are a few roan antelopes. This country is very uneven, consequently very fatiguing; there are ravines, river-beds, with perpendicular banks, hillocks, hills, and mountains to wind round or to climb, making you think that you are hunting chamois or bears rather than rhinoceros. The rhinoceros, however, are fond of

---

[1] See *Mes Grandes Chasses*, pp. 134, 135, etc.

these wild and tranquil places, and, if they do not venture on to the mountainous parts, at least they frequent the hillocks whose stony soil, whether it be sparsely or thickly covered with vegetation, suits them equally well.

For several days we follow, without any result whatever, rhinoceros' tracks made during the night; these animals continue their march in the morning because of the cloudy, rainy weather, describing interminable circumvolutions and incessant detours. On account of its wandering habits, its continual passing to and fro, the rhinoceros has been styled by the natives by the name of *pembere,* a word which comes from the verb *kupembera*—that is, "to turn." Having noticed that several tracks finish almost regularly in the direction of a range of very wooded hills situated two hours' distant to the north of our camp, we pass a night there so as to be on the spot at daybreak. Setting off in the morning we soon find fresh footprints, which we follow for half an hour and then abandon to follow others which we see on the way, belonging to an animal a little larger than ours. Happy inspiration! In a minute we discover the fresh, unbroken dung of a rhinoceros:[1] when the dung is found unbroken the animal cannot be far off, his habit being never to leave the places where he has deposited excrement without returning there a short time afterwards to scatter it in every direction with his horn. Why does he

---

[1] This dung resembles that of a horse, but it is much larger, like that of the hippopotamus and elephant.

do this? Through instinct of self-preservation and because he knows that these traces left behind him make known his presence? I am totally ignorant. The fact remains that he never neglects to perform this little act. Sometimes he does not do it at the very time, he walks about in the neighbourhood; but he returns invariably to the place where he has left these traces and never leaves it until he has crushed them.[1]

As the rhinoceros cannot be far away, I consider it prudent to be on my guard. I believe, in fact, that the rhinoceros is the only animal which rushes at man without provocation. According to certain hunters, it only "seems to rush at you": it does not rush at you, they say: "it tries simply to run away in any direction in its fright caused by your smell." That is playing with words. Nobody has ever been able to analyse the sensations of a rhinoceros at the psychological moment when he charges; but I have noticed several times that when a rhinoceros has scented you, he beats the bush around you like a pointer, and makes for you as soon as he has got wind of you. During our stay at Niarugwe Camp a rhinoceros charged us twice consecutively. Sometimes also, it is true, the animal has gone off without charging; but that is the exception.[2]

We shall have to return to the habits of this strange animal, and those of other denizens of the forest; but

---

[1] The natives say that the animal is so vicious that it even gets into a rage with its own dung.

[2] That was the opinion of Sir Samuel Baker. See *The Nile Tributaries of Abyssinia*, small edition, p. 246.

I have said enough to make it clear why, seeing the unbroken rhinoceros' dung on the ground, we thought that a meeting with the animal was imminent. It is well we are on guard, for five minutes have not elapsed before a well-known snorting is heard; but it is impossible to know whence it comes. Kambombe, who climbs up a tree, has no sooner looked around and fixed his eyes upon something, than there comes over his face that nervous expression which I know, and he slides down in haste with the words, "Quick, this way!"

The rhinoceros is behind us! Through extraordinary luck he has not yet scented us, though we believe the wind to be in our faces. We hasten to change our position to a place seven or eight yards on one side. The spot is not much sheltered : there are few trees, but many thick bushes, similar in appearance to oleanders, clustered one against the other. Some of these bushes reach to our waist; but others are taller, and here and there block out the view. Within a radius of ten yards these bushes form a curtain, and (this is one of the peculiarities of the African bush) one can see nothing beyond. This kind of vegetation is very favourable for tracking an antelope, but it is not very suitable with a rhinoceros. Its height is great, it is true; but it holds its head low down, and its vital parts are a yard from the ground.

The dung is on our left on a small empty space, and, consequently, between us and its owner. My intention is not to fire immediately the animal appears. I want to watch attentively how it proceeds, for I believe that the purpose for which it has returned is to occupy its attention, and that it will give us a little example of its habits. The wind is now in our favour. I must add that the ground is stony, and slightly slopes towards the side whence the animal is coming. I load the 303 with two solid bullets, lest I shall have to shoot at the head ; Express No. 1 with solid bullets will do for the body. When this is done we wait hidden behind a bush.

The rhinoceros has not scented us : otherwise, in all probability, it would have charged. The snorting we heard is not repeated. It was very fortunate it snorted at all, because it warned us, and although the sight of dung already announced its return, it was a good thing to know the exact moment. The animal is a long time in appearing : it eats quietly, and draws near little by little. At one moment its back appears ten yards away. . . . One cannot imagine the agreeable emotion which a hunter feels in thus seeing a dangerous animal approach without suspicion.

The head is invisible; however, at a certain moment, it is raised with a distrustful air, and remains motionless. The animal then snorts, continues on its way, and again snorts, showing that it has smelt that we have been there, but has not yet got wind of us. If only it will not take to flight, if only it will not move about too much, and thus enable me to shoot with certainty ! The idea occurs to me to get in front of it in order to hasten the end ; but my men restrain me, as the rhinoceros continues on its way and draws near. Never have I seen the terrible animal so well as on this day. It scratches the earth with its right foot, and with two or three blows with its horn, which are given automatically and with the regularity of a pick-axe, unearths roots, which its prehensile lips tear up and its teeth crush ; its ears move with its jaw, and its small tail swings to the right and left, with the object, on the face of it useless, of driving away the flies. On its back, neck, and flanks, are insectivorous birds which call out, fly, run, and cling like magpies, in search of the many insects which are on the thick skin of the pachyderm. The presence of these birds is the most annoying thing which can happen to me : if one of them flies away or another arrives, we shall be discovered; a cry of danger from one will cause all the others to take to flight, and perhaps also the rhinoceros. So, without further delay, and renouncing the hope of seeing the manner in which it scatters its dung, I raise my Express slowly and aim at the heart. . . . The birds fly away at the report, and with a long neigh, almost a whistle of pain, the rhinoceros mounts the slope of the hill right of the wind at full gallop, without leaving me time to place my second bullet. For some seconds we hear it breaking down the bushes which it encounters, while the stony ground resounds under its feet. As usual, we follow its track immediately. I see soon that, in spite of all my care, I have missed the heart, the blood which we find being fairly abundant, but frothy, which shows that it comes from the lungs. Night comes before we have overtaken our wounded animal. We camp on the very spot where the pursuit is stopped, near a pool of rain-water, and we decide to continue our search at dawn next day. The night is passed with the small comfort which can be obtained from a saucepan, a blanket, and a handful of rice, things which are inseparable from long elephant hunts. And, as there are no lions to be feared, and it is late when we abandon the pursuit, we simply lie down under a tree in the midst of the bush, after lighting fires, which we keep up all night. That is the usual way of resting in these regions when on a journey : encampments with stockades are only established in dangerous countries where an attack is feared, if wild animals are to be dreaded, or if one is going to make a stay sufficiently long to merit the trouble of pitching it—that is, four or five days at the least.

Dawn next day found us on the track of the rhinoceros, and it was not until about nine o'clock in the morning that we discovered its body on the edge of a pool. It must have died on the previous evening almost at the time we were obliged to stop. Its horns were worn out, and its size was ordinary : so, considering the labour it had cost me, I was only half satisfied with my conquest. Rhinoceros in the full force of their strength have horns in perfect state because they grow quicker than they wear away ; but when old age begins, the growth of the horns appears to stop, and they grow shorter and shorter with time. I have killed a very big old female rhinoceros whose horns were completely worn out and only a few inches

SPORT IN THE RHINOCEROS COUNTRY.

long. It is rather a bitter disappointment for a hunter when he sees that he will have nothing to keep belonging to an animal which he has killed. Fortunately, this has not often happened to me, and one of the finest specimens which I have in my collection came from the very region of this last hunt. I spent a fortnight there, and killed four rhinoceros, two of which were very remarkable for size, and had horns measuring, respectively, 23 inches and 12 inches, 25 inches and 13 inches. In the matter of other game, I killed only two or three roan antelopes, a wild boar, and a klipspringer.

This country made a deep impression on me, like the recollection of a region of giants, imposing in its beauty and solitude. One cannot describe the grandeur of certain landscapes in these countries. At the foot of huge mountains are gray rocks of all sizes, scattered over an immense inclined plane; between them is vegetation which grows in the greatest profusion; and in the midst of this wild nature, far from the rest of the world, rhinoceros trample with heavy step those quiet places which their extinct ancestors trampled thousands of years ago. And is not the rhinoceros itself already almost fabulous? Its ugliness, its ever-increasing rarity, its quiet habits, and its unsociability—all contribute to making it a mysterious and strange animal worthier of figuring among mythological monsters, in Scandinavian tales, or in Buddhist fables, than in reality.

Contemplating the calm, majestic nature of that country with its giant two-horned animals, as I have often done, I have imagined myself transported to a legendary world, or else to prehistoric times when cave-dwellers hunted the mastodon for food, and I have thought that soon it will no longer be possible for the hunter, even the richest and bravest in the world, to find himself face to face with these giants, and to inscribe their names on the list of his triumphs.

Those parts of the earth not yet trodden by the foot of man, where nature is left to itself, are becoming more and more rare at the end of the nineteenth century. Future generations will only find in fossils traces of those gigantic animals which an unknown law is sweeping little by little from the face of the globe, giving preference to races smaller and better adapted to lack of space and to the ever-increasing invasion of humanity.

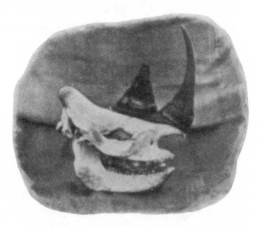

RHINOCEROS SKULL.

A WILD SPOT IN THE BUSH.

CHAPTER VII

SEASONS AND SPORT — AN EARLY MORNING ALARM—
IN THE TALL GRASS

Native information—Absence of elephants in the Undi country—At Mpeseni
—Nocturnal noises—Hyenas — Elephants crossing a river—Alarming
proximity—Trial with the 303—Female animal's rage and charge—
Her death—Capture of a young elephant—Shooting at the head—Last
fruitful elephant hunt in 1895—In the tall grass—Varieties of tall
grass—Death of the little elephant—Difficulty of rearing animals in a
moving camp—Change of country.

WHEN you ask a native upon reaching a village if
there is sport in the vicinity, the question is never
understood in the sense in which you put it. He
answers invariably, "There are waterbuck, koodoos,
elands, wart-hogs, bushbucks, sable antelopes, etc., in
the woods." "Thanks: I know that. But in the
neighbourhood—in fact, near this—is there anything
(nyama)?" "Near here, yes. There are, in the

direction of ——" And a place, generally thirteen miles at the least, is indicated to you with a vague gesture.

Do not insist: they will not tell you any more. So I have given up asking natives for information. The nature of their answers arises from their ignorance of sport, ignorance to which I have alluded already, and also from their desire to be agreeable to you without being able to be so.

In many places where our renown as hunters precedes us, they enter upon this subject even if we do not touch upon it. They think they are flattering our *amour propre* by announcing to us that there are many *nyama* in the neighbourhood. Without giving them time to finish, I begin the sacramental enumeration, in which my men join, in unison: "There are waterbuck, koodoos, elands, wart-hogs, bushbuck, sable antelopes, in the woods." And, without paying attention to our bantering air, they say almost always: "Inde! Inde!"—"Yes, in fact"— looking at each other as much as to say, "They know it already."

It is useless, therefore, to seek for information from that source. However, as it is desirable to know in what to believe, it is my custom to ask first of all in a village if there is a hunter. I summon him as well as other hunters in neighbouring villages if they tell me of them; and, according to their information, either I take them with me as guides, or I send them away with a small present.

As guides they receive good payment if their

report is accurate; but if they have drawn upon their imagination they receive food only—not to count the jokes which the men of the expedition make about them when they see they are disturbed for nothing. When you are a stranger in a district any native can guide you from one point to another; only hunters can show you the places frequented or likely to be frequented by game.

We were rather badly off in the matter of sport in the Undi district. Formerly animals were very plentiful everywhere, but to-day their traces disappear in proportion as you get away from the Zambesi. This country has been explored by thousands of natives, who were sent out in all directions every year by the Tete ivory merchants, the result of this war without quarter being that elephants have departed for ever from this dangerous zone. With the exception of a few rhinoceros and a dozen antelopes, our journey was fruitless.[1] I will take the reader, therefore, to the end of the rainy season —that is, in June—on the return from that journey.

We are on the Upper Kapoche, a few days' journey north of our former Niarugwe camp on the territory of the chief Mpeseni. As the dry season is approaching, elephants will be fewer and more difficult to follow. The character of sport is about to change completely.

From the hunter's point of view the seasons are divided in these regions, that is, south of the equator, into three well-defined periods, as follows :—

[1] See *Mes Grandes Chasses*, p. 275.

December, January, February, and March: rain and tall grass. Animals are invisible, lost in the dense vegetation; water is abundant; everywhere are streams, rivers, rain-water pools, and marshes. Antelopes are very rarely seen; big animals travel little; elephants linger in marshy regions. It is the time when the elephant, the rhinoceros, and the buffalo are hunted in preference to other denizens of the woods.

April, May, June, and July: showery weather and tall grass, more or less dried up. It is impossible to walk in the bush without making a noise by brushing against the grass. Despite all precautions, you announce your presence; moreover, being ignorant of the position of animals, you run the risk of being scented. Elephants begin to travel; rhinoceros get under shelter at dawn; antelopes are invisible. This is the most disagreeable and least fruitful period for sport. Rain-water pools and marshes have disappeared, and rivers begin to go down.

August, September, October, and November: dryness. Fire clears the greater part of the country and burns the grass, leaving everywhere only trees, bushes, and shrubs, surrounded by a carpet of ashes which changes in November into a green carpet.[1] Animals can be seen distinctly; large animals seek wooded places, impenetrable to the light, which the fire has spared; antelopes collect in districts where there are drinking places. Water becomes scarcer and scarcer, especially towards the end of November, and night-watches can be made with success. During the

---

[1] See *Mes Grandes Chasses*, pp. 122, 202, 237, and 241.

day the absence of leaves and of shade makes the heat overwhelming. This is the time for hunting antelopes.

Having, therefore, hunted the elephant and the rhinoceros during the rainy reason, I prepared during the dry season to collect for the Paris Museum, preferably antelopes and small animals. As seen, you can succeed or fail completely according to the time chosen for such or such sport. One may say that elephant-hunting during the dry season is only accidental. Excessively toilsome is it, too, the animal only travelling at night and early in the morning; it is during the heat of the day, when it is resting, that its track must be followed. It will be seen that we had a few examples of this; but I will not anticipate. I return to the Mpeseni country at the end of the rainy season, and at a time when it is covered with grass, no longer green but half dry and rustling, —where I have no great hope of success as far as pachydermata are concerned.

After exchanging presents and compliments with Samba Mropa, one of King Mpeseni's ministers, whose residence is near, I camp on the banks of a small stream, the Ntsatso, which flows into the Luiya. Our stay in this district opens with a period of the most abject failure, during which my men eat all my sardines, for I am obliged to give them something in place of meat. I must ask the reader to excuse my passing over these few days of bad luck [1] which is

---

[1] Some friends reproached me, upon the publication of *Mes Grandes Chasses*, for having mentioned successes in my narratives without speak-

inexplicable, because the region is deserted and quiet. True, the season for *fulas* and *matondos* is over; but there remains the *migbalamgbw*, or fan-palm (hyphœnœ), loaded with fruit, of which the elephant is very fond. We snare a few guinea-fowls, which keep the pot boiling; and we fish a little in the Luiya, hardly 400 yards from our encampment.

One morning about half-past three o'clock, and the moon shining brightly, repeated elephant trumpetings ring out in the direction of the river. When they play at the edge of the water and think they are in security, these animals express their joy by cries which may be likened unto cavalry trumpet-blasts.

Awakened with a start, we hastily fit ourselves out and proceed through the tall grass in the direction in which the cries seem to come. Unfortunately, upon arriving at the edge of the Luiya we perceive that the elephants are on the opposite side; we cannot see them, because of the vegetation and the steepness of the bank; but we hear them distinctly. The river being very deep at this point and its breadth exceeding 100 yards, what is to be done? Swim across, you are going to tell me. Impossible. First of all,

---

ing of the checks and inconveniences which I must have necessarily experienced. I must admit that I did this designedly, because to enumerate all the animals I have missed would have made the book too long. The following rule may be made in this matter : A good hunter, however careful, adroit, or well seconded he may be, must count one out of every two animals which he pursues as lost, owing to the many difficulties of his profession. This is the minimum, for how many wound or miss three or four animals before killing one ! It would, therefore, be absurd to describe all the hunts, marches, and counter-marches which have ended in nothing.

we have rifles, which are injured by water; and
then, African rivers swarm with voracious, silent
animals, very unengaging in appearance—crocodiles.
It is wise, even, not to stand on the sandy
bank gazing at the sky, for you may be awakened
from your dream in a most disagreeable manner.
So, without lingering on this spot, we return and
decide on a means of crossing. There is no canoe;
but some distance up-stream there is a ford by means
of which we crossed the day before, or the day before
that, in search of game. We proceed thither without delay, as may well be understood, almost
running; and at daybreak we reach the place where
the elephants are. A crashing, a crackling of broken
branches, tells us that they are still in the neighbourhood but lower down stream. In fact, we hear them
moving about noisily in the reeds which border the
river. As the wind is coming up the valley, we keep
ourselves always above stream and follow the elephants for a time; but they out-distance us, owing to
a large pool which obliges us to make a detour, and
when we arrive on the bank again we see them
in the middle of the river in the act of crossing it,
more than 150 yards from where we stand. It would
do no good to fire; besides, at a certain moment, the
elephants bury themselves completely with the exception of their trunks, and walk on the bed of the
river. The spectacle offered us by these trunks, similar
to large snakes whose heads alone emerge and turn
all in the same direction, is exceedingly curious.
Slowly the enormous animals walk, leaving a track in

the current. In a few minutes, the bed sloping upwards, they reascend and reappear one after the other, black and streaming, on the bank. I count seven of them, including two old males and a young elephant. The last-named springs into the river when nearly all the others have landed, and its mother supports it with her trunk while it swims ahead of her.

We remain where we are, waiting to see which direction the elephants will take. If they remount the stream we have lost them, because they will scent the camp in ten minutes; if they descend, our resource is to follow them until we have found a ferry. But, far from pressing themselves, they seem to take a pleasure in tarrying in the wet reeds at this early hour.

Sighting a somewhat narrow part of the river down stream where the large stones which encumber the bed are a little closer together, we have rather violent exercise in jumping from one to the other. Taking a partial bath, we ourselves cross the river and rejoin at full speed the track of our elephants. We are in such a hurry that we find ourselves (in the reeds) in the very midst of the animals, without, however, seeing them. These reeds, about three yards high, have pointed leaves which tear the skin, and we have great difficulty in making our way through; their bed is made of lianas and dry entangled reeds, hanging from which are the delicious *tchitedze* (mucuna pruriens) or nettle-beans, which you cannot brush against without remembering it. It is impossible to see six yards before us; the noise made by the elephants clearly indicates that they are very near, but I do not suspect that they surround me when, suddenly, behind me to the right, almost within arm's length, an enormous gray serpent winds itself around the reeds, tears them up, and carries them away with their roots full of sand and earth. At the same time I make out the head of an elephant quietly taking his breakfast! Never in my life have I seen one so near and so distinctly. I see his brown eye, the hairs on his lower lip, and his tusks, which are white, polished, and a fair size. "It is the male," says Tambarika, in my ear: "let us be quick, he will scent us!" At the same moment I myself think that we cannot draw back: I must aim at the head. Besides, if I recede a step I shall no longer see him. In half a second, and while the elephant swallows the armful of reeds as though it were a baking of macaroni, I substitute two solid bullets for the hollow ones which were in my 303, and, having cocked the 8-bore, place it in the hands of Msiambiri within arm's reach. When bringing my rifle to my shoulder, I say to my men, "Which way shall we run after the shot?" "That way," they answer, pointing to the Luiya, "and then to the right." "Good! . . . Here goes for the eye and the opening of the ear: . . . there, right in the middle . . .!"

While we run at full speed towards the river bank, where the ground is more open, a trumpet-blast on our left and the crackling of broken reeds warn us of a charge. . . . Hardly have we reached it and turned to the right than an elephant appears on our heels, and, carried on by its momentum, enters the water, in which it flounders, continuing, with ears erect and trunk twisted, to cry out, and endeavouring to recover our scent, which it has lost because of our sharp turn to the right. Instinctively we have plunged into the reeds as soon as it entered the river, so as not to be discovered; but we are only imperfectly hidden. . . . We observe that it is the female which charged us, doubtless to protect her young one, which it thought in danger. She is alarmingly near, and yet if we move she will see us! . . . She retreats and then advances towards us. . . . Ah! she sees us! . . . It is a choice between two dangers: better fire at her at once. As I have my 8-bore still in my hand (I took it immediately after firing), I fire a shot which misses the heart, wounds her on the shoulder, and increases her anger. She turns straight in our direction, facing the smoke, and this time really sees us. If she charges it will be impossible to flee into the entangled reeds. . . . "Fire again, *sapristi!*" I say to myself, and my bullet, passing under her twisted trunk, strikes her full in the breast at the base of the neck. . . . She turns aside, stunned. . . . I see that she is wounded to death. . . . Poor beast! . . . Never have I been able to contemplate so near the death of an elephant in all its details. She is lying eight yards from us in the full sunlight at the edge of the water, which is tinged with red, and we look on in silence while life leaves the enormous body; her flank

FEMALE ELEPHANT ABOUT TO CHARGE.

heaves, blood flows from breast and shoulder, her
mouth opens and shuts, her lip trembles, tears flow
from her eyes, her limbs quiver; with her trunk
hanging down, her head low, she sways to right and
left, then falls heavily on one side, shaking the ground
and spattering blood in every direction. . . . All is
over !

Such a spectacle is enough to make the most
hardened hunter feel remorse.   It seemed to me that
I had done a bad action.   Several times have I said
to myself, upon seeing these splendid animals suffer,
that I ought to place my rifle in the gun-rack for
ever.

But this time, at least, it was the animal which
provoked us.   If I had had a one-barrelled rifle only,
we were certainly lost : I had not the time to change
it, and to move would have been to betray our position.   Immediately the first shot was fired was she
not inclined to charge on the smoke ?   My two bullets
fortunately followed each other at two or three seconds'
interval; otherwise the animal would have been upon
us in two strides, and would have trampled one
of us under foot while the others plunged into the
reeds.   I do not really know which is the more
terrible alternative in those moments—to run at the
risk of bringing down upon your head the rage of the
animal which is looking for you, or else to remain
quiet with a very good chance of being discovered,
and not escaping from the fate which awaits you.
One must always beware of female elephants
which are feeding their young, especially females

without tusks,[1] because they charge almost always, and sometimes without other provocation than a shout or the report of a rifle. I did, indeed, think of that for a moment when we entered the reeds; but the sudden appearance of our old male had surprised me, and, in great danger of being smelt, forced me to act immediately. I had forgotten that the female was perhaps a few steps away; which was the case, since she entered the thicket the last of all.

As soon as the female falls we think of going to see the result of my first shot, or rather my two first shots, because I fired two at the head of the male elephant; but the idea suddenly strikes us that, although the elephants have fled a long time ago, the young one will not perhaps leave its mother—it will return assuredly. Above all things, we must decide upon a means of capturing it. The fan-palms are not far away and their leaves will furnish us with a first-class rope : so I send all the men to cut them, advising them to go by the water's edge in order not to disturb the young elephant if he is in the reeds. Hardly have my men left than I hear an animal walking and breaking the reeds, first behind me and then on the left. It is the young elephant, which arrives at the water's edge and stops before its mother's body.

Its appearance is somewhat comical. Its skin appears to be much too big for it, and to fall in folds everywhere; one would say that it had put on the coat and trousers of its elder brother. Its ears

[1] See *Mes Grandes Chasses*, p. 290.

appear, I do not know why, bigger than necessary, and its little trunk makes a thousand contortions, does not stop for a moment; at each side of its mouth are two white points as thick as the finger, indicating future tusks; and its eyes are light. There is something comical and sportive in its physiognomy which I cannot express. This roguish fellow, whose height I took later, measured 3 feet 10 inches.

Without understanding why its mother is thus lying on the sand, it comes to her side, enters the water, comes out again, and plays all kinds of tricks, throwing water, wet sand, and gravel in every direction. Two or three crocodiles, attracted by blood, appear near the bank. If only the heedless young thing does not again venture into the water, and fall a victim to some nasty trick! Suppose I show myself? But how will it take my presence? If it wants to flee I really shall not know how to prevent it. Meantime my men at last appear, and after having stopped a moment to contemplate from a distance the orphan's gambols, they begin to make a rope, hidden by a bush. We must bring the business to a head. I imitate the cry of the sparrow-hawk, a call understood between us; and one of the natives comes to me skirting the reeds, the young elephant seeing him distinctly, but, being unable to scent him, appearing not to mind his presence. Seeing this, instead of continuing to conceal myself, I leave my hiding-place and walk about on the sand to leeward; finally I sit down, so as not to frighten it by my movements. Once it looks at me, raises its trunk as though to scent me, and draws near a few steps, its ears open ; then, changing its mind, it turns its back on me and continues to amuse itself.

At last the rope arrives, and the attempts to capture the animal begin. Young as he is, the tender nursling easily knocks us over with its head ; as to its feet, they are as heavy as those of a horse, and must be carefully avoided. But I believe that at bottom he wishes more to amuse himself than to escape, and he submits to it with a good grace. We end by passing a strong rope round its neck and forefeet, and tethering it to a tree. I send to the camp for condensed milk and the additional staff.

Let us now see what has become of the first elephant. Returning into the thicket, we advance with precaution towards the place where I opened hostilities. In the midst of the broken reeds lies a gray mass stretched on its right side, and in its temple are two minute holes, clear-cut as though by a punch, from which flow two small streams of blood. The dead elephant is enormous, and its tusks (weighing fifty-two pounds and a half each), are very fine.

Not often have I had such an occasion of firing at the head with success. How many times in succession have I not tried this shot without other result than bleeding the animal or exasperating it ! A rather interesting study is to be written on the question of the shot at the head, and I intend to return to it in one of the chapters which follow.

This elephant hunt was the last of the rainy season of 1895, or rather the last which was successful. A few days later, in fact, we were destined to find ourselves again in terrifying proximity with elephants, amid circumstances which I will relate briefly.

Fairly late in the morning, we strike a track two or three good leagues above the camp, and we only come upon our game about four o'clock in the afternoon, after a forced march of twenty miles. The country into which the hazards of the chase have led us differs from that where we are encamped; it is a succession of wide plains covered naturally with tall grass, and we reach it by a gentle slope. There, on the edge of the plains, we discover dung which the men find by feeling it with their feet to be still warm. Attention! Elephants are not far away. We march through grass more than 8 feet high, in which the elephants (ten or twelve of them) have made parallel paths. It is impossible to see, and we walk through the grass exactly like blind men. The wind is unfavourable. At a certain moment we hear, at first indistinctly, then very clearly and near to, a powerful rumbling, then another, resembling a boiler which is getting up steam. The natives believe that it is the elephants' stomachs which make this noise; I do not know. I confine myself to relating the fact. This rumbling, or powerful roar, is intermittent. Is this the means by which elephants communicate with one another? I cannot say; but it is only when quite near the animal that you hear it. We are, therefore, literally between their legs. I get on Rodzani's shoulders, and hardly are my eyes on a level with the top of the grass when I cry, "Run, *sapristi!* we are too near! They have scented us!" In fact, elephants are in movement a few yards from us on all sides. I saw their backs on a level with the grass, nothing more; but I know that the alarm was given. We withdraw just in time not to be stamped under foot by the herd, which is in flight. Unknown to us, elephants were on our right, and they scented us at the very moment I put my head out.

Here, then, was a herd of twelve elephants in the grass with us at our very side, and we had not seen even one of them, with the exception of the few backs of which I caught a glimpse. Deny that nature protects animals of all sizes! In the brushwood of African forests the elephant is as well hidden as a mouse in the lawn-grass.

After reflection we thought one other thing contributed to awaken the elephants' suspicions — the nature of the grass in which we were walking. From the month of May it is very rustling, and you cannot walk through it without betraying your presence. We were very near the elephants; they must have stopped, and their ear, however imperfect it may be, must have heard the rustling of the dry stalks. The natives call this grass *tchigonankondo*—that is, "where warriors sleep" when they fear being surprised by the enemy.

Do not think that the expression "grassy plain" means flat expanses covered with a species of uniform grass, or you will belittle the richness of these countries. The grasses are various, and hunters

are obliged to know the different species, because
they all have peculiarities more or less troublesome. Thus the *tchigonankondo* makes a noise
which is heard a long way off; the *nsandje* also,
but it is not so long, rarely exceeding the height
of a man. The date of an elephant track is
most difficult to recognise in the *nsandje*. The
niumbo, with which the thatch of roofs[1] is made, is
very tall, but makes little noise; the *kadiambidzi*[2]
has a long, thin stalk, and grows in little tufts 2 feet
high, with spaces between them, leaving the earth in
view; the *tsekera*, or *tchipeta*, which has a large stalk
as thick as a penholder, grows 8 feet high in wet
places. The latter is fire-proof. The *sont'e*, a short,
broad, cutting, supple grass, is much liked by buffaloes;
the *ruba* is a small, red, rare grass which grows in
sandy forests; the *nsidzi* leaves a multitude of small,
prickly, bearded burrs sticking to your skin or clothes,
which must be taken out one by one from the
cloth; and the *lincotche* is sought for by guinea-
fowls. There are many more, which the man of the
woods will get to know.

Our little elephant was completely domesticated
after four or five days of camp life. It required
on the average eight tins of condensed milk a
day, and my stock was not long in running out.
I sent to headquarters for other tins; and to feed
it until they arrived—that is, during a period of ten
days,—I tried to buy one or two cows from Mpeseni.

---

[1] Hence the native name for hut, *niumba*.
[2] That is, "which zebras eat."

But they came too late. After trying paste, which did not suit it, then chopped grass, which suited it still less, I gave it Liebig, biscuits, flour, everything which I could make it swallow; but it needed its mother's milk, and died before our eyes. Moreover, it was suffering from inflammation of the bowels when captured, and all my endeavours to cure it were not equal to the precautions which its mother would have

BERTRAND AND THE BABY ELEPHANT.

taken. It died one night to my great regret, having lived with us for twelve days. It was beginning to understand very well when the men called it *ndjovo*—*i.e.*, elephant.

How many times have Bertrand and I not given all our care and attention to the rearing of animals? We have never succeeded. Excepting monkeys, all have died. I have had zebras, hartebeests, reed-bucks, blue-bucks, lions, civet-cats, wild-cats, etc. It was useless! Something fatal always happens to them, which arises from the fact that one cannot take care of them as they ought to be taken care of. They must be spared marches, fatigue, and transportation, — precautions which cannot be taken on an expedition.

The Luiya camp was abandoned as soon as the biltong was dry. Until the period of fires it was necessary to look for a country less thickly covered with vegetation. I decided to proceed to the north of Makanga, into the *mitsagnas* (mopanes) woods, where the grass — the *ruba* to which I have referred — is short, and game remains morning and night. This was to help us to await the dry season, and to allow me to collect for the Museum certain rodents which are found in this kind of forest only.

CHAPTER VIII

NATIVE DOGS IN LION-HUNTING—THE AFRICAN WOLF —EUROPEAN DOGS—JACKALS AND HYENAS

Attempts to train native dogs—Services which they have rendered in Austral Africa—Uselessness of the horse in these regions—Effect of a wounded lion on my pack—End of the pack—African wolf enemy of the lion—Wolf's stratagem with crocodiles—Its method of hunting—Uselessness of the European dog—Jackals and hyenas.

AT this period, about the middle of 1895, I was already engaged in looking in the district for dogs intelligent and brave enough to assist me. With this object I offered large prices for sporting dogs, so as to induce natives to bring me animals which showed the required qualities. The natives of Makanga, Magandja, and other countries in this region have always used dogs for hunting the agouti, and some even for the wart-hog.

The agouti, which is the size of a rabbit, lives on grassy expanses; at the time of the first fires dogs are used to dislodge it, and it is then riddled with arrows. Agoutis being very plentiful, this sport is much liked by the natives, who, moreover, are very fond (well they may be) of the flesh of the *tchenzi*, as the animal is called. The native dog is small, with straight ears and pointed muzzle of the Kabyle type; it follows the agouti with pleasure. Hunting the wart-hog consists, on the contrary, in forcing it to pursue and to hang on to the animal's ears. Dogs which are capable of this are very rare. Very rare, also, are those which know how to track antelopes. It was for dogs coming under these last two categories that I had offered a large sum. Several were brought to me, which I did not buy, of course, until after a trial; and, at the time at which this chapter opens, I was possessed of a pack of four dogs which were, without a doubt, the best in the district.

They were far from realising the qualities of those which one finds in Austral Africa; but I counted upon making them of service by force of patience. They were excellent for tracking an antelope, especially if the animal was wounded; but we did not need them for that. On the other hand, they made a noise, snifted, and announced our approach. My men and I could follow the track as quickly as they and without all these inconveniences. What I wanted to teach them was to beat the bush without noise and to warn us of the presence of dangerous animals, or else, if they were incapable of discovering them, to assist us in finding them again when wounded. I spent much time and patience in training them, awaiting the occasion to make them acquainted with the game which preferably I intended them to hunt.

Five hunters and four dogs make a becoming retinue. Alas! as we shall see, I was far from having realised my dream—at the most my dogs were good for ornamenting the camp. They were unable to walk for two hours without hanging out their tongues, and water was to be carried expressly for them to revive them *en route*. This would not have mattered if they had been of service; but how wretched was the behaviour of my pack, and what a miserable, though well-merited, end it met with! I shall have to return to the matter. Several months went by before I was able to convince myself of the uselessness of my labours, and to demonstrate that the dog of Central Africa resembles his congener of the south in nothing.

Gordon-Cumming, Selous, Kirby, and many others have obtained inestimable services from the latter in Austral Africa. The first-named even used it in elephant-hunting; the second owes a good number of lions to it; the third says that he never shot a leopard without the assistance of his pack. Moreover, in those flat countries they were always on horseback, which considerably reduced distances and fatigue for them. I myself could not use a horse, for various reasons: first of all because of the uneven character of the ground (everywhere were ditches, *crevasses*, hyena and ant-eater burrows, and wild-boars' holes) ; then because of the density of the vegetation, which would have prevented a quick pace, the low branches, roots on a level with the ground, etc. ; and, finally, the prevalence of the tsetse fly.[1] Without uselessly exposing the dogs to the bite of the tsetse by taking them with me into infected places, I could have wished to count at least on their help in case of need, and then for important and dangerous searches I should have sent for them to the camp.

I had been in possession of my dogs for nearly three months, and I had great hopes of them, when the time at which the season is at its driest came.

As soon as water is very scarce I profit by it—as I have said above in speaking of the seasons—to lie in watch for animals, preferably at night. Furnished with my electric projector, I take up a position on the edge of a pool with my back to a tree, to leeward if possible, and a little higher than the surface of the water. Then I wait for the animals to come. One night, the tenth which I had passed in that manner, two lions came to drink; but, the projector working badly, I was unable to fire with ease, and at the risk of placing my men and myself in the most dangerous position, I managed only to wound both animals. In the morning the first was found dead fifty yards from the pool ; the second had de-camped after losing much blood. I sent immediately

[1] See *Mes Grandes Chasses*, pp. 29, 30, 31, etc.

to the camp for the dogs to pursue it, rubbing my hands like a man certain of success.

As soon as the pack arrived I gave orders that the dogs should be leashed, and put on the scent. I might as well have let them go, because they had no sooner smelt blood and saw the kind of game with which we wished them to come to close quarters, than, in perfect accord, they put their tails between their legs and slinked behind those who held them. Exhortations and petting were useless, like everything else; the more they were made to smell the track the more they showed signs of fear; and they would have been dragged by the neck rather than advance a step. After expending so much patience on them I was seized with anger. I would willingly have killed them one after the other. They were then taken near the dead lion, where, terror-stricken, they tried to run away, and began to bark, and to roll over in an ignoble exhibition of fear.[1]

We had to do without their assistance. As to the wounded lion, we were, to our great regret, never able to find it, notwithstanding a pursuit full of danger through the dense and dark vegetation. Judging from the blood on the track, we thought it would be strange if it survived its wound. It is annoying to lose an antelope, but you can find another; to lose a lion is an irreparable misfortune for a hunter.

---

[1] A few days afterwards the scent of a wounded leopard, on the track of which they were put, produced the same effect upon them. At night, if lions or other wild beasts prowled around the camp, far from barking they hid themselves in their terror in a tent or behind the men's legs. They were useless even to keep guard.

As soon as they were recognised to be useless the dogs became superfluous mouths at the camp, and I decided to get rid of them. Two saved me the trouble. One of them was snapped up by a crocodile one morning when he was imprudently drinking on the banks of the Revugwe, and disappeared for ever with a piercing cry ; the other died from the bite of the tsetse. The two survivors became the property (fortunate possessors!) of the natives of a village, until a nocturnal leopard finished them, as happens to the majority of dogs in certain mountainous regions. Hence, perhaps, their instinctive repulsion for great carnivora.

If the dogs of these countries are useless for pursuing dangerous animals, what marvellous hunters, on the other hand, are their elder brothers the African wolves! What boldness, perseverance, and tenacity they show! Nothing is more interesting than to see them hunting on their own account, and at their own risk and peril, without horns, or red coats, or whippers-in.[1]

During my last stay in these regions I had occasion frequently to see them at work. I was present at only a few of their hunts; but I learnt some new and curious details about them, which I will add to the information already given about these animals, completing the very striking portrait which the pencil of M. Mahler has drawn in *Mes Grandes Chasses dans l'Afrique Centrale*.

Experience has shown me that they attack not only

[1] See *Mes Grandes Chasses*, pp. 166, 167, 200.

all animals of medium size, but also the lion itself.[1]
They wage terrible battles, in which the lion suc-
cumbs to number, though not without having ripped
open some of the enemy. But the survivors in their
turn soon tear it. Consequently, the large ravenous
beast has a salutary terror of them.[2]

One twilight evening after an elephant hunt which
we had abandoned, my men and I found ourselves
in an unknown and uninhabited region. Fauna, consequently, were abundant. Near a pool of water
where we had decided to camp were many spoor
of lions. I was too tired to try a night-watch; in
spite of all the lions of the earth, I should certainly
have fallen asleep. So, in a few minutes, we made with
a hatchet a small entrenchment, inside which we got
ready to pass the night; a camp smaller than that
which I have already described—that is, a stockade and
a rustic door (for there were only eight of us). While
cutting branches and trees my men perceived a bees'
nest fifty yards from the camp. As these insects
are much less enterprising at night, the natives prefer
to await that time to dislodge them, and take possession of their honey without suffering too much from
stings. When the camp was established (night had
come, and the fires were lit) Rodzani, Tchigallo, and
Msiambiri took dry straw and firebrands, and went
out to gather in the coveted booty. I had remained
at the camp with Tambarika and the two bearers of

[1] I believe even that the wolf is the only enemy of the lion.
[2] There is, therefore, only the buffalo, rhinoceros, and elephant which
have not to fear it.

food and water ; and while the men were conversing
in low tones we heard outside the distinct and regular
blows of the hatchet upon the tree trunk. Our honey-
gatherers had almost finished their work when all of
us heard noises, about which a trained ear could not
have the slightest doubt—they were made by lions.
. . . There were four or five of them. We heard them
distinctly walking in the dry leaves with which the
ground was strewn. Sometimes they exchanged low,
deep mews in various tones ; at others, roars peculiar
to them, by which, I believe, they communicate with
one another.

Almost at the same time my men outside made the
recognised signal to us by whistling. Looking at the
arms rack (a forked stick driven into the ground), I
saw that they had taken only one rifle with them, and
this they had probably left at the foot of the tree
while they climbed into it. "Return !" I shouted to
them. "Impossible : they surround us." "Then remain in the tree." But they shouted that they were
going to fall, that the branch was slipping.[1] Then we
must not hesitate a moment longer. Out we go ! I
gave the straw torches to a bearer while Tambarika
and I, our rifles ready, left the camp, our way lit up
from behind. The night was as black as pitch, and
we did not distinguish the trees until upon them.
Lions prowled around us, and one of them roared
within alarming proximity ; but we could not see
them ; we heard them walking in the leaves on all

---

[1] Blacks simply lean a branch against a tree, and climb on the top
of it with the assistance of their hands.

sides. . . . Reaching the tree we found one of our companions with the rifle cocked, another trying to relight a half-extinguished torch. . . . Still the lions walked. . . . We guessed them coming and going in the darkness.

At that moment Tambarika whispered to us the advice to imitate the *p'umpis* (wolves) in the distance. So we immediately began barking and shouting, "Hu! hu! hu!" in an undertone, as though the pack was still at a distance, while the man at the camp made the same well-imitated cry. The effect was instantaneous. There was a rapid gallop in the dry leaves: the lions decamped. The more or less well-imitated approach of a pack of wolves rid us of them for the whole night. We returned to the camp with our honey, and nothing troubled our tranquillity until morning.[1]

This is what probably happened. I believe that these lions simply wished to drink, and that they prowled around and examined us more or less in a bad temper. My men, on their side, fell from their tree, being unable to remain in it, and, their light having gone out, they were in a rather trying situation. As to myself, though I did not find this sortie on a night as black as a forest and with lions around me at all to my taste, I could not fail to go to my men's assistance. I was even morally obliged to do so. My feelings, when one of the lions roared and I could not see three yards before

[1] Hunters generally use the wolf cry for calling to one another in the woods.

me, were far from agreeable, and I do not recommend
it for people with delicate nerves. But in bush-life
danger becomes familiar ; in those moments men must
support one another, and I should no longer have had
the right to expect my men to risk their lives at my
side if I had abstained from helping them when I was
able to do so.

The African wolf is, as I have said, the only
enemy of the lion, a fact which my men and I
knew well; but, as often happens in such a case,
none of us thought of it—with the exception, of
course, of Tambarika, who once more showed his
presence of mind and made use of his knowledge of
the habits of animals.

Wolves sometimes show proofs of intelligence and
reasoning. For example, when traversing the country
in every direction in search of game, they continually
cross rivers, and, knowing that the water hides one of
their worst enemies, the crocodile, this is the method
they adopt to avoid it. Assembling at the edge of
the water, they bark so as to attract the crocodiles ;
when this is done they set off at full speed, either up
or down stream, and when a hundred yards away
throw themselves into the water and cross the river
in a body in the deepest silence. Very often have
we heard them barking, for they can be heard a
very long distance ; and one day we witnessed this
trick. It is stated that dogs use similar strategy, but
I have never seen an example. Besides, the dog has
hardly sufficient reason for wishing to cross streams,
and when he does so it is generally in the arms of

its master, who loves it, or in his canoe. The African wolf alone undertakes singly to overcome an antelope the size of an ass; it follows it at full speed, generally attacks it in the stomach, and, by biting it almost in the same place, ends by disembowelling it. One day I was present at the end of one of these hunts, in which a female wolf had just killed a water-buck. After dashing it to the ground, its enemy had strangled it; then, hanging out its tongue, the wolf lay down to rest by the side of its victim. The water-buck was in a state which indicated a long race; the poor animal's coat was entirely plastered down with perspiration; the under portions of its four limbs were spotted with blood; and its open stomach left to view the half-protruding intestines. For a moment I thought of killing the wolf and taking her young; but where were these to be found? My men took possession of the buck in spite of the growls of the dispossessed vanquisher, who, with hair on end and teeth showing, did not wish us to approach. She moved away, however, upon seeing us walk towards her. I required that a great part of her prey should be left, since she had so well earned it.

In the case of the zebra, which kicks and makes any approach from behind dangerous, wolves go to work differently; they pass it and try to attack it in front by biting at its knees and breast. Once the zebra is kneeling down with a cut tendon, it is lost.

The lion and the leopard are great hunters; but they hunt by craft and by watching, whilst the wolf backs its speed in full daylight against that of the animals it covets, overcoming them by quite exceptional force of resistance and tenacity. Once the animal is down it is devoured in the twinkling of an eye, and the pack rests until hunger once more urges it to the fight.

Those are the animals which must be captured young and trained for lion-hunting. With six wolves one could track, drive, and bring to bay, every lion in a district, whatever might be their lairs, cunning, and daring.

It is useless, I fear, to think of acclimatising our European dogs in these countries; heat and skin diseases would quickly kill them, and especially the tsetse, which swarms there. When you speak of lions you mean big game, and where big game is you may be certain there are tsetse - flies. In temperate countries and on the mountain plateaus of Africa dogs may be used for partridge and small - antelope shooting, but those are almost always destitute of other animals. The rat terrier lives fairly well in warm climates, but he would not support life in the bush : only persons living in towns or in comfortable houses can possess him.

It must be well understood that for lion-hunting it is unnecessary to have large savage dogs; a common mongrel, whatever its breed and size, is quite sufficient provided it is not frightened, and that it barks round the lion, at the same time carefully avoiding it. It is sufficient to discover the retreat where the wild beast is crouching, and, once the dog has seen it, it occupies it sufficiently with its barking to enable you to approach without being noticed. Three or four dogs are indispensable for attaining this object. On the other hand, pure-bred dogs full of courage are killed immediately by wishing to get too near the beast.

The jackal also inhabits these regions, but, contrarily to what one sees in Algeria, does not go about in packs; one meets with isolated animals or pairs only. It frequents preferably flat parts of hilly countries. It is about the size of the fox, and its colour is a tawny-gray. It utters a particular cry, is very timid, and feeds with hyenas on the remains of animals left by lions and hunters.

A few words more on the hyena of these regions,[1] to complete this chapter devoted to the dog family.

The only one which exists north of the Zambesi is spotted. In daylight nothing is uglier than this animal, and its strange habits have given rise to certain superstitions among the natives. They say, for example, that after its death its sex changes, a belief which arises simply because of its special conformation and the difficulty one has in telling its sex. It is also stated that hyenas sometimes speak from the bottom of the holes, from which you try to dislodge them, like persons complaining of being ill-treated. This story has been told to me several times. I have sometimes dislodged one of these animals from its hole by means of sulphur rockets; but, apart from uttering a few feeble mews, the hyena has never addressed anything to me. The other variety, the

1 See *Mes Grandes Chasses*, pp. 128, 129.

striped hyena, is met with south of the Zambesi and in the north of Africa—that is, in temperate parts.

The burrows in which the hyena lives are generally old burrows abandoned by ant-eaters. It does not often make one for itself. At nightfall it scours the district in search of food, uttering at intervals a mournful cry. If lions are making a

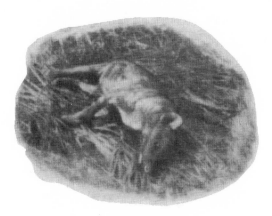

A SPOTTED HYENA.

meal the hyena arrives immediately, enticed by the smell. It waits patiently at a distance until the guests have withdrawn, to throw itself in turn upon the remains. It finishes the carcase, or else prowls round villages and camps, and, driven by hunger, steals whatever it can find—bones, pieces of skin, feathers, etc., even dogs and goats, if it meets with them. There are cases, people assure you, in which it would even attack human beings during their sleep.

When hyenas prowl around my camp, and are too enterprising, I throw pieces of meat to them containing strychnine, and the next day we sometimes find one or several of the wretched animals lying dead in the vicinity.

VULTURES PUTTING HUNTERS ON THE TRACK.

CHAPTER IX

ANNUAL FIRES—AN AGITATED NIGHT—BIRDS OF PREY

African landscapes—Bush fires—Fires and animals—Torrid heat—Preparation of specimens — Varieties of elands — A double shot — Antelope-
hunting—An improvised night-watch—A wounded lion—Hunters overturned — A hunt by torchlight — Sudden conclusion of the hunt—
Measurements of an adult lion—Vultures and their habits—The gift of
Akrassus—Varieties of vultures—Marabouts—The Nyangomba.

I HAVE already indicated the division of the hunting
seasons. We have reached the dry season of 1895 at
the time fire will sweep the country.

Scattered over the country in France you can find
in summer scenery which faithfully represents African
landscapes, and will assist those who have never
seen them to form an idea. Instead of expansive
fields of yellowing corn, place any kind of grass having

the same appearance and covering hills, valleys, and the banks of streams ; in the place of clumps of trees or poplars carefully arranged in straight lines, substitute wild trees, growing somewhat at random, with dry foliage, because it is winter ; and you have before you to a certain extent the grassy countryside of Africa. For woods replace the pines of the Fontainebleau forest, for example, by exotic trees growing haphazard on a surface covered with short grass and small plants, upon which neither road nor footpath is traced, and you will understand the ordinary African forest. Quite different is the equatorial forest, that through which Stanley passed ; it is darker, larger, more obstructed with lianas; the surface of the ground is covered with roots, and humidity is everywhere.

But here we are still far from the equator, and west of Lake Nyassa those masses of vegetation are rare. In addition to a forest here and there and grassy plains, imagine other regions with shorter grass, about 3 feet in height, covered with stunted and deformed trees 4 or 5 yards high, nearly resembling apple-trees, but, alas ! fruitless.

These three aspects, with an infinite variety of views, are almost the only ones—the grassy or wooded plain, the grassy or wooded hills, forests here and there.

Now, in August it is exceedingly difficult to traverse the country. Native footpaths are half covered with grass ; everything is dry and brittle. It is then that fires, called bush fires,[1] are lit by natives in the

[1] See *Mes Grandes Chasses*, pp. 122, 202, 237, 241.

SABLE ANTELOPE IN THE DENSE BUSH (BEFORE THE ANNUAL FIRES).

vicinity of the villages, by travellers on footpaths, by
hunters in the woods. The wind fans the flames with
its powerful and continuous breath, and the fire
spreads. Generally started in the evening, it spreads
the whole night through with a noise like the
rumbling of thunder, licking the trees with its tall,
flaming tongues, and advancing with terrifying
rapidity. Smoke rises in clouds heavenwards, bearing
burning straw, whilst on the ground is a crackling like
a fusillade of bursting stems and plants. The wind
moderates or increases the roar, and the unbridled
element thus sweeps over plains, climbs hill-sides, and
rushes across immense stretches of country. Sometimes, several days afterwards, a wreath of blue smoke
rises in the midst of the mass of black, gray, or white
cinders, and of dead tree trunks which have caught
fire, showing that the fire smoulders, and that it is
slowly continuing its work. Rarely does it cover
great distances without being stopped. The natives
burn the grass in the vicinity of their villages before-
hand to protect them, so that the flames, finding
nothing more to burn, stop short. Forests destitute
of grass, damp places, and sandy or stony spots also
arrest combustion.

As a rule the speed of the flames on a grassy
plain is in direct ratio to the wind. I have seen
them sweep along with terrible rapidity, perhaps
thirteen miles an hour; at other times, on the
contrary, they were travelling at barely three or four
miles.

If surprised by a conflagration when on the march

in a dry country and when the wind is high, not a moment is to be lost, especially if the grass stretches a long distance in all directions. We have several times found ourselves in this situation, and it has needed all the care of which we were capable not to suffer from the scourge. Whenever you hear the fire—and you can hear it a long way off—you have only, if you are on its probable path, to set fire to the grass to leeward, tracing a line stretching to right and left. The flames start thence and move away from you, since they cannot spread against the wind, thus clearing a space where you must hasten to take up a position as far away as possible from the edge of the grass still unburnt. When the great conflagration arrives it naturally stops short where you began yours.

Quantities of *buchangas*, birds as black as the smoke in which they fly, follow the fires, catching on the wing the grasshoppers and insects which the flames arouse on their path.

Warned of the approach of the scourge by scent, before they are able even to hear it, animals leave the dangerous zone either by fleeing before the fire, or by escaping to the right or to the left.

Once the flames are passed, the country has assumed a different aspect: the yellow grass has disappeared; the trunks of trees—freed from vegetation —seem to have become longer; leaves—scorched, twisted by the flames and scattered behind them— strew the ground, and the eye can stretch far into the distance in every direction over a black carpet which

RESULT OF A DOUBLE SHOT AT WART-HOGS (IN THE BUSH AFTER THE ANNUAL FIRES).

somewhat resembles a mass of seaweed mixed with twisted branches and cinders.

The heat is fiercer on this blackened ground deprived of shade ; but, on the other hand, how much more is the hunter at ease upon it, and how much better his eye can see the smallest objects ! If, for the same reason, it is more difficult to approach animals, there are cunning methods of hiding oneself, whereas there is no way of avoiding being heard in the dry grass.

The reader now being acquainted with the changes which have come over the country, I resume hunting.

At the end of August most of the rivers are low or dried up, but water is still sufficiently abundant in the country to permit animals to change their drinking places often. One must, therefore, be in the neighbourhood of these drinking places and give oneself much trouble in killing one or two heads of game a day, the heat and the total absence of shade making sport especially fatiguing. On the other hand, in October, after two months of torrid heat the number of drinking places is considerably diminished and often reduced to one or two for every six square miles. It is then useless to disturb yourself; you can lie in watch, and shoot near these pools during the day and night all the animals of the district which are obliged to come there to drink.

It is during the dry season that Bertrand and I have prepared each year the largest number of mammals for the Paris Museum. Abundance of animals allowed of selecting only fine specimens, and the temperature was admirably suited for the preparation of these large specimens, which are so apt to spoil. We have always at the camp ten or twelve children from neighbouring villages, who, at our request and paid by us, collect small animals. These young hunters set out every morning under the direction of a man with cages, traps, and boxes, and return in the evening with their prey. Thus, we have added to our collections varieties of tortoises, birds, small mammals, and insects, which we should otherwise have never been able to obtain.

At the time in question I had occasion to notice an anomaly among the elands met with in the mitsagnas (*mópane* or *bauhinias*) woods. The males, instead of having a tuft of hair at the base of the horns and on the forehead, have short hair like the females, giving them quite a different appearance. I attribute this peculiarity to their thorny habitat, unless it be they belong to another variety of *oreas canna*.

One day I made a very pretty double shot in these *mitsagnas*. Some elands having set off unexpectedly and passed before us at full gallop thirty yards away, I fired and killed two of them, one after the other. As luck would have it, I had fired a little too much in front each time, and struck them on the neck, which is fatal to them. To bring down an animal as big as an omnibus horse with each barrel, to roll it over as though it were a rabbit, is a pleasure which one does not often experience. That day I used the Express No. 2 because this weapon was the first which came to my hand at the noise of the gallop. Following the herd, I killed a male also, making a total of three. None of them had a tuft of hair on the forehead.[1]

I killed antelopes in August and September— elands, koodoos, waterbucks, sable antelopes, reed-bucks, bushbucks, etc. I pass rapidly over these days of sport, which I have already described, to speak of my first night-watch of the season in the middle of September.

I had seen lions' spoor on the shores of a pool in a large plain. This did not trouble me. But when returning the same way a little before sunset we saw something which, upon drawing near, we recognised to be the body of a zebra, which had been dead barely an hour. It must have been killed by a lion—or rather by several lions, because of the many wounds on its body. It was lying in the middle of a red pool; its face was one large wound; and from one of its empty sockets, from its open throat and swollen breast, blood, with which it was spattered all over, was pouring copiously. The fight must have been a terrible one!

We immediately inspect the neighbourhood, convinced that the lions have decamped upon our approach; but we notice nothing more than a few small insignificant bushes. I decide to try my luck that night, and, as the camp is barely a mile and a half

---

[1] I preserved the finest of these three elands; but it deteriorated, and I was unable to send it to Paris. Through one cause or another, we lost more than thirty magnificent specimens in the course of 1895-96.

away, I send there for something to eat, for my field-glass, and for a blanket to pass the night in.[1] I keep only Msiambiri with me. We take care to keep away from the zebra, because the lions must not be put on their guard and suspect that a trap is being set for them by scenting our tracks near their game.

I examine the surroundings. They are excellent as a place for shooting, the country being fairly open, and the moon will be almost at its full this evening; but thére is not the smallest tree against which to lean one's back, not the smallest mound which will allow us to hide ourselves. We must, therefore, make a small entrenchment; and, without losing time, we go to cut some trees which are a certain distance away. We will decide on a place afterwards. Our companions soon return and assist us, but night is falling and we are unable to cut sufficient trees to shelter all six of us. Therefore, I send three men to perch in a tree 60 yards away; the two others remaining with me at the edge of the pool. We hastily construct, with stakes fastened together at the top, a kind of conical hut, which we cover with grass and earth, making it resemble a termites' ant-hill. Night has fallen when the watch begins, and each one is at his post.

I profit by this interval of rest to swallow hastily some *riz au lait*, a full saucepan of which Bertrand has sent me, food which I generally take with me

---

[1] The temperature at night from June to September is low in comparison with that of the day—*i.e.*, only 51° to 59°.

A MALE WATERBUCK.

on my night-watches, because it is easy to eat—you have no need of bread, salt, plate, or glass: only a spoon. My meal over, I remain motionless.

I am placed in such a position that the moon illuminates the ground to my left where the pool and the tree, upon which are my men, are situated; the zebra is opposite me about 30 feet away. Three irregular openings, sufficiently large to pass the head and shoulders through, act as outlooks. I must add that our installation is more intended to hide than to protect us, for a lion jumping on to it would suffice to overturn it. There is some risk in thus venturing; but it must be remembered that this night-watch was decided upon in a few minutes by taking advantage of circumstances, and in this kind of sport, especially with the lion, which is so difficult to meet, an opportunity must be seized or it may slip through your fingers for ever. "Nothing venture, nothing have," says a proverb, and never has its application been more apt.

I am convinced that the lions will not be long. The somewhat rare fact of them having attacked and killed an animal in open daylight shows that they were hungry. Momentarily disturbed by our arrival, they will doubtless return as soon as quietness is restored. Twice we hear in the distance the braying of a zebra, weeping for its dead or absent companion; crickets begin to chirp; and in the distance, every now and then, is heard the cry of a bat.[1]

---

[1] A large fructivorous bat whose cry exactly resembles the noise of blows on an anvil.

Stillness must have reigned for about half an hour when the hoot of an owl (a cry which is Kambombe's speciality) tells us that our companions have seen something from their tree ; and a second afterwards the same signal is repeated. Opening our eyes very wide, we look in all directions through our port-holes, but see absolutely nothing. And yet it is relatively light. The moon gives the country a uniform silvery-blue appearance, and upon it the bushes stand out in dark blotches. There, by the side of the water, in which the stars are reflected, is the body of the zebra, having the appearance of a black mass. Field-glass to my eyes, I examine every yard of ground, this precious instrument, which has rendered me inestimable services in similar cases, allowing me to distinguish details admirably. I examine each bush, every plant, the banks of the pool, and the zebra. There is nothing. I conclude that our comrades are pointing out something which is outside our range of vision, and I resume my immobility with ears on the stretch, bringing my glass to my eyes each time that I see something unusual.

In regard to rifles, I have put my 303 on one side, because too great precision is needed to use it successfully. The Express with its shorter sight, for which I have substituted a large white pea-sight, is better suited to the circumstances. My six - shot Winchester loaded with buckshot I keep within reach in case of too dangerous proximity on the part of animals. My two companions are armed with the Express No. 2 and with the 303, which they are not to use unless they are defending themselves. The men in the tree have no firearms.

Another hoot is heard, and again I carefully examine the surroundings. Changing my position, I peer through the left-hand side outlook, then through that at the back, but without success. I return to my post. At the first glance the zebra seems to me to be larger than it was a few moments before : one would say that it was raising its head. The poor animal being stone dead, I tell myself that something new has happened : in fact, my glass shows me that an object is at its side. But what is it ? I cannot distinguish. After all, what does it matter ? If it be a hyena, nothing is to be done ; if a lion, there is no need to hurry.

A gentle wind springs up from the left, and a few clouds obscure the moon from time to time. I make out plainly the animal which is on the zebra—the upper part of its body is above the carcase, we see its head and shoulders,—but it is impossible to say what it is. My men are unable to use the field-glass, and by its aid I see the object better than they do.

The motionless animal is soon accompanied by a companion. There is no doubt that they are looking in our direction, probably puzzled by this eminence, which they have not noticed before. One of them leaves the zebra, and walks towards us with head on high and the whole of its body visible. . . . There is no deceiving oneself this time : they are really lions.

Hastily putting down my field-glass, and cocking my two triggers, I lower my barrel slowly. At this moment I experience keen emotion, a sense of pleasure mingled with fear, and as the clear-cut silhouette of the animal advances towards our hiding-place, my heart beats so furiously that I hear it distinctly. The lion stops shortly after passing the zebra, its head raised, evidently engaged in inspecting the sham ant-hill, which puzzles it; unfortunately, one cannot distinguish the expression of its physiognomy, one can see only its light tawny coat slightly lit up on its back and head by the moon, while the rest of its body is blended with the bluish obscurity of the ground. After having looked for a moment, during which time we have retained the most complete immobility, the lion lowers its head, smelling the ground to find an indication which confirms his suspicions. Once only have we passed over that spot, and our track must be effaced, because he raises his head once more and again advances. . . . A thousand thoughts whirl at this moment through my clear brain, which forms a striking contrast to my beating heart. If it promenades around our hut, I say to myself, it will scent us, and I shall be unable to fire at it; if it makes off after having scented us, our night's sport is compromised. Better fire, therefore, before it moves too far to the left, where the position of my outlook would prevent me from seeing it.

At a certain moment the lion again stops in front of us to look in our direction. It is about twenty-four feet away; but the ground is very dark, and the animal does not stand out against the sky. Hence I cannot fire with certainty; I only see it partially.

Instead of going towards the left, as I thought, it draws a step nearer, and, smelling the earth, gives a deep and short growl, which we understand as plainly as its companion, meaning, "Attention — there is danger here!" It raises its head, looks in our direction, then immediately begins again to smell about.

Now it turns slightly to its right, and follows our track towards the edge of the water, taking two or three steps, and at that moment presenting to me its left flank. I thrust my barrel outside lightly, noiselessly, inclining it a little so as to see my sight, and seeking in vain for some seconds for the spot at which I must aim. These seconds seem like centuries to me. I have grave fears of making a bungle of the business, and still greater fear of seeing my adversary decamp without my having had time to fire, indecisive as I am between the desire to wait for a better opportunity and the fear of not finding such a good one again. At last, guiding myself by the shadow of the lion's back made on the ground by the moon, I take careful aim . . . and press the trigger. . . .

A terrible roar bursts forth; an enormous projectile seems to strike our shelter, which collapses, covering us with earth and sand, while we see between the disjointed motionless stakes, the smoke still suspended in the damp night air, and the cloud of dust which rises from the ground in consequence of the fall of our hut. We are in a very awkward position beneath, occupied in supporting with our hands the pieces of wood which nearly fell on our heads, looking outside to see what has become of our wounded animal, for I am sure I have hit it. If he were by our side, to move would be dangerous. At last, as nothing moves, I put out my head, then an arm, and scrutinise the surroundings in the somewhat comical position of a man who tries to extricate himself from a heap of sticks under which he is buried. My men do the same, and, as none of us sees anything, we disengage ourselves from the ruins without other injuries than a few insignificant scratches.

What happened? The lion, blinded by pain or maddened by surprise, must have run against our improvised shelter when in flight, or else it grazed it with its foot, and, because of its slightness of construction, our building fell. After we have shaken ourselves and extracted the rifles from the ruins, we look around us. The zebra is still there, and only it. We call to our companions, who descend from their tree and report to us. The first hoot was to warn us of the arrival of the lions which passed under the tree in which our scouts were stationed. Walking round the pool, they remained for a long time looking in the direction of the zebra and the hut. The second hoot announced their progress towards the zebra. After the rifle shot, my men, seeing one lion only decamp at a slow trot by the way that it had come, and stopping several times to look back as though it were awaiting its companion, thought that the other had been killed on the spot when I called to them. Unfortunately, that is not so : our lion has disappeared.

We light a few blades of grass in order to see the

track. At first we see upon it only the animal's spoor made at the moment it sprang forward; but quickly we come upon a large jet of blood three feet beyond the hut, the very stakes of which, on the side against which the animal ran, are spattered with blood. It is fairly common to see a lion upon receiving a shot spring forward, the beast, doubtless, wishing to defend itself against attack, and its most natural movement being this pretence of a charge.

We believe that the animal is wounded fatally, and that it is impossible it has gone far. But how look for it without straw or torch? Moonlight is quite insufficient for such work. Even in daylight there is no more dangerous work than looking for a wounded lion: so I leave you to imagine the pleasure one must take in the task in darkness, which makes every shrub suspicious—there are twenty chances to one of finding nothing and at the same time risking your life or the lives of your men.

By common accord we were going to postpone the search until the following day, when an idea strikes me: if the lion is dead the hyenas of the district will leave only the bones to-morrow morning. This idea arouses my men—because no skin, no reward.[1]

So we hold a meeting in consequence of which it seems to me that the most reasonable thing to do is to wait a little while, for the longer we wait the more chance there will be that the lion, if wounded,

---

[1] As encouragement and reward my hunters received a small sum agreed upon beforehand for each elephant, rhinoceros, or lion killed. For other animals they received nothing.

will die. Two of us will, therefore, remain here and smoke a pipe, while the four others are gone to camp and have brought back some Bengal lights. I write to Bertrand by the light of a match to ask him for them, and for straw and some assagais. A few additional men will bring firebrands.

As soon as our companions are gone and everything has become silent, we hear, twice, in the direction of the plain a noise like a complaint. Is it a night bird or else a hyena on its round? We cannot say. The noise is not repeated. Almost an hour passes without incident. The moon begins to decline, and it is perhaps one o'clock in the morning when voices and firebrands announce the approach of reinforcements; our men have returned.

We set out in front with torches to follow the traces of blood, and from time to time I have a Bengal light raised on the end of a stick, lit behind us to light up the plain, which I explore with my glass. Fortunately for us, fire has cleared everything away with the exception of a few stunted trees and withered plants.

Blood is abundant but intermittent, and we have the greatest difficulty in following the traces. This group of men with torches, these dazzling lights brilliantly illuminating the trees and the details of the plain for a certain distance, whilst the remainder of the landscape is in shadow, produce a strange effect: one would say it was some culminating point in a melodrama, and I do not think the lion has been often hunted under these conditions. Not to wish to lose its skin is very wise; but to follow it at night when it is perhaps still alive and maddened by its wound, is risking your own skin. It is even madness.

We have taken thus an hour to cover about two hundred yards. I shall always remember what happened at that moment. In the glare of a light I have just explored all the surroundings without seeing anything, when we hear before us a distinct growl which changes almost immediately into a terrible hoarse roaring as though the beast which made it is choking, but a roar of rage which gives warning of the spring, attack, and vengeance of a maddened animal. Every one understands that so well that in a moment everybody vanishes. The torch-bearers scamper away, the lights go out and leave us in darkness, and the most complete silence reigns save for the hiccups of the lion, indistinct noises, and moans, the crackling of shrubs and leaves barely fifty yards away. Then the moon sets, leaving everything in darkness.

At the time of the panic-terror—natural on the part of beings who, like us, cannot see at night—I run a few yards to the left, fearing the animal's pursuit; then, hearing nothing more, crouch down very low, rifle in hand, in such a way that if anything approaches I shall see it against the sky. It is then that I hear the lion groan, first of all on my right and then in front of me, but as though it is making off instead of drawing near. I give a low whistle, which is answered by a similar one, and a black mass which I might have taken for the lion if it had not whistled approaches me on all fours; then another comes, and yet another, until my men and I find ourselves crouched in the midst of complete darkness without a match and without a fire, with a wounded lion dragging itself along twenty yards away. It is imprudent to move away, because the animal can see distinctly, and one might attract its attention. The best thing is to remain quiet and to listen. So the night passes, the dampness and the dew keeping us agreeably cool, and the lion's intermittent groans preventing us from falling asleep. Towards morning the comrade of our wounded lion returns and passes within terrible proximity to two of our men who have taken refuge in a small stunted tree, so frightening them that they nearly fell from their perches. It skirts the plain and roars around us in a very unpleasant manner. I would have given much for the sun to rise that morning sooner than usual. At last dawn whitens the horizon, then colours it, and soon the eye, limited at first in the vicinity, is able to see over the plain. Over there is our collapsed hut, the pool and the zebra; before us are some bushes.

The hunt begins again; but this time we can see, and very well too. I take my 303, and, wiping its dew-covered barrel, start to follow the track carefully. Everywhere are pools of blood where the animal rested: here is the place where it tried to spring on us, and there are furrows made by its claws. The bloody trail leads to a big thicket where it must have taken refuge, and thirty feet in front of that I stop.   Clods of earth are thrown at it. . . . Then the bushes bend, and we see that the lion is leaving the other side : so I make a detour, and we find ourselves face to face. . . . But a glance is sufficient to convince me that the poor animal is to be feared no longer; its mane clothed with blood, it drags itself along with difficulty, feebly growling, looking at me with its mouth wide open and its ears flattened. . . . I finish it off with a shot from the 303.

Its skin covered with dry clots, the unfortunate lion must have lost its blood even to the last drop.   It was smeared with it all over.   Entering above the heart, the bullet had traversed the lungs and come out at a hole as big as a five-franc piece.   The animal measured 10 feet 4 inches ; it was in the full strength of its age, and fairly fat.   But what a night I had had to spend, and what emotions I had experienced !   The previous day had been very tiring.   So I went to sleep at the camp, to which, a few moments afterwards, the lion was carried by eight men.

You cannot obtain a very good idea from menagerie specimens of the size of one of these magnificent lions when in an adult wild state.   Imagine an animal with withers about 3 feet high, 6 feet in length exclusive of the tail, from 13 to 15 inches across the chest, and weighing between 440 and 500 pounds.   It makes a fine mark for a rifle, but it is dangerous and rare.

The lions which had killed the zebra were four, and they hunted in company.   During the whole of the time of our stay in the district the three

survivors continued to beat the vicinity of the plain;
but we did not meet them any more, in spite of
another night-watch which I organised near a buffalo
which they had killed and partly eaten; for two
nights they prowled around the carcase, but either
because we let ourselves be scented, or did not
hide ourselves well enough, they did not draw near
to it. Doubtless there was another reason for their
distrust, for I have observed that nothing prevents a lion drinking or eating if it feels the
need. It was amid rather curious circumstances
that I discovered this buffalo's body.

One morning four or five days after the death of
the lion we see some vultures describing circles
in the sky — an indication that they have found
an animal or its remains. As it does not take us out
of our way, we go to see the object of their desire,
and without making a noise reach a very bushy spot
surrounded by trees, upon which other vultures are
already sitting. Something, doubtless, prevents these
birds from settling on their prey. Knowing that we
may meet large carnivora unexpectedly, we advance
with great precaution, rifle cocked and finger on
trigger, stretching our necks to try to discover the
animal or its remains, which lie in a clearing there.
. . . There is a low roar, a rustling in the shrubs,
and we hear animals making off. . . . Upon approaching we discover a buffalo, the abdomen of which has
been emptied, and the thighs partly devoured. Three
lions, the spoor of which we find, were occupied in
feasting when the slight noise of our advance frightened

THE *COUP DE GRÂCE*—FINISHING OFF A WOUNDED LION.

them away.   Although rather late, we hide ourselves, and several hours slip by in the deepest silence, much to the disgust of the vultures which still remain waiting on the trees.   So much the worse for them !   They will be there at their own expense, for, intending to watch at night, I cover the buffalo with foliage, and build a shelter stronger than that of the plain at the foot of a tree.   But, as I have said, the lions do not return, and we leave the vultures free to dispose of their find.

This species of bird plays a very important part[1] in the life of the African hunter, because they tell him by soaring in the air where are to be found the animals which he has sometimes wounded and lost. They are everywhere without your seeing them, and no sooner does an animal fall than a vulture immediately flies through the air as though by chance, ever ready as they are to devour your game, if you leave it without hiding it under a heap of leaves or grass.   In the case of an elephant nothing is to be feared, their beaks cannot penetrate its skin.   Nor can they penetrate that of the large antelopes ; but they go about their business in a different way then, attacking the anus and the soft parts of the abdomen, where the skin is tender, and making an opening through which they drag the intestines.   When these are eaten they enter the cavity, and devour all the flesh of the ribs inside, sometimes seven or eight of them getting inside the body for that purpose, while the others eat the eyes, tongue, etc.   So it happens that when you

[1] See *Mes Grandes Chasses*, p. 246.

arrive in haste, your antelope, which has the appearance of being intact, is nothing more than a skin stretched on a skeleton, emptied and cleared out inside. One after another, the vultures come out of the aperture, and, gorged with meat, heavily fly away.

This variety is called the turkey-buzzard because of the rosy caruncles which ornament its head. When they fight around a carcase they utter cries which resemble those of a turkey; and, like this bird, they have a way of waddling in their walk which is very comical.[1]

This reminds me of a little trick which we played in Dahomey on an Italian naval captain. We sent him in a cage four of these vultures, called there *akrassus,* which act as scavengers in the district, calling them turkeys of the country. He ate them heartily, and replied to our letter asking him how he liked them, " Un poco dure, ma buonissime "—(" a little hard, but very good "), adding that he was keeping two of them to celebrate Christmas at Castellamare, Naples. This incident remained legendary, and we used to say, to express the *ne plus ultra* of a feast, " There will *even* be a truffled akrassu."

I, too, should have very much liked to be able to eat these turkeys; that would have been a precious gift in times of hunger; but they give off a repulsive smell like all the flesh which they touch, and are generally only skin and bone.

There is another species of vulture which, for

[1] The native name is *magora.*

want of another name, I shall call the "white-breasted vulture." It is a little larger than the turkey-buzzard, and its head is bare; but it has white feathers on its neck, breast, and wings. The spread of the wings of the turkey-buzzard may be five feet eight inches; that of the other, six feet and a half. The female turkey-buzzard has a head covered with short, grayish feathers; that of the white-breasted vulture has a bald head.

According to a somewhat widespread error, these birds have a very keen scent, and by that means discover their quarry; the natives say even that they guess where it is to be found. I have studied them a long time to settle the question; and I am persuaded that they smell absolutely nothing, but that, in compensation, they have an extraordinarily sharp eye. The proof of this is that they never discover an animal when you have taken care to hide it from them by means of leaves or straw. Lions know this so well that they drag the bodies of animals which they cannot finish eating at night under dense thickets, so that on the following day the vultures will not forestall them. They soar at such a height that the naked eye or the field-glass hardly distinguishes them; but the smallest red ray or bleeding débris makes them flock from all points of the compass.

There is another bird which feeds on carcases in all stages of decomposition, the marabout, a wading bird very common in certain regions, especially in flat countries. It is to be found everywhere in the basin of the Zambesi. Under the tail near the rump are the feathers with which fashionable ladies trim their hats. Three marabouts are necessary to make a becoming hat, one of those enormous structures which permit us to enjoy a play at the theatre without being troubled by a sight of the stage. Ostrich feathers have taken the place of those of the marabout, and that bird does not at all complain.

When the marabout lacks carrion it fishes in pools and at the edge of rivers, a resource which the vulture does not possess.

Each of the three birds which I have just enumerated flies in the air at different altitudes: the marabout is the highest flier, soaring far from human sight; the white-breasted vulture comes next; and lower down, but still hardly perceptible, is the turkey-buzzard. When they discover prey, the buzzards, more courageous than the others, arrive first, describing large circles in the air for a long time; above them appear the white-breasted vultures, more distrustful and long in coming to a decision; and finally, the marabouts, sure of their superiority. But as soon as they alight the order is reversed—the vultures are forced to leave, pursued by the enormous-beaked, long-striding marabouts which quietly eat the first, while the birds of prey respectfully keep at a distance. Then the waders let them have their turn. Marabouts are not always found with vultures, because the latter are much commoner; but that is what happens when the three species are assembled.

Another curious bird which upon this occasion I

added to my collections is the *nyangomba*, which exchanges an interminable "Diti, diti, dutou, dutou" with the female.[1] I have watched it with the object of observing its habits, and have seen that it feeds not only on shells but also on tortoises. As these latter are hard to break open, the bird places them under its claws and with its large beak strikes with the regularity of a steam-hammer always on the same spot. By this means it makes a hole in

CORNER OF OUR CAMP.

the carapace, and by enlarging it, devours alive the unfortunate tortoise.

It is the size of a turkey. Black all over, the head ornamented with red in the case of the male, and with gray in the case of the female, it possesses a large brown eye, much resembling a human eye and having the same expression and softness which is given by long eyelashes. It frequents long grass

[1] See *Mes Grandes Chasses*, p. 176.

and stony places, and is known to naturalists as *bucorax cafer*.

A volume is to be written on the curious habits and history of all these strange animals, so numerous and so varied in Africa. Not having the necessary space at my disposal here and only being able to mention them incidentally, I leave to others the task of making this interesting addition to our Buffon.

CHAPTER X

NIGHT-WATCHES IN 1895—SUCCESSES AND MISADVENTURES

Period for night-watch shooting—Information service—Organisation—Installation—Risks and dangers of this form of hunting—Emotions of nocturnal watching—Average of successful nights—First *chassés-croisés*—Animals frequenting the pools—A lion hunt—A fruitless night—Precautions to be taken with the rhinoceros—A night-watch at the small south pool—A nocturnal charge and flight of the hunters—Hide-and-seek in the darkness—Death of a rhinoceros—An unlucky night : three lions missed—Tardy improvement of the electric projector—Arrival of the European mail—An unexpected visitor—Hunting a rhinoceros in slippers—Extraordinary penetration of the Express No. 1—Night-watch at the large south pool—Lion lost and found again—The delicate sense of smell of the blacks—The largest lion of my collection—Day-watches—Animals which do not drink—Habits of various animals at drinking-places.

WE now reach the most exciting period of the year, that which I reserve exclusively for the lion, leopard, and rhinoceros, for which I await at night-time in

11

places where they are obliged to drink. I do not include the elephant. For it I am always waiting; but it has come only once in eight years.

When the year has been very dry—that is, when rain stopped early in October,—drinking-places are reduced, as I have said already, to a few small, muddy pools of water scattered over the country. By working systematically it is then you can know the fauna of a district accurately.

I had organised my nocturnal hunts in the following regular manner :—

I began my watch at nightfall at one point or another in company with two of my men, each in turn. For example, one night it was Rodzani and Msiambiri, the next Tambarika and Kambombe, then Tchigallo and a man selected from the most intelligent in our *entourage*. In the morning I returned to the camp (that is, when no animal was pursued), took my bath, breakfasted, and, selecting a quiet, shady place on one side, put down my mat, and went to sleep under guard of two men, who relieved each other alternately until I awoke, generally about three o'clock. When my toilet was performed I occupied myself with one thing or another until four o'clock, which was the fixed hour for dinner, so as to give me time to get to the place where I was to watch, and to be ready before darkness set in. Certain years I have done this for forty to fifty days in succession.

I had one body of men, or several bodies, according to the number of drinking-places, to collect information, setting out at dawn, and making a daily report to me upon my awaking.

At the time at which I have arrived in my narrative I was in the south of the Angoni country, in a region swarming with game, with *only four drinking-places within a radius of thirty-three miles.* There were forest lands, plains, hills, sandy or stony ground,—in short, the kinds of country and vegetation suitable for all animals. My camp was near one of these pools, and was placed almost in the centre of the group. To avoid the native names of these pools, names which are difficult to pronounce, I shall designate them by their position. One was north of the camp, about an hour and a half's journey away ; [1] the others were to the south, distant the one from the other, and different in expanse,—namely, the large south pool, which was within three-quarters of an hour, and the nearer to me, and the small south pool, which was two hours' march from our encampment. During the early days of our occupation we visited all the pools, and measured all the spoor with pieces of straw. Animals' feet are like human faces—there are no two alike. Each day the men came to tell me where animals had been drinking, and what kind of animals, in case of doubt bringing their straw measures. In a week's time we knew these animals exceedingly well. What makes this kind of work interesting is seeing with what perspicacity and high spirits the natives are always ready to assist you. My assistants were naturally selected from among

[1] About six miles.

hunters in the villages, or professional assistant hunters, and all recognised a track very well. Moreover, as the same men visited the same pool each day, they saw all the better the changes which had happened during the night. If there were something extraordinary they had orders to come back posthaste and awaken me.[1] Apart from this contingency, they returned to camp, some about ten o'clock, others about noon, according to the distance they had to come. Upon waking I summoned them before me, and sometimes there were contradictory reports.

"Well, what fresh?"

First group—"The small rhinoceros drank last night. There is nothing else. The lion did not come."

Second group—"He came to us, and the small rhinoceros also."

First group—"Impossible, since he went in an opposite direction to you, and we followed him as far as the hills."

Second group—"He came notwithstanding, and we recognised him distinctly." (Sceptical smiles and chuckles on the part of the first group.)

I intervene by saying, "Where are the straws?"

"Here they are."

I compare them, and find that the measurements are of the same animal.

Second group, triumphantly—"Ah! now you see.

[1] For example, if elephants had visited the pool late enough at night to give one a fair chance of overtaking them, or if my emissaries made some discovery, such as a lion sleeping in the shade, the retreat of a rhinoceros, etc.

Only *you* can recognise spoor. Fine sportsmen you are ! "

First group, with disdain—" Your tracks are not to-day's : they are yesterday's. That is all ! "

Second group—" What ! not to-day's ? They are this very morning's." (Sensation.)

" Very well, now," I say. " Tambarika, see who's right."

Third group—" The lion drank last night for the third time almost at the same place. He killed in the vicinity a waterbuck which the vultures finished this morning. We have seen an enormous *palap'ala* (sable antelope), extraordinary. . . ."

I know how much to accept of the blacks' exaggerated stories. I put down everything which precedes, according to my daily custom, in one of my notebooks. During the afternoon Tambarika returns with his report. The first group is right—the tracks are of the previous day. The second group is hooted, called *azimba* (savage), and excites general laughter, especially, as always happens, on the part of those who are incapable of distinguishing whether a track is a day or a fortnight old. The day in question, for example, I decide to try my luck at the pool where the lion has drunk three times in succession. Unfortunately, he does not return.

The habits of the lion and the rhinoceros are not the same : the former will drink at the same place for a long time ; the latter will never visit a pool more than once or twice in succession if it has another drinking-place.

Once having decided to hunt in a region, I had a night-watch shelter prepared at each of the pools, a shelter which consisted either of a hut, like the one I have described already, or of a small earth or stone entrenchment, so as to protect us, especially in the rear. More generally I used one of the ant-hills which abound at the water's edge and form elevations there. I cut out a seat[1] in it, and surrounded it at the back with thorns in order not to be surprised from that side. Other conditions are indispensable for the establishment of a shelter: for example, you must be leeward of the drinking animal, not too near nor too far off, as a rule outside the line by which it arrives at the water, and, above all, not too high; otherwise you are obstructed in firing. Sometimes, when there were no ant-hills and I could not do anything else, I have taken up a position on a tree; but, in return for the one advantage of not being scented, this position presents serious inconveniences, the first of all being the impossibility of moving or changing your place according to need. A tree is hardly any security: you cannot climb into it unless it is small (large trees being out of your reach), and any animal can spring into it—witness that wounded leopard which one day nearly reached our perch and sent us over *pêle-mêle* at the risk of breaking our necks and receiving us on its back. On that occasion the animal was frightened by what it had done and made off.

---

[1] On this seat we usually spread a piece of thick canvas, or an old sack.

Emphatically a tree is not equal to dry land. Of course, there is no contesting the fact that it is dangerous to wait for redoubtable animals on a dark night; but you retain the possibility of flight, and notwithstanding the doubtfulness and difficulty of this action, the thought reassures and gives you confidence; you are able to hide yourself behind your ant-hill, and even, if need be, choose before-hand a near tree in which to take refuge; you can change your position according to circumstances, and, besides, are at liberty not to fire, not to reveal your presence if you feel the danger is too imminent.

And then you must remember that in this form of hunting the man has the advantage of the surprise; he it is who waits in ambush and the animal is without suspicion. If at first I felt unnerved and full of apprehension, I soon got used to night-watches. Manifestly the emotions which result are much more violent than those which day-encounters produce; in the absolute stillness a falling leaf, a shadow, a breaking branch startles you, and the heart beats more than once upon the approach of an unknown animal which turns out to be but an inoffensive antelope.

If hunting in daylight is often a matter of taking in the situation at a glance and of rapidity of judgment, night-hunting, on the other hand, is *a question of coolness and calculation.* You must always beware of your senses, for many are the errors which one commits; the habits even of animals are different at night from what they are during the day, the beasts examining suspicious objects for a long time, prowling slowly round them, and thus giving you time for reflection. Moreover, you have several things in your favour: the stifling heat of the day, which makes animals thirsty, the absence of other drinking-places in the neighbourhood, and the very strong temptation which the wild beast will have to drink even if it suspects danger. Add also, as in my case, an electric projector which will send into the darkness a flood of light, and perfected weapons which are terribly destructive if well directed.

One will be inclined to think that, with so many precautions, this method of obtaining information, and this perseverance, I must kill, wound, or at least miss, an animal at every night-watch. Not so. According to an average for the years 1892, 1893, 1894, 1895, and 1896, I have passed 185 whole nights, from sunset to sunrise,—that is thirty-seven nights a year,—from October to December.[1] Out of these thirty-seven nights I have had on the average :—

Sixteen nights without any result, having heard and seen nothing: that is, almost half.

Six nights during which I have seen something without being able to fire.

Seven nights during which I have fired, wounding or missing animals which I have not been able to find.

---

[1] 1892, twenty-one nights ; 1893, thirty-two ; 1894, thirty-five ; 1895, forty-five ; and 1896, fifty-two.

Eight nights during which I have killed on the spot, or found the animals dead the next morning.

Eight successful days out of thirty-seven! That was sufficient, however, for I killed animals which amply repaid me for my trouble. But what feelings of discouragement I have had also, what moments of real anguish! How many times have I said to myself on returning, tired out by my night of waiting, during which fever was my only visitor, "I shall return there no more!" Yet I was there again in the evening. There is a host of sensations in the life of a nocturnal hunter which would need a more skilful pen than mine to describe them adequately. Some day I may try to relate them in detail, because all the incidents have been carefully noted down. For the time being I wish to relate a few only of the night-watches of the year 1895. The reader, assuredly, will find it more natural—my relating to him some of the eight nights which were crowned with success rather than the twenty-nine others which were without result. That is what I thought. I cannot too often repeat that, in the course of this book, I have designedly avoided telling him of all the inconveniences, checks, and disappointments with which I have met, because it would have been no longer a book of sport, but one of adventures which did not come off. I lay stress on this point: that, though I save the reader from the weariness of them, I have had, like everybody else, twice as many failures as successes.

My first nights in 1895 slipped by in a *chassé-*

croisé, which I shall place to the account of my adversaries. The evening I go to the north pool the beasts all drink at the south pool, and when I lie in ambush at the edge of the latter, absolutely nothing comes. Among the animals frequenting these drinking-places are two rhinoceros, strangers one to the other, an enormous solitary lion, two lions in company, and another family of three of these animals, two females and a male. Up to the present they do not seem to me to have any special pool; they wander about the country at night, and, from what I see, are well acquainted with the existence of the four pieces of water. They drink anywhere. I leave things to chance, therefore, and it is the pair of lions that I meet first of all.

I am hidden with Tambarika and Kambombe at the large south pool. The moon will not appear until about nine o'clock, and between the setting of the sun and the rising of the moon the darkness is intense. Our hiding-place is at the foot of an ant-hill, left of the pool and about thirty feet from its edge, around which is a gentle slope of one yard. I have with me the Express No. 2 loaded with two expansive bullets for the lion, the projector,[1] and the luminous sights fixed to the barrel, in addition to the Express No. 1 loaded with two solid bullets for the rhinoceros. Near at hand is the Winchester loaded with buckshot, to be used for firing point blank in case of imminent danger, such as a hand-to-hand

---

[1] For description of this projector and these sights, see *Mes Grandes Chasses*, p. 311.

struggle. My men have the 303 and a Martini rifle
in view of the same eventuality. The electric battery
is behind me securely fixed to a stake, so that a sudden
movement will not upset it.

The darkness has been intense for a quarter of an
hour. The field-glass, so useful for moonlight nights,
is not the slightest assistance in this black night.
Only the pool of water which reflects the sky is a
little lighter than the rest. All around we neither
see nor discern anything, although there are, alternately, bushes and bare earth, trees and stones. There
is not the slightest noise. Every now and then, however, a silure leaps out of the water and disturbs the
calm, some crickets chirp in the distance, and the
sharp, trilled notes of the goat-sucker (*rumbe*),[1] resembling the notes of our nightingale, strike upon the
ear. . . . Suddenly, without warning, another noise
comes from the edge of the pool, "Koom! koom!
koom!" . . . We nudge one another's elbows and our
hearts beat violently. . . . A lion is drinking! . . .
This "Koom! koom!" is made with his throat,
slowly, at intervals of a second, and for several
minutes does he drink thus. . . . The eye still distinguishes nothing. . . . The barrels of the Express
decline in the direction of the noise . . . there is no
need to hurry. . . . I turn on the switch, and a
dazzling ray shows us two lions, almost white under
the jet of light, in the position of crouching cats
which lap up milk, and at the same side of the pool
as ourselves. At this moment they turn their heads,

[1] *Cosmetornis vexillarius.*

and, without changing their position, look fixedly in our direction with blinking eyes. . . . Unfortunately, my projector is not well adjusted : the line of sight of the electric sights, similar to two small pieces of burning coal, does not accord with the centre of the patch of light : thus I am aiming at the neck, and the part illuminated is the stomach. . . . We experience a second of anguish ! . . . What is to be done ? Put out the light ? Impossible ! Let us try to aim by guessing . . . and I pull the trigger ! . . . A snarl answers to the rifle shot, and, with intermittent roars in my ears, I see a lion in the midst of the smoke and the diffused light roll over, suddenly rise, and try to climb the gentle slope of the pool. Again I fire, but badly ; he manages to climb up, and disappears in the darkness. . . . By moving my projector I try to see over there, but with the exception of a few bushes nothing is visible. The lion continues to growl at a short distance. . . . I put out the light, and with beating hearts anxiously we keep our ears on the stretch, our eyes having become useless. . . . There is a roar of pain . . . then another quite near behind us. We listen attentively with fingers on the triggers of our rifles. . . . Is it by chance turning round towards us ? . . . No. . . . An hour passes. We hear still another feebler groan, but almost at the same spot. . . . How fortunate the animal is still there ! . . . It is, therefore, unable to escape ! . . .

You may imagine, as I am not yet thinking of committing suicide, that I am careful not to move.

A NIGHT-WATCH: LIONS UNDER THE RAYS OF THE ELECTRIC PROJECTOR.

The moon rises. Some antelopes which come to drink take to flight, doubtless having scented the redoubtable personage who is near to them. The night passes without further incident. Every now and then the lion feebly moans, thrilling us with emotions until morning; about dawn we cease to hear it.

At daybreak my men try in vain to discover the whereabouts of the lion from the top of the ant-hill, and, as soon as it is full daylight, we leave our post, and, winding round the elevation, advance with precaution to a small tree into which Kambombe immediately climbs, to report to us that the lion is lying against a bush twenty yards away. He can only see its tail and hind paws; nothing moves. I make a detour, and, stifling the noise of my feet, get within thirty yards of the animal. Its head is hidden, but I see the remainder of its body lying on its right side. So, hiding myself behind a thicket, I use my field-glass to see if its flank rises and falls, but two minutes pass without my observing any movement. I throw a clod of earth near the animal, my weapon ready to bring to my shoulder if it rises. But it will never rise again : the lion is stone dead.

We draw near, and I have the pleasure of looking at a magnificent maneless lion stretched in a pool of blood. The bullet has broken the spinal column, or at least must have injured it sufficiently to make it snap when the animal took a few steps; the top of the lungs is shattered, as well as part of the liver. There is no trace of the second shot.

When finishing our examination we see a group of men in the distance, and find they are from the camp. In spite of the distance, the night has been so silent that they were able to hear the gun-shots, and Bertrand has sent to see what news there is. This reinforcement arrives timeously, and the lion is soon brought to the camp. Two hours afterwards its skin, carefully treated, is stretched on steel pegs in the sun.[1] Its skull is buried so as to get rid of the flesh; the carcase, after the examination of the stomach, which contained zebra, is taken a long distance from the camp and left to the vultures.

Two or three fruitless nights follow that which I have just related. One evening the rhinoceros approaches us at the north pool, round which it promenades, and, after having excited us to hope, makes off without drinking. Its suspicions were stronger than its thirst. As it is moonlight, I have a good mind to go in pursuit; but the prospect of being charged, even in the soft and poetic light of the moon, makes me renounce the idea, and I let it go. The rhinoceros makes off quietly, now and then sniffing with distrust, as much as to say, "Emphatically this place does not please me!" We have all our night's trouble for nothing.

Doubtless, it was the morning tracks of our men which this animal had scented. One has to avoid

---

[1] At the end of this book I give, for the benefit of hunter-naturalists, some indications on the manner of preparing animals' skins and other trophies.

walking round a pool where a rhinoceros is awaited :
its sense of smell is keen. So it was that my " information brigade " had orders to arrive in single file and
to enter the water, making a circuit of the pool, and
examining the edge with their feet in mud the whole
time. They came out at the same point they had
entered and followed the same path by which they
had come, so as to leave only one trace of their
passage.

One evening we took up our position at the small
south lake, which is very long and narrow. To be
within equal distance of all parts of it, we had to
place ourselves in the middle of one of the long sides,
profiting by an ant-hill which was there. This
position presented the serious disadvantage of allowing us to be scented by everything which would
come to our left. To possess a means of retreat in
case of a charge, we made steps at the foot of the
ant-hill so as to get down easily to the water, because
the edge of this side of the pool, which it overhangs
by nearly two yards, was perpendicular. Facing us,
on the other side, a gentle sloping bank led to a
plain devoid of obstacles, with the exception of
a few clumps of bushes scattered here and there.
In case of danger we had to let ourselves down into
the water, cross it, and make off over the plain, in
front of which, at a distance of 150 yards, was a
large tree in the low branches of which we could take
refuge. The rhinoceros, being unable to jump over
two yards of water, would be obliged to walk round
the pool ; which would give us a start. This little

plan had been made by Rodzani at our installation. We were there five or six nights without anything happening. The few animals which had broken the monotony of our waiting — buffaloes and antelopes for the most part — had gone down to the water on the side which was not steep. These animals do not like to descend a steep slope to drink, because it prevents them, when at the bottom, from seeing the surroundings, and they fear surprises. But you must always beware of the rhinoceros, and we had done well, as will be seen, not to trust to chance.

The evening, then, as I have just said, we take up our position. The first hour passes very quietly. Though there is no moon, the night is very clear, and the sky is sown with stars. Two hundred yards behind us is the dry bed of a river strewn with dry leaves, which have constituted a precious means of warning to us. For the last four days our pachyderm has not paid the shortest visit to these regions. This silence, this monotony of waiting, and my immobility produce a certain torpidness in me; I have the greatest difficulty in the world to keep awake; I rub my head and drink water, so as not to fall asleep. My men, silent as statues as usual, listen, and vigilantly keep their eyes open. From time to time they nudge me with their elbows to point out something which attracts their attention. I take my glass, and by the animal's gait, its method of proceeding, rather than by direct vision, I recognise it. Sometimes it is a hyena, which is recognisable by its sloping cruppers, and also by its lapping; sometimes an antelope, advancing without the least noise, like a shadow, remaining motionless for several minutes before resuming its walk.   Then everything disappears, and calm reigns once more.   One of my greatest privations on these night-watches is not to be able to smoke.   Ah! the hours would be less long if one could pass part of the time that way; but we smell quite enough already to animals, and also, it appears, to Chinese, without the still stronger emanations of tobacco smoke.

Suddenly, about eleven o'clock, we have plain proof that we give off an aroma very disagreeable to the delicate nose of certain wild beasts.   We hear at first a sound of sweeping in the dry leaves of the river-bed behind us. . . . Fully awake, with all my presence of mind about me, I listen with keen emotion, for there indeed is the step of a large animal. . . . It crosses, then comes out on our left, and immediately a snort as powerful as a jet of steam from a locomotive resounds in the silence of the night. . . . We recognise the angry bicornis for which we have come to look; but, to tell the truth, we expected it from another quarter. . . . We ask ourselves, with a feeling of anxiety, which may well be imagined, whether or not we have been scented. . . . In a few seconds we shall be quite certain about that. . . .

In fact, the approach of a furious gallop, an intermittent noise as of a small trumpet, and of heavy breathing, a fracas of broken bushes, tell us that not a moment is to be lost, and we decamp by our back door,—that is, we hastily climb down the embankment, plunge into the water up to the stomach, reach the other bank by large strides, and scamper over the plain at the moment our assailant reaches the ant-hill mad with rage, blowing and snorting like a steam-engine. We stop a few steps from the protecting tree to listen and to look round with wide-open eyes. We must make a very funny picture with our small packages; one of my men carries my cape, water-bottle, and electric battery; the other, like myself, has a rifle in each hand. Needless to say, we are ready to throw down everything which impedes us; but danger is not imminent for the moment, for upon reaching our ant-hill the rhinoceros must have lost our scent. Where is the animal? That is what we must know without delay, and only our ears can tell us.

Another snort and the noise of branches inform us that it is skirting the pool to the right of our watching-place. . . . We must come to a decision without a moment's delay. We decide to return immediately to our ant-hill, because the animal cannot scent us now: only, it has stopped perhaps, and is on its guard : so we must not make a noise. Consequently, we judge it wise not to cross the water, but to make a circuit of the pool in the direction opposite to that taken by the rhinoceros, in order to reach the ant-hill on the left. We put this idea into execution without accident. Hardly have we returned to the place where we sat than we hear the pachyderm, which has also passed round the pool, but the opposite way,

snorting on the plain which we have just left. . . . A
few minutes longer and we should have met it again!
My field-glass shows me only a gray, very indistinct
shadow which advances over the plain, but too far
away, owing to the darkness, to be fired at. . . . The
only thing to do is to wait. . . . During the space
of half an hour the animal makes us experience
many emotions: irritated beyond measure, it comes
and goes, returns on its steps, always invisible and per-
petually snorting.   At one time it must have arrived
near the tree at the place we stopped to listen, because
it breathes with still more anger and precipitation.
My men say, " It isn't a rhinoceros, it is a steamer,"
pronouncing the last word *stima*.   In fact, it is a
whistling, blowing, and snorting machine, which beats
the neighbourhood, and looks for us in all places
where its little brain suspects us.   We fear above all
that it will return on the left, and will again charge
us.   This little game may be allowable in open
daylight, but in the very middle of the night, when
you can hardly see to direct your steps, playing at
hide-and-seek with an angry rhinoceros is a pastime
which I do not recommend to people with delicate
nerves.   Your incapacity to see exasperates you
beyond measure; you start at the slightest crack
or sound, and at last your ear even deceives you
as to the real position of the animal which you
hear.

The noise ceases at last, and we believe that the
rhinoceros has gone.[1]   More than half an hour passes.

[1] The next day I saw that the rhinoceros had not left the plain for

I am considering the night as wasted, and our encounter as bound to have no other result, when my men and I suddenly see a shadow coming straight towards us from the other side of the water, and I recognise it to be the rhinoceros, slowly and noiselessly walking along. If I were not acquainted with the animal's habits I should think it saw us and was going to cross the water; but its quiet air and raised head show absence of suspicion; its mistrust is set at rest, and it is coming simply to drink. There it is at the edge of the water, where it stops facing us, listening and appearing so plainly to look at us that I cannot prevent muttering to my men, "It sees us!" "No, no, it doesn't see us; it is going down to drink. Wait until it is at the water's edge," they whisper in my ear. But a final suspicion comes over it; it stops at the edge and turns to look behind it, presenting its entire profile as a mark for my rifle. Distinguishing it clearly, I wish to profit by its position, and without using the reflector take good aim at its shoulder, firing two shots with the Express, one after the other. . . . We hear the violent impact of the bullets.

Hardly has the report rang out than the noise of a gallop dies away in the plain, and the usual questions are exchanged between us, " Have I missed or slightly wounded it?" "Oh no; your bullets went home, and it did not utter a cry. We shall find

an instant; it had stood motionless in the middle against a thicket, doubtless waiting until some noise or breath of wind informed it of our movements.

A NIGHT-WATCH: RHINOCEROS AT THE EDGE OF THE SOUTH POOL.

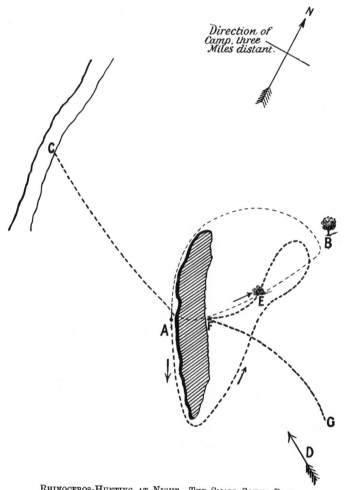

RHINOCEROS-HUNTING AT NIGHT—THE SMALL SOUTH POOL.

A, Our night-watch ; B, Isolated tree ; C, Dry bed of river ; D, Direction of
wind ; E, Bushes ; ⋯⋯⋯⋯, Path followed by hunters ; -------, Path
followed by rhinoceros ; F, Spot where it was shot ; G, Spot where it was
found dead in the morning.

it perhaps a long distance away to-morrow. We shall know the truth when it is daylight."

When daylight comes! . . . That is the only answer to the uncertainty of the result of these nocturnal hunts when your weapon is hesitating, your eye indecisive, and you lack confidence. Those hours separating you from sunrise appear interminable.

At daylight we start on the trail, on which there are here and there spots of blood, followed by spirts and large clots. When we see that "the heart laughs," as the natives express joy, and victory is almost certain. Two hundred yards from the pool, in fact, the rhinoceros is found to have fallen flat on its stomach with its four legs bent under it. It is the large rhinoceros reported by the research brigade — a female animal with a very fine pair of horns. One of the bullets pierced the heart, the other passed a little above the lungs; and both went right through the animal, stopping at the other side under the skin, where they formed protuberances.[1]

The death of a rhinoceros always brings joy to the camp. Its feet and heart, like those of the elephant, are almost the only parts which a European can eat; the rest is hard and at the most only good for making *pot-au-feu* or biltong for the natives.

[1] These bullets, and those with which I have killed my principal victims, I extracted from the body and preserved in a small collection which I look upon with a certain pride. Flattened, crushed, twisted, and deformed, my "celebrated bullets," as I call them, bear labels recalling their histories.

Two days afterwards, when at the north pool, I meet with the most terribly bad luck which I have ever known. Lions come twice; and the first time I miss two of them, shot after shot, the second time once more. Having seen three lions at the pool in one night, I return to the camp thoroughly beaten. Was not this the fault of the projector? I thought to have remedied the defect already pointed out, but the place upon which the luminous centre is brought to bear continues not to accord with that of the line of sight. Resorting to another expedient, I separate the projector from the rifle and attach it to a stick, which one of my men will hold. Henceforth it is he who will direct the flood of light on to the animal by following its movements, so that I shall be able to take aim at my ease. This improvement was very satisfactory: why did I not think of it sooner?

Out of the three lions, I believe, I have wounded only one, and that very slightly. The two others will return surely, but when? And where shall we meet again? How many nights will be necessary to make up for this lost opportunity?

A week slips by still with alternatives of discouragement and hope, but without the least success. At this time an attack of fever forces me to take two or three days' rest at the camp. We are, I repeat, a few yards away from the edge of a pool, and leeward of it, sheltered by a clump of large bushy trees whose shade makes us decide to establish ourselves here. Around is an abatis of branches and thorns; inside are pent-houses in which the men sleep in the shade.

On the morning of October 29 the European mail arrives with four months' letters and newspapers. At night, already, while Bertrand sleeps, I am stretched in the open air on my mat (I use neither a tent nor an iron bedstead during the dry season) with my feet bare, but otherwise dressed. By my side, on a stone which serves as a table, is a lantern, and I am reading the *Figaro*. Around me are a few half-extinguished fires, and men asleep; it is about nine o'clock, and moonlight. Suddenly, Msiambiri, who is taking a bath outside, runs in half-naked and streaming with water, saying, " *Pembere, mzungo, pembere!* " ("A rhinoceros, sir, a rhinoceros!")

I jump into my slippers, buckle on my cartridge-belt, which is within arm's reach, and seize my Express, while Msiambiri takes the other; and half a minute afterwards we are outside, advancing at the edge of the shadow of the trees. . . . I see a motionless gray mass at the edge of the pool; but it is too far away. Ordering Msiambiri to remain behind, I advance in the shadow to within twenty yards of the animal. I kneel down; but it is impossible to fire, as I cannot see well enough. . . . I drag myself forward again, crawling on my hands in the aquatic grass, until within ten or twelve yards of the animal. The rhinoceros begins to be suspicious; perhaps it even sees me; slightly turning, it completely faces me, at the same time snorting a little. . . . It

will charge, I say to myself: there is no drawing
back.   Pointing my rifle in the direction of its
chest, I fire the right barrel, reserving the left.
With one bound I spring into the grass out of the
way of my smoke, while the rhinoceros charges
almost to the very spot from which I fired, making a
tremendous noise with its feet, which slip on the
pebbles.   Then it stops, turns round, and disappears
at a slow trot before I am able to get into position
and fire again. . . . Once more am I very uncertain of having seriously hit.   I distinctly heard
the bullet strike and the animal cease its noise, which
it resumed afterwards as though I had caught it in
the wind ; but I shall not know the truth until to-
morrow.

How did this rhinoceros come almost leeward of
our camp, where there were thirty men, without
seeing it ?   It is very abnormal, and, on the part
of so distrustful an animal, is difficult to explain.
It is probable that, departing from its habits, it
came to leeward, and then, quite by chance, encountered the pool.   It was unable to scent the pool
without scenting us at the same time, and it is
probable, even certain, that, in that case, it would
have charged the camp, passed through the stockade,
and trampled under foot everything which it found
inside, while we should have escaped *pêle-mêle* on to
the plain.

However that may be, this unfortunate pachyderm
was very badly inspired in visiting us, for it cost it
its life.

At daybreak, on the following day, they came to tell me, to my great satisfaction, that the pebbles of the bank of the pool are spotted with blood. Lest there should be a pursuit, perhaps a long one, my men and I equip ourselves, and take with us food and water. But hardly are we *en route*, and have entered the plain, than Tchigallo exclaims, "There it is!" . . . and we see the rhinoceros lying on our right. It must have died a few seconds after receiving my shot, which, though fired almost at random, was most lucky amid the circumstances. But none the less what a terrible wound it made! The animal almost facing me, the bullet made a deep furrow along the right jaw and entered the neck, traversing the whole length of the fleshy mass, then pierced the upper part of the heart, and at last fell against the diaphragm, after having twice perforated the skin and followed an almost horizontal line through three feet of flesh and muscle. A few days before an animal was pierced through and through. What more can you expect from a weapon? But these are only two examples among many of what I have done with my Express No. 1.

This rhinoceros, which came to kill itself near the camp, was the one we called "the little one," the one which generally drank at the north pool, and on a previous evening was impolite to us by not coming to drink. Though its marks were much smaller than those of the female, it was, nevertheless, a very big animal, differing from the other by a few inches only.

DEATH OF OUR NOCTURNAL VISITOR.

It had fallen in the midst of charming scenery: a plain sparsely covered with grass, but here and there scattered with clumps of large *mitsagnas,* and in the distance a range of high hills, one of those European landscapes lit up by the rising sun. I have preserved this picture, like many others, by means of photography, and the reader may judge from the accompanying reproduction. The camp was about one hundred yards to the left. After the death of this animal, "rhinoceros," as my men used to say, "are finished." In fact, there existed only these two in the district, and the "information brigade" henceforth saw no more traces of them. Lions remained, five of them, including three which would never figure in my collection. I now come to my encounter with the two others.

It occurs at the beginning of November at the large south pool, which decidedly is the favourite with lions, for it is there that I killed one a few days before. Our position is the same as on that particular night, and it is also Tambarika and Msiambiri who accompany me. Only the moon gives us light until about twelve or one o'clock, and nothing comes up to that time. About three o'clock it is a starlight night. Lions are heard roaring in the distance, and I think "they have just eaten and are coming to drink." The roars draw near and then cease. The characteristic roaring by means of which, I suppose, they converse soon announces their arrival; they pass on our right, wind round the pool, and proceed down the other side—that is, in front and to the right of our hiding-place. The distance is from ten to twelve yards, the side of the pool about a yard high and preceded by a gentle slope from the water. Assisted by the ear, the eye distinguishes dimly the wild beasts' coats, which stand out and pass before surrounding objects, but we guess rather than see them. . . . They walk at the water's edge and at last stop. . . . Immediately the " Koom ! koom ! koom !" . . . with intervals between, begins. . . . " Now is the time, hunters ; let us try to do better work than the other day. Attention ! . . .

Tambarika holds the projector, which he directs towards the animals ; Msiambiri has his finger on the switch ; and I point my Express with its two luminous sights . . . I mutter a quick order, and the ray of light flashes out and strikes the astonished animals. . . . I do not lose a moment in looking at them while they raise their heads towards this improvised moonlight ; I aim at the first I see. . . . I aim at its shoulder-blades, which form, in its crouching position, two humps on its back. . . . Fire ! . . . The other lion makes off by climbing the bank, followed step by step by the reflector. . . . Bravo, Tambarika ! . . . I fire at its shoulder and it falls back again. . . . I fire once more . . . it rolls over with a growl, a harsh and continuous roar. . . . At last it rises, jumps on the bank, and disappears, roaring this time with all its force. . . .

Its companion is mortally wounded ; its head dips in the water, and it has fallen over on its side. As I cover it with my reloaded rifle its limbs give a final quiver. . . . All is over. The wounded lion groans once or twice on the plain before us, and the remainder of the night passes without other incident. A hyena and one or two antelopes approach, but all scamper away mad with fear as soon as they scent the lion. The hyena returns shortly afterwards; but, as I have no desire that it should spoil the magnificent skin which is there, that of a maneless male, I have the light projected on to it, and send it a bullet which wounds it, I believe, in the stomach. The hyena turns on itself like a dog trying to catch its tail, uttering howls and grunts of mingled rage or pain, and makes off, every now and then waltzing in the very comical manner described.

As soon as it is daylight Bertrand, who has heard my rifle-shots, sends my other hunters and men as upon the last occasion, lest there should be an animal to carry back. We perceive that the lion which has made off is the big solitary one whose spoors we have noticed more than once. Seriously wounded, it has made many stoppages on the plain and left small pools of blood everywhere ; but the whole morning is taken up in pursuing it, and a long, perilous pursuit it is, because its traces on the blackened earth are hardly perceptible, and only isolated drops of blood appear on plants or bushes. My men have climbed more than fifty trees in bushy places in the neighbourhood to look round. At last we lose the track completely ; the hemorrhage seems to have stopped, which often happens when a clot of blood naturally closes a wound. We abandon the chase about noon—to my great vexation, for I bitterly deplore the loss of this magnificent animal. Returning to the camp, I write my letters for the European mail instead of resting, the men who have brought my correspondence having to leave at dawn the next day to take it to De Borely, who is at a village six days' journey away. I send him with our letters, as I do upon every occasion, some packages of biltong and the natural-history specimens which encumber us. That night, therefore, I sleep at the camp. About ten o'clock the next morning two strangers are pointed out in the distance coming towards us. Yes : there can be no doubt they are coming here. They ask to see me, lay their weapons, rifles and assagais, against the stockade, clap their hands in token of welcome, and sit down at my feet like people who are in no hurry. At my request, one of them explains : " We are people of Bwana Marungo, and this morning we met on the Mafsitis' path[1] your two letter-carriers. We told them that we had seen vultures in the east, in the woods near the Mtudzi. Your carriers then told us that it was a *nyama* which you had lost yesterday, and that you would perhaps give us a present for coming to tell you."

"It is the lion ; it is the lion !" cry my men, who had surrounded us to hear what the strangers had to say. I give the two natives a present of cloth and a package of biltong, and they go on their way rejoicing. We, ourselves, set out at once as quickly as we are

[1] A footpath which led from Tete on the Zambesi to the Angoni country, a former slave-traders' route.

able. The place where we gave up the chase yesterday is south-west of the camp, and just before arriving there is the dry bed of the Mtudzi, a small river which flows in a southerly direction, and passes at a short distance the Mafsitis' pathway which we know well.

Now these natives, in coming this way, saw the vultures in the east, near the Mtudzi, and there is every likelihood that what they are after is our lion. In case we are right I take everything necessary to prepare the skin on the spot—steel pegs, a bucket, skinning-knives, arsenical soap, etc.

We reach the spot where we abandoned the chase yesterday, and, as the large trees hide the sky in the distance, we make a detour towards the Mafsitis' pathway. Half an hour afterwards we see the birds of prey, and we soon arrive on the spot above which they hover. We force a way through the thick vegetation, which the fire has left untouched, clouds of white and brown vultures flying from the surrounding trees at our approach. At last we distinguish a brown animal lying on the ground, half hidden by a shady bush. The quantity of flies show that it is quite dead. Let us approach. It is really our lion, but, alas! already much injured by hyenas, which have eaten the paws, and its swollen skin indicates decomposition. After having cleared away the bushes and grass, I photograph it; it is dragged into the shade; and my men hold it while Tchigallo proceeds to take off the skin. All have the calm bearing of men whose noses are philosophic in regard to smells: they surround this carrion and bend over it as we should over a basket of flowers. But this is nothing. When the intestines are removed they burst, and gases escape which put me to flight; but my men say simply and without conviction, " *Alle kunnuk'a* " (" It smells nasty "), exactly as we should say, " It is fine to-day."

As soon as the skin is removed I dip it, without touching the hair, into an alum bath prepared in the bucket, in order that when drying the hair will not slip; then I stretch it in the sun immediately, on a spot which my men have previously cleared. Assisted by Tchigallo, I measure the lion's carcase, at the same time holding my nose, and drag the body farther away, after which we go to rest in the shade and in the wind, while the skin dries, and the vultures feast at their ease on the body. Thanks to the care which I have taken with it, the skin, which has a splendid mane, almost black, is saved ; unfortunately, the paws had to be sacrificed. But I gather together most of the claws, and since then I have made souvenirs with them for my friends.

Here was a lion upon which I counted no longer, and I do not regret the presents given to the two natives who enabled me to find it again. According to its measurements, it is the largest which I have ever killed. It measures 11 feet 9 inches from the tip of its nose to the tip of its tail, and its skull is 1 foot 5 inches, one of the largest which I have ever seen. The advanced state of decomposition does not permit me to examine the body carefully. I believe that one of the bullets entered obliquely and pierced the upper part of the lungs, and that the other was lost in the back.

Three hours' torrid sun are sufficient to assure the preservation of the skin, and we set out for the camp after rolling it up with the hair outside, and passing a stick through it, which two men carry.

The vultures have long since finished their work, and a few well-picked ribs are waiting for the hyenas to-night.

The unexpected manner in which we have entered into possession of our wild animal is the subject of conversation for several days. I take a little rest; then, with the object of varying my pleasures and also to get some specimens of animals ordinarily difficult to approach, I spend a few days in hiding at the edges of my pools. Only in daylight I do not wait for animals to come to drink; if they approach within 100 yards it is sufficient—the 303 easily reaches them. I thus add to our collection two magnificent koodoos, an enormous baboon (*cynocephalus*), a fine specimen of a zebra, a curious monkey with a reddish back, etc.

Several times at the close of night-watches, when I had lost all hope of seeing large animals, I have killed smaller but very interesting nocturnal animals, such as lynx, civet-cats, tiger-cats, and a wild-pig (a rather rare animal), which must not be confounded with the wart-hog, which has large tusks, whereas the wild-pig has none. The wild-pig (*kumba*) is larger than our wild-boar; it is essentially nocturnal; its flesh is excellent, and its bristles are reddish brown.

I have kept its skull. I have killed a scaly ant-eater, an animal partly protected with scales, very curious and very rare, which the natives hardly know. This strange animal did not come to drink; I do not think it ever drinks. It was rummaging about near our hiding-place, and disquieted us for two reasons; its noise was unknown to us, and I did not manage to reconstitute its identity. At dawn one morning I sent a bullet at it, and we heard it no more. We found something afterwards, somewhat similar to a large fir cone, which turned out to be the scaly ant-eater rolled into a ball with its scales raised. It opened out when *rigor mortis* was over.

Among animals which do not drink, or find underground resources of which we are ignorant, I will also mention *en passant* the ant-eater, the tortoise, the snake, most species of rodents, the agouti, insectivora, etc., the squirrels of the "mitsagnas" (*baubinia*), hares, etc.; and among those which one never sees at the water, which undoubtedly drink in places known to them alone, partridges, francolins, klipspringers, etc.

What proved to me that nowhere was there water except at our four pools were the two daily visits which birds made to them. In the morning and evening all the small species came, quantities of doves and guinea-fowls; at noon, vultures, marabouts, crows, and sparrow-hawks. By remaining for several days at your observation station you could see them appear with great regularity; some at the time of the first and the last rays of the sun, others

THE KOODOO: THE HANDSOMEST OF ALL THE ANTELOPES.

during the hottest part of the day. Animals which hardly ever wander from water, such as water-bucks, reed-bucks, wart-hogs, hartebeests, etc., generally drink about nine o'clock, coming back again about four in the afternoon; those which go far afield, such as elands, zebras, sable antelopes, and nswalas, have no fixed hours, and come when they are able. Buffaloes appear at sunset, or, if travelling at night,

EN ROUTE FOR THE CAMP.

generally reach the drinking - place early in the morning. Monkeys, large and small, show themselves about noon.

Ordinarily, lions slake their thirst after sunset and before sunrise, but they are not very regular, everything depending on the result of their hunting; if they have eaten well at night they are certain to come to drink at daybreak, before retiring to digest their food. The rhinoceros comes to the water about ten o'clock—

that is, two or three hours after nightfall—or in the morning before daybreak.

There are, however, many exceptions to these habits; and one can never foresee very clearly what humour, instinct of self-preservation, or distrust, will inspire in these animals.

AN "INYALA."

CHAPTER XI

GIRAFFE-HUNTING—HIPPOPOTAMI ON LAND AND IN THE WATER—ELEPHANTS

Life in the midst of insects—In the Barotses' country—Tracks of giraffes and
their pursuit—Death of one of them—Colour of the coat and measurements of a male giraffe—Differences between wild specimens and those
in zoological gardens—Hippopotami-hunting—Hunter in the water and
hippopotami on land—Rapidity of this animal—Method of hunting it
in the water—Specific weight of flesh—Its eatable quality—Flesh of
felines—A hunter's bill of fare—Elephant-hunting—Females without
tusks—Man injured by an elephant—Death of a solitary elephant—The
"pneumatic" elephant—History of a bomb-shell—Vultures assembled
—In Moassi's country—Snakes—Python dance—Insectivorous birds—
The Inyala—Catching fish with dynamite.

In the wilds of Africa you accustom yourself to
living with a multitude of small enemies. For
example, a piece of firewood which you pick up is full
of pleasant surprises; as soon as one end is on fire you
see crawling from the other bluish scorpions and very
venomous scolopendra, which immediately seek refuge

in the nearest object, whether it be a heap of straw or your own bed. The lantern, by the light of which you are eating your *soupe*, attracts and causes to fall into it either wood-lice which poison it, or lady-birds which colour it. Or, a dung-beetle, the sacred insect of the Egyptians, after having rolled about among the filthiest things (even where butterflies and bees settle),[1] and promenaded around the camp, walks across your face or over your biscuit. Your sugar is always covered by a small red swarm of minute ants whose speciality is sugar, fat, oil, butter,—in short, everything which you would especially like to be without ants. Water is sometimes full of leeches, or else contains larvæ, which leave you one fine day in the form of guinea-worms. White ants emerge from the earth on all sides, and, respecting iron only, eat into your packages. Bugs, imported by the Arabs (longer in shape and more slender than the European kind), invade certain villages to such an extent that the blacks desert their huts, sleep outside, and end by burning their hamlet and everything they possess before going elsewhere. Fleas, larger than those which infest our dogs, are rarer, but none the less hungry; they attack the body, while their still more voracious sisters, the jiggers, penetrate the flesh of the feet, which they devour, and in which they lay thousands of eggs. If you eat by lamplight your plate is full of insects; if you take your meal in the dark, strange, new, and indescribable tastes tell you that you eat them all the same, although in smaller

[1] See *Mes Grandes Chasses*, p. 277.

quantities; you cannot open an egg without finding a chicken there, or certain fruits without discovering worms inside; native figs (*nkuiu*) are always full of black ants and meat of maggots.   Insects are everywhere.   Tsetses, wasps, stinging flies, and gnats, occupy themselves with you in the daytime, whilst at night mosquitoes pay you their attention.   Charming existence, and one full of surprises, to which, however, you grow accustomed, so much so that when you return to Europe, and have none of these inconveniences, you miss them, and solitude *almost* weighs heavily upon you!

Life swarms everywhere in these countries, and possesses wonders for the student.   I have neither the time nor the pretension to enlarge on this subject. I have contented myself by showing that the hunter has not always to attack big animals.   On the hunter returning to camp a swarm of animalculæ shares, as you see, in spite of himself, his life . . . and his food. I now return to hunting.

About the end of December 1895, the expedition, continuing its scientific work, had crossed the Aroangwa and was in the Barotses' country, very far from the scene of my first hunting exploits.[1]

On the other hand, the country has almost the same appearance; the grass, which is late, is a foot high, and at this period—equivalent to our spring in Africa—everything is a tender green.   We have

---

[1] The end of November and the beginning of December had been fruitful in results; but, for want of space, I have not been able to mention them.   I now come to a new sport, giraffe-hunting.

not yet resumed the semi-aquatic life which we lived at the Kapoche camp; but we shall soon, for storms follow one another at short intervals, accompanied by deafening claps of thunder, and rain cannot be long in falling with abundance and regularity.

Meantime my men and I again cross the country. The dry season was a time of rest for our legs; now begins again the period of long marches up hill and down dale, over forest and plain, in search of game.

Twice already we have seen traces on the ground which are unknown to us. Tambarika himself is unable to inform us, and though I am doubtful as to what animal made the marks, which resemble those of a buffalo, but are much larger and more elongated, I guess we have to do with giraffes. Having seen these animals in zoological gardens, I describe them to my men. They look at me with an air which leaves no doubt as to what they are thinking: the glances which they exchange say as plainly as words, " Up to now we should not have thought the master such a joker. A great change must have come over him."

I question the first native we see about our discovery, and describe a giraffe to him, which he corroborates in every point, even giving me the name of the animal in "Barotse," a name which I had forgotten.

Supplied with information, and accompanied by a few native hunters lent me by the chief of the country, I find myself, a few days afterwards, in the region frequented by giraffes, and doubly desirous of meeting with them, first of all because I have never killed one, and then to show one of them to my men.

Among my new assistants I notice one who appears to know his business well. He is a man who can read a spoor admirably, climb a tree and descend quicker than a monkey, and moves through the grass like a snake. He has the reputation of having killed giraffes, and of being acquainted with their habits.

As a fairly large company of elephants frequent the district regularly, probably because the natives have no firearms, we have a double chance of success. I notice also two species of antelopes, which are new to us, "pookoos" (*cobus vardoni*), and "letchwes" (*cobus leche*), both varieties of water-bucks, the first small and broad-backed, the size of a light-bay ass, the other gray, with a white stomach, and their horns very much resembling those of the water-buck with which we are acquainted.

Large rivers, such as the Aroangwa or the Zambesi, mark out well-defined limits which certain species of game never exceed. That is why fauna differs according to the banks one visits.

At this time of the year the wind is no longer certain, and its continual changes sometimes do us a bad turn by putting animals to flight,—one day particularly, when it warned a herd of giraffes of our approach. From their fresh spoor and dung we see that they have smelt us, and fled only a few minutes ago. Perhaps, also, their sight being long, they saw us. I do not know for certain. Trees are climbed, and the horizon is scanned; but nobody sees anything.

A few days afterwards we see a herd of five or six giraffes four hundred yards away. The telescope, which I have expressly carried with me for several days, enables me to see them splendidly as they stalk up and down with their long legs, and swing their long necks backwards and forwards. We throw ourselves to the ground, although a long distance from them, and, while my men remain, the Barotse hunter and I drag ourselves forward on our stomachs, from time to time risking a glance, to disappear again in the grass. When we find plants a little taller we get on to our feet, and, bent double with our chests against our knees, and our heads low, we glide between the bushes. As soon as the bushes cease, and the short grass reappears, without anything to hide us, we begin once more our slow snake-like movement on our stomachs. We crawl thus for about one hundred yards. During this time the giraffes continue to walk about quietly among the trees, stopping from time to time, several of them eating the leaves of the trees in which their heads are hidden or buried.

A bare space now comes, as difficult for us to cross as a fathomless torrent: so we drag ourselves over it with great care, letting some trees farther away interpose like a screen between our position and the large animals. This snakish movement is very tiring in the sun, for every yard you have to stop with your chest against the ground, get hold of your rifle, which you have left in the rear, and place it in front of you, to crawl up to your weapon, and then to begin the same movements again. You do not regret your trouble if everything succeeds, but if when two hundred yards from you the giraffes scamper off you are not at all pleased. That was what happened to us the day in question.

The Barotse hunter assures me, and with reason too, that we were seen, but how not be, unless possessed of the ring of Gyges, on open plains habitually frequented by these animals, whose necks serve them as belvederes? He adds that we have the best chance in the evening, and that he often proceeds as follows: first of all he examines the giraffes' position at sunset, and at dawn he is able to approach them without being seen, or scented, or heard.

My misadventure on this occasion is repeated several times; once when within two hundred and fifty yards, another time when within three hundred yards, the giraffes make off as we crawl along out of breath, and with perspiration pouring from us. I become convinced that they always saw us from the very first, some time even before we saw them, but that they flee only when they believe danger to be imminent.

One day, however, when we are leaving a dense thicket for the plain, we catch sight of giraffes. Immediately, like one man, all of us draw back into the shadow to consult. It is decided that we remain under cover of the thicket, and, as it winds round the plain, we can draw near the distrustful animals. Consequently, we turn back, and, following an old elephant track, walk rapidly and noiselessly for ten minutes. Halt! The Barotse returns from the edge of the thicket, where he has been to look out, and leads us there with many precautions. I then perceive, at a distance of at least two hundred yards, seven or eight giraffes quietly browsing in various positions, some walking slowly about, others standing in the shade of the trees. . . . There is no means of drawing near in a straight line. The animal which seems larger to me than the others, perhaps because it is the nearest and most clearly seen, presents its cruppers to me. It is busily eating from a tree four or five yards high, above which its head towers, and from the top of which it seems to be choosing the young shoots.

I take my 303, not relying very much on the precision of the Express at this distance, and load it with two decapitated solid bullets. The point only of the bullet is filed off. Bullets treated in this way give animals a more violent shock than hollow ones, and at the same time without going through them.[1]

Carefully I bring my weapon to my shoulder. The sharp report of the 303 makes the giraffes start and rapidly assemble, their long necks motionless, and stretched in the wind like ducks which are about to take to the wing. Not knowing exactly whence the

---

[1] When you have nothing better you can thus make good projectiles for large animals out of solid bullets. The nickel point must be filed away until the lead is well in view.

shot came, they hesitate for a moment. . . . I take advantage of this to fire once more at the same animal, which upon the first shot jumped forward, and feel certain that my two bullets have struck hard. This time the herd dashes off at a gallop, in the midst of a cloud of dust, and as we emerge from the thicket at a run I see the wounded giraffe following painfully. We proceed to examine the tracks. At first there is no blood at all, but its stride has that tired and flagging appearance we know so well, indicating that an animal is seriously wounded ; a little farther on a few drops of blood appear, and, led by the Barotse, we follow the track at a quick trot.

Suddenly our leader throws himself to the ground, and we imitate his example. The giraffes have stopped two hundred yards away, all assembled in various positions, with their necks stretched out in our direction, all so motionless that at a first glance I thought they were a clump of dead trees. Again I fire ; I hear distinctly my bullet strike one of them, and the herd again sets off. But soon we see a giraffe, still moving, lying on the ground, hidden by a hillock which had shielded us from the herd, and with a haste easy to be imagined we get over the two hundred yards of ground and look upon our victim. My men utter exclamations of astonishment at the curious shape of this animal, which they see for the first time. Leaving it in charge of two of them, I set off in search of the one which I have just wounded.

As no trace indicates a wounded giraffe, and as it is four o'clock in the afternoon, I decide to abandon the chase after covering two-thirds of a mile, and return to the dead animal. It is a male of great size : never should I have believed that this animal could reach such dimensions. Here is its complete description, very different from that of the pale and sickly specimens of our zoological gardens, which are mostly born in captivity, so different, in fact, that for a time I thought I had discovered a new variety of the camelopard of naturalists (*camelopardalis*).

The ground colour of the coat over the whole body is chestnut or nut-brown, almost black on the back ; the spots are darker than the ground colour, hardly perceivable on the cruppers, invisible on the back, more distinct on the limbs ; the stomach is a little lighter ; between the legs the animal is light bay ; its hair is very stiff, and shines in the sun like copper ; the skin on the back and shoulders is thick, nearly one inch and a half, and exceedingly heavy, as heavy as a rhinoceros' ; the horns are surmounted by a little tuft of hair, the eyelashes are long and silky ; the tail ends with a big bunch of long and supple hairs. Its general aspect is coarse, suggestive of strength and constant strife rather than of slender delicacy. The meat, which gives off a strong smell of musk, appeared to me uneatable, with the exception of the tongue, which, by the bye, is immeasurably long. We obtained excellent marrow from its bones. As to its size, it measured not less than 17 feet 3½ inches from the

A MALE GIRAFFE.

top of its horns to the bottom of its hoofs; and this is not the maximum, male giraffes having been killed in South Africa measuring 18 feet and 18 feet 11 inches.[1]

I should have liked to preserve this magnificent beast for our museum, but it was practically impossible to dry a skin of this thickness and size during the rainy season; besides, transporting it would have been no small matter, judging from the fact that, while even the skin of an eland weighs more than sixty pounds, a giraffe's skin exceeds one hundred pounds. What losses to science occurred during this expedition owing to lack of means of transport! Many elephants and other large animals were killed whose skins or skeletons would have been invaluable for our museums.

On other occasions I wounded two giraffes, but I was never able to overtake them. When one recollects that hunters in South Africa, even on horseback, and pushing their steeds to the top of their speed, do not always overtake these animals, one can easily understand the chance I had on foot. I consider having killed one as very satisfactory.

During these two or three weeks we study the habits of the giraffe, and I find out that it inhabits, preferably, flat countries where, lacking *acacia giraffae*, which is its favourite food south of the Zambesi and is little met with in the Barotse

---

[1] Females are, according to their age, rather lighter in colour, but I have never seen any which were the colour of those in our menageries.

country, it eats various leguminous plants of the same species. It takes the young shoots of the tree, and leaves *débris* strewn on the ground wherever it has eaten. When pursued it dashes into the thickest forest with an ease which seems incompatible with its shape; its head is lowered and passes under the branches; its long legs adroitly avoid the thousand obstacles in its path. In the act of running it makes with its neck a very regular, combined, upward and forward, downward and backward movement like that of some jointed toys, at the same time ceaselessly switching its tail. Finally, it only goes at a walking-pace or gallop, without intermediary speed, and, though seeming not to multiply its steps, really proceeds with considerable speed. The toughness of its skin, which I cannot better compare than with the hide of a rhinoceros, requires heavier bullets than the Expansive, and the Express seems to be the one for shooting this strange animal.

The more or less dark chestnut colour of wild giraffes makes them very difficult to distinguish in the distance, owing to their legs and neck being exactly the same shade as the tree trunks with which they blend. When on the *qui vive* these large animals also keep perfectly still, completing the illusion; if one thinks of looking at the top of the trees instead of underneath, one can sometimes see their heads. An almost completely black back is a feature of old male animals.

The day on which I killed the giraffe described above, the whole expedition—composed, in addition to my hunters, of natives, the majority of whom were from the east bank of the Aroangwa,—wished to defile before this colossal quadruped, and the cutting up of the body was not performed until next day. I shall profit by the few days' rest following this task to relate a hippopotamus[1] hunt a short time before, on the banks of the Aroangwa, amid circumstances not often experienced, which merit the telling.

In the immediate neighbourhood of the great river were shallow pools, and around them banks of sand partly covered with reeds. Having seen five hippopotami lying in the sun on one of these banks, I was struck with the happy idea of cutting off their retreat by coming upon them through the pool, the bottom of which I could see. Advancing, therefore, by the river bank, my 8-bore in readiness, I entered the water, and silently advanced with the intention of making ravages in the herd of monsters.

Nothing is so ugly as a hippopotamus on land. It would seem as if Nature, by creating this deformed animal, wished to ridicule beauty, regularity of lines, harmony of outline. Moreover, it is to be noticed that large animals of the past or present have had the privilege of ugliness. While giving myself up to these philosophic-æsthetical reflections, I draw near to this kind of " Mille Kilos " Club, and I deploy my men, giving them orders to fire if the hippopotami charge them. I imagined that this animal moved slowly on land ; how wrong I was will be seen.

[1] For the habits of this animal, and how to hunt it, see *Mes Grandes Chasses*, pp. 58-64, 70, 221, 239.

When within ten yards, hidden by reeds, we rise slowly and look at the animals. One of them is awake; it moves its measly eyelids; and its little eyes, turned towards us, blink. . . . I select the oldest male, which sleeps well in profile in the middle of the group, as though, before going to sleep, he had told them some story of mediocre interest, and when I fire my men deploy with much noise to drive the hippopotami in the direction of the land. All but one rise like a single animal, and while two of them come to meet us, two others make off to the right along the sand-bank. The one which remains, the old one, struggles on the ground with a shattered shoulder. I finish it off afterwards by putting a bullet in its head with the 303.

Seeing the two hippopotami making towards us, my men fire at them; but this provocation only increases their rage, and they open their enormous red mouths, armed with gigantic teeth, mouths the lower jaw of which seems as big as the cot of a ten-year-old child, and from the depths issue formidable roars. Increasing their pace they continue to proceed straight upon us. But my men and I, without thinking of playing at this improvised *jeu de tonneau*, quickly make off, while the other two hippopotami, which have skirted the bank, enter the water down stream with loud plumps. In less time than it takes to say so, these pachydermita have gone one hundred yards, and have disappeared in the deep, protecting waters of the Aroangwa.

You cannot imagine how quick these massive

animals can run unless you have seen them. Without galloping, they trot very quickly with their big, waddling bodies, and get over much ground without seeming.to do so. I am sure that an agile man would have difficulty in outrunning them.

A few days afterwards, however, having noted their position, I construct a barrier in the form of a big net of palm-tree fibre stretched down stream, and kill three of the hippopotami in the water with my 303.

This form of hunting is very simple; it only requires a little patience. All you need is a steep bank at the part of the river where hippopotami come up to breathe, and at the side nearer to them from which you can fire down upon them. You hide yourself, and take advantage of the moment all the animals have disappeared to take up your position on the bank, where, by retaining perfect immobility, you will not be seen. To change your place or position, to raise your rifle, or to move in any way, you wait until the hippopotami are under water. When they emerge you carefully select one of them, and aim between the eyes if the animal is facing you, under the eye and on a level with the water if it is in profile, between the two ears and on a level with the water if its back is towards you. The brain is touched with a solid nickel-cased bullet from the 303; often even the head is pierced from side to side; and death is instantaneous. In this case the animal falls backwards with its mouth open; its two fore-feet appear; and a little froth and blood rising to the surface are the only signs to show the place where it lies at the bottom. On the other hand, if it rolls over, and its four feet beat the water, the swirl indicates its position, and it reappears several times, agitating the surface. Owing to the difficulty of shooting with accuracy amid these conditions, several bullets will be needed to kill it. Once dead, the animal sinks to the bottom, but the distension of the intestines gradually raises it to the surface in three to six hours,[1] according to the temperature of the water. As soon as it begins to rise, the current carries it away, and in deep rivers the hunter loses his quarry. That is why I place very broad nets made of palm-tree fibre, with stones and floats attached, across the river down stream, these restraining the body when it drifts.

Blacks are very fond of hippopotamus flesh, which they prefer next to that of the buffalo. All these dried meats are very much alike. In the opinion of Europeans they are only fit for improving *soupe*, they do not supplant fresh meat; but native hunters recognise very well by the taste of biltong the various animals which have been used in its manufacture. I distinguish the various kinds almost as well as my men, but it is by their density. As a matter of fact, these meats, when well dried, are quite different in weight, this doubtless arising from their more or less close fibres and the proportions of water which they contain. The lightest is that of the elephant; the water-buck, reed-buck, and sable antelope come next; then, in smaller proportion, the rhinoceros,

---

[1] A slightly less average than given in *Mes Grandes Chasses*, but which experience of recent years has shown me to be correct.

zebra, wart-hog, koodoo, and bush-buck ; and, finally, the heavy meats, such as eland, hippopotamus, and buffalo.

In these countries the flesh of a young eland will be found by a European to be equal to the best butcher's meat ; small antelopes, in addition to wild-pigs and wart-hogs, come next in order as choice food ; large antelopes are only just eatable ; and the flesh of young hippopotami is fairly good cold.   As to buffalo, elephant, rhinoceros, and male giraffe, they are the food of the famished negro ; and those fine shots of ours do not improve the hunter's fare—at the most they result in a good *pot-au-feu.*

Felines are excellent in every way, the lion, leopard, serval, and wild-cat supplying a white, tender flesh without unpleasant flavour, which resembles veal or fresh pork.   The populations of the basin of the Zambesi do not eat them, but those of the great lakes rightly consider them as a treat.

Young crocodile is eatable if you know how to skin the animal without tainting the flesh with the musk, and when in Dahomey we made some succulent stews with it.

Finally, to complete this brief description of new food-stuffs, I will add white ants,[1] grasshoppers, which take the place of shrimps, land and water tortoises. As game I will mention the iguana, python, monkey, squirrel, agouti, and other animals which we Europeans do not eat, because our forefathers have not accustomed us to them.

[1] See *Mes Grandes Chasses*, pp. 139, 144.

It would not have been difficult for me, if I had had guests at the camp, to draw up a menu after the following fashion :—

MENU

SOUP
Consommé of buffalo tail.   Eland soup.

HORS D'ŒUVRE
White ants, grasshoppers on the point of laying.

ENTREES
Jugged wild cat, elephant's foot à la poulette, giraffe's tongue with caper sauce.

VEGETABLES
Mushrooms, Bonongwe with eland's marrow, Runi, Mtanga with ground nuts.

ROASTS
Elephant's heart larded with wart-hog fat, rolled rhinoceros fillet, monkey en papillotte, agouti stuffed with tortoise.

SALAD
Matako ia tsano.

DESERTS
Fulas, matondos, mtudzi, tchendje, and various others.

WINE AND BEER
Moa or pombe and fresh Chiromo nchema.

Unfortunately, you generally lack ingredients with which to prepare all these good things, and neither

Bertrand nor De Borely had a passion for exotic cooking. Willingly would they eat meats, but they were by no means enthusiastic over white ants, small rats roasted *en brochette*, spinach of the region, and a host of other dishes of the same kind.

For my part, I can only repeat what I have already said elsewhere : [1] if we made a list of everything used for food in various parts of the world, vegetables apart, we should come to the conclusion that everything living which nature has placed on the earth is eatable, and that people fond of it may be found. Was it not with this object that animals were created, like an interminable bill of fare, from which man is free to choose what pleases him ?

All these considerations have made me forget the giraffes : so I return to them.

Seeing that I was wasting my time and trouble in pursuing them, I decided to change the kind of game and again search for elephants. So, leaving the countries of the plain with their sparse vegetation for hilly ground covered with thick thickets and grass which promised to be tall, I came to other parts. I was fortunate enough to kill nine elephants there, most of them females. The majority of these hunts, however, were not marked by any abnormal incidents. Naturally, we were charged several times; but there were no accidents.

I now reach a day on which we came across four female elephants and their small families. The pursuit having been long, we overtake them at the

[1] See *Le Dahomey*, p. 151.

hottest part of the day, when they are shading themselves under a clump of trees. The Barotse hunter, who has not left us, has brought a compatriot with him, a hunter like himself, named Katchwa, who committed several imprudences on preceding hunts. Armed with a flint-lock in which he had great confidence, he drew disquietingly near to elephants, and his gun often missed fire. I had a great desire to leave these two men at the camp or to send them home, but every hunter is a little superstitious. I attributed the return of good luck to their presence, and should I not have made the luck change by sending them off? That was the reason I took them with me each morning; and each time we met elephants.

Now, the day we come across the four females, we have no sooner clapped our eyes on them than we see that two of them are tuskless, and my men mutter, "*Niungwa,*" the name of tuskless elephants, as though as to say, "By Jove, it's going to be warm work!" . . . Immediately, and not without difficulty (because he does not understand me very well), I advise the native hunter not to throw himself among the elephants' legs, as he has done several times already, as soon as the first shot is fired.

As far as I am concerned, I do not see anything to be gained in the affair; two tuskless females are going to charge; and the tusks of the two others are insignificant. My first impulse is to leave them alone, but when you are in the presence of these enormous animals it is difficult not to shoot, and to turn tail foolishly. However, I keep at a respectable distance, about sixty yards, whereas in the case of a male animal I place myself at fifteen or twenty. Aiming at the shoulder of one of the females, I fire.

The country is relatively open. The report has no sooner rung out than two trumpet-blasts announce the charge, and one of the females (not the one at which I have fired) dashes to the right. As she is going to scent me, I withdraw fifty yards. At the same time I see the native come up with the intention of cutting off the animal's retreat. She immediately scents him, which is only natural, and we witness a mad race between the man and the furious elephant which pursues him. He cleverly escapes, and the animal loses his scent, but another trumpet-blast rings forth, and the second female, which was on the watch, in turn throws herself upon him. Notwithstanding two bullets which I send into her head, one of which strikes her violently, she passes on our right a few yards behind the unfortunate fellow, almost touching him. . . . The two fresh reports have attracted the attention of the first animal, which again charges the smoke from my rifle, while we decamp at the top of our speed, only thirty yards ahead of the animal. . . . But she loses our wind and goes off to rejoin the other in the distance, both of them then disappearing in the direction whence their companions, including the wounded animal and a small one, have already gone.

Where is Katchwa? He is bleeding from the

mouth and nose, stretched on the ground. After bringing him round I feel him all over, and find that, in addition to serious bruises, he has two ribs and an arm broken. As well as he is able, he explains to us that the elephant gave him a kick. He does not know himself how that happened. I believe that he must have been dashed against a tree by the elephant's trunk, or else, in trying to walk over him, it was carried forward by its inertia, and gave him a kick which sent him several yards away. My men carry the poor fellow to the camp, where I bandage him up, postponing until the following day the search for the wounded female, which, owing to my bullet having struck home, cannot have gone far.

In these countries it is common for a native to be caught by an elephant. Msiambiri knew two of his father's comrades, and I can mention three or four men of coolness and courage, all elephant hunters, who were killed in this way between 1891 and 1897. This often arises from the fact that blacks get too near the animal; having confidence neither in the range or the precision nor in the penetrative power of their weapon, they fire almost point - blank, so that they have not always time to avoid a charge if it is made immediately.

The following is a list of similar accidents which happened, to my knowledge, to members of my expedition, or else to neighbouring natives, during the last seven years in the course of my hunts or "battues":—

1891. Kapoche.—One man killed by a buffalo. Two men killed by elephants, one of them on the spot.

1892. Tchipeta.—One man wounded by a buffalo. One wounded by an elephant.

1893. Tchipeta.—One man wounded by a leopard. One trampled under foot and killed by an elephant. Two wounded.

1894. Makanga.—One man wounded by a buffalo. One wounded by a lion in camp.

1895. Angoni.—One man wounded by a lion. One killed by a lion during a "battue." One bruised by an elephant.

1896. Moassi.—One man seriously wounded by a lion. Msiambiri carried off by an elephant.

1897. Congo.—One man wounded by a leopard.

Total.—Five men killed, including three on the spot ; and eleven wounded, one of whom has remained lame, and five of whom were very seriously hurt.

Our hunter had well avoided the first female, but unfortunately fell in with the second, which kept a treacherous immobility until the wind told her of the presence of the enemy. He might think himself lucky in having got off so well.

I improvise with bamboo a rough - and - ready apparatus to keep his arm rigid, and all danger of complications seems to be over after a few days. The two Barotse hunters then return to their country by short stages.

The day after the accident we go in search of our wounded elephant, but on the way we come across the track of a male elephant which is quite alone. This animal being large in size, we once more postpone the search for the female, and follow the solitary animal.

In Africa, solitary elephants (known as "rogues") are easier to kill than others. Naturally, they cannot guard themselves as well as a herd of several animals; and, moreover, though generally on the *qui vive*, they are easy to approach. It is the same in the case of buffaloes. Several times have I killed isolated males, and it is infinitely less dangerous than looking for the head of a herd sometimes in the midst of females. I emphasise this point, because all hunters are not of the same opinion, and solitary elephants are generally given a character for wickedness and ferocity which they do not deserve.

We follow our elephant, which eats as he walks. The wind, fortunately, is in our favour. We overtake him in the tall grass while he proceeds slowly on his way. Those colossal gray cruppers which move away in front of me hide the tusks, but, according to the dimensions of his foot, I believe they are of large size. Waiting until he again stops to eat, we keep at a distance; but he seems to be no longer hungry, and, as the wind may change, I begin walking parallel to him, hiding myself behind the bushes. At a certain moment, when I am twenty yards to his right, and my men are a little in the rear, he stops, and whether by chance, or whether he is suspicious, stands exactly opposite the bush which hides me.

At this moment he is magnificent to look upon, with his large ears open, his two short, white tusks shining in the rising sun. Has he seen or scented me? I get ready my Express (which I had brought with me that day, as on every other day of the week, leaving my 8-bore at the camp) in case of a charge.

. . . But he turns and continues in his first direction. I run a little forward and stop to await him, my rifle barrels already searching for his heart under his gray and wrinkled skin, which moves when he walks like the folds of an accordion. . . . At last I have it, and my first shot is fired, the bullet striking his body with a dull sound. . . . I had kept the second shot with which to defend myself, but seeing the elephant keep straight on, I fire from where I am when he is a few yards farther away.   Hastily recharging, I skirt the bushes at a run, without showing myself, in the same direction as he. . . . Suddenly he stops, and, in the middle of the plain, thirty yards from us, again turns round in my direction.   Notwithstanding the danger and the imminence of the charge,—for I clearly perceive he is trying to see or scent his enemy, —I cannot help admiring him.   How splendid he is thus! His head on high, his trunk raised, and his ears—like large shields—stretched out, he resembles one of those powerful and dignified bronzes of colossal dimensions which sculptors place on monuments. . . . But the bullets will soon do their work, and before I have fired again he makes off with bent head, takes a few more steps, his trunk hanging down, with a sad, downcast gait which sadly contrasts with that of a short time before.   After stopping and oscillating for a moment, like a tottering house, he slips down on his hind-quarters, then falls over heavily on his side, throwing his trunk in the air as though to make a last appeal to man's clemency.   At the very spot where a minute before there rose, in all its savage beauty, this majestic conception of nature, the largest and the most powerful of the animals of the earth, nothing more than a mass of gray flesh appears in the blood-spattered grass.[1]

The solitary elephant out of the way, I set to work on the following day to search for the female which I lost two days before. We are not long in discovering her. She fell one hour's distance from the spot where our hunter was injured, and during these forty-eight hours has undergone a transformation hardly to her advantage. The enormous quantity of gas generated after death has completely distended her skin; she looks quite round and blown out, and resembles one of those gigantic elephants made of gold-beater's skin which toy merchants sell. The skin is so thick that the gas is so far powerless to burst it, and no odour can be smelt outside. Maggots, deposited by flies, swarm in her mouth and at the commissure of the lips. Her face is swollen like the rest of her shapeless body; never was a "pneumatic" more blown out. When the skin bursts under the pressure of the gas it will not be pleasant in the neighbourhood, and I fear that under the burning sun this catastrophe will arrive soon.

Msiambiri, who is never at a loss for a joke, immediately tells us of an extraordinary occurrence which happened amid similar circumstances. The elephant in question had eaten a large quantity of

---

[1] This elephant was the largest I killed in those regions. Its measurements will be found in the table at the end of this work. As will be seen, its tusks weighed seventy pounds each.

the fruit of the fan palm-tree, fruit which is the size
of the fist and very hard.   When the animal burst
the fruit was projected into the midst of the crowd
of men around it like the contents of an immense
bomb, strewing the ground with dead and wounded.
. . . Everybody doubles up with laughter, while the
narrator affirms the absolute truth of this event.   It
is a fact ! Fearing that a similar fate may be reserved for us, we draw away from this barrel of
gunpowder with already lighted fuse, making up our
minds to come back in two or three days' time to get
the tusks.   Needless to say all the trees in the
neighbourhood are covered with vultures ; powerless
to penetrate the skin of the body they wait until
decomposition has done its work.   The elephant's
skin is quite white with the dung of these birds,
which have ceaselessly walked over it, doubtless
conversing about the expected event.

We avoid visiting this neighbourhood the following day, but the wind informs us at nearly two miles'
distance that the explosion has occurred.   Not wishing to go myself, I send two men there to know
whether felines frequent the place, and also to bring
me back the tusks.

At this season (rain has started to fall for some
days past) it is probable that all lions, leopards,
and famished hyenas within a radius of several
miles have been attracted around the elephant's
body.   However, my men see nothing but vultures,
and no tracks whatever in the neighbourhood, showing that this country must be very poor in felines.

Rhinoceroses are not found here; it is probably the same with the lion.

January, February, March, and April of 1896 pass without extraordinary occurrence. In May we again find ourselves with the expedition in the Angoni country, where I had some interesting fishing and hunting. This month is the one for snakes; it is about this time they look for a place to deposit their eggs in order that the sun may hatch them. At the same time, birds and a few small insectivorous mammals[1] which feed on these eggs, watch for the reptiles, and destroy the greater part of their offspring. Certain waders, such as the serpent - eater and marabout, and certain gallinal, such as the guinea-fowl, eat the snake itself, taking care to break its head before doing so. Owing to all these enemies, the reptiles do not multiply freely. That is much to the benefit of hunters who go about in the bush with bare feet and legs.[2]

One day when I was sitting on a fallen tree waiting for antelopes I sáw one of these hideous animals. It passed a few inches from my legs in the shadow of the trunk without my suspecting it; all that I had heard was an inexplicable rustling of dry leaves when the snake appeared from beneath my tree and made for a place full in the sunshine. Perceiving that it had not seen me and that it was moving away, I did not move. It twisted itself

---

[1] Civet-cats, ichneumon, badger, etc.
[2] For the habits of snakes, and accidents caused by them, see *Mes Grandes Chasses*, pp. 66, 67, 299.

about here and there on the sand. I did not know what to think of this dance executed, in my honour perhaps, by a very large python. Were these, perchance, the preliminaries of an attack? So as to be on the safe side, I decapitated it with a bullet in the neck from the 303. Upon examination I recognised that this reptile was a female, in the act of laying in the sand a string of twenty-six eggs, joined by a membrane, whence would have issued twenty-six charming little pythons a short time afterwards. This snake measured no less than 24 feet, and in the middle was the thickness of the knee.

I saw a python skin at Lake Nyassa which measured not less than 30 feet, and, when the reptile was killed, was found to contain a large kid half-way down its stomach. Although inoffensive as far as the bite is concerned, snakes of this size are not very agreeable to meet with, for you never know whether or not they are going to try to embrace you.

There are about twenty other kinds of snakes, not exceeding 2 yards in length, the bite of which is more or less poisonous; these are very common, especially in the rainy season, when the water drives them from their holes; but in these countries, where you are so accustomed to looking where you tread, accidents are very rare. In fact, on the ground are thorns which have fallen from trees, carnivorous ants, different kinds of creeping brambles, a species of very irritating nettle, and a thousand other very painful things, so that everybody accustoms himself to scrutinising the ground before setting foot down.

I was obliged at first to suspend my marches because of the thorns which pierced my feet through the thin india-rubber soles of my shoes. The thorn breaks in the wound, inflammation sets in, a gathering forms, and your only means of healing yourself is to extract the thorn and rest. That was the reason why I was obliged to accustom myself, like the natives, to looking where I was walking, and now, after years of practice, I do it quite unconsciously. How many times have we not seen motionless snakes, looking like dead branches in the grass or on the ground heated by the sun, and how many times have we not narrowly escaped stepping on them! But, ever on the watch, we saw the danger, and the reptile was killed or allowed to escape.

In addition to reptiles there is a swarm of strange or noxious insects in the African bush, especially on the vegetation, which would require a volume to describe. In the case of birds, for instance, the nomenclature of those which are truly curious for their habits, song, and plumage would be interminable. I will only say a few words *en passant* on the subject of insectivorous birds, those which we often saw on our game, and which perch on the backs of buffaloes, elands, old koodoos, wart-hogs, and rhinoceroses, searching for parasites. These birds looked black or uniformly brown, but, having had the good fortune to see them closely, I was surprised to find they were brilliant in colour, —some light-brown with pearl-gray beaks and red eyes, others gray with bright-red heads. It is very difficult to study these birds, because they will not let you approach them; but one day when they were perched on a dead eland I was able, hidden behind a bush a few feet away, to examine them at my ease. They ran about in all directions on the animal, descending and ascending vertically with ease. Their song somewhat resembles that of the lark.

No less difficult to study are certain antelopes, among others the "inyala" (*tragelaphus angasi*), whose tracks one always sees, but which you never meet. Its habits are strange, and quite different from those of its congeners. Instead of feeding on grassy plains and sleeping there, it eats leaves and lives entirely in dense thickets without ever leaving them, disappearing at the sound of the least crack, or the rustling of a dry leaf. You can imagine what chance a man has amid such circumstances of getting near it. Its capture is so difficult, that, although this antelope has been fairly plentiful in Zululand, and notwithstanding the myriads of hunters who have beaten the country, Cape Town Museum did not possess a specimen in 1897. In the region north of the Zambesi it is found only on the chain of hills which passes behind Chiromo, and stretches as far as Lake Nyassa, under the name of the Kirk Mountains.

As I wanted to procure a few fine specimens, I set to work in that region, where, in 1895, I had made a first unsuccessful attempt. It was necessary to employ cunning and stratagem. I took more than ten days to find where these mysterious animals drank—a small pool completely hidden in the centre of the forest. I took up my position there, and, after two days' waiting, saw an inyala for the first time. This strange animal's appearance no more resembles that of other antelopes than its habits resemble theirs. The male is dark iron-gray; its height is about 4 feet; and under the neck and stomach it has long, hanging hair, which much increases its size seen from a distance, and makes it look as though its neck and shoulders and short legs were those of an ox. Its elegant head and straight nose somewhat resembles that of the ox, so that at a distance you believe you are looking at one of small size. The female is smaller and of another colour, which is rare; it resembles the bushbuck, owing to its tawny hair, spotted on the buttocks with white, and also owing to the shape of the hind-quarters. Moreover, the koodoo, bushbuck, inyala, and situtunga are of the same family.

From the time of firing the first shot at the pool, a shot which cost the life of a male inyala, these animals no longer appeared in the daytime; but they continued to come at night. I waited for them with the electric projector, just as in the case of lions, and was able thus to obtain a few specimens of the "boô," as the natives call it. The horns of this antelope, which are exactly the shape of a lyre, are very graceful. The accompanying photographs show a front and back view of this beautiful and rare animal.

Other antelopes are, as I have said, very difficult

BACK VIEW OF AN "INYALA."

to see at this time of the year,[1] on account of the
height of the grass. Awaiting the good season and
our departure for the north-west, I did some fishing
in the rivers. I possessed nets and hooks, but I
preferred to use dynamite for this purpose. Upon
finding a deep place where the current is not strong,
I throw there during the day a quantity of chopped
meat, maggots, cooked corn-flour, boiled rice, etc.,
to attract fish. Encouraged by this free distribution,
they soon swarm within a narrow limit, and greedily
dart at each handful of ground bait. At this moment
I take one or several dynamite cartridges, according
to the depth of the water and the number of fish,
and having lit the fuses with which, in addition to
detonators, they are supplied, I throw them into the
water with a fresh supply of food.

While the fish are confidently feeding around the
cartridges a little smoke rises to the surface; then,
after about a minute, a deep, violent explosion up-
raises the water within a radius of fifteen yards, shaking the ground and surrounding rocks; a multitude
of bubbles rise from the bottom, and fish appear
from all sides, some floating on their bellies, others on
their backs. Twenty men dash into the water, and,
with hand-nets already prepared, gather in the
unfortunate victims which still struggle enough to
make them unseizable with the hands. At one sweep
I have thus captured 103 fish weighing between three
and eight pounds each. Generally there were always
twenty of them of good weight. Silures (cat-fish) are

---

[1] The rainy season.

the only fish which, killed or stunned by dynamite, remain at the bottom of the water; all the others rise to the surface, at least momentarily,—the reason why you must make haste to seize them.

The effect of the explosion on the fish which are very near to the cartridge is to pulverise the bones completely, and only pieces of them can be found. The damage done is in direct ratio to the distance they are from the dynamite, but all, as a rule, have shattered viscera, — liver, heart, bladder, intestines, etc.

This method of destruction is more expeditious and more advantageous than line fishing, especially when you are not a fisherman and you have to feed an expedition. I have thus made some really miraculous draughts in the large lakes of Central Africa, such as Lakes Nyassa and Tanganyika.

THE "PNEUMATIC" ELEPHANT.

TSESSEBE. CONGO BUFFALO. LETCHWE.
POOKOO. SMALL FOREST ANTELOPE.
SPEARS USED BY KATANGA ELEPHANT-HUNTERS.

CHAPTER XII

SOME ANIMALS OF THE CONGO [1]

Fresh animals—The Congo buffalo—Various antelopes: pookoos, letchwes, hartebeests, tsessebes, small brown antelope; *tragelaphus*: inyalas, situtungas, koodoos—Absence of rhinoceroses—Leopards and their depredations—Elephants—Denizens of the forest: monkeys, wild-boars, and large monkeys—The "soko" or chimpanzee—Its portrait—Supposed habitat of the gorilla—Parrots and birds—Aquatic animals—The Congo regarded as a hunting ground.

BEFORE reaching the concluding chapters which deal with the elephant and lion, I ask the reader's permission to pass in review a few excursions which I made towards the end of my journey into the Tanganyika

[1] By Congo I mean all the territories, French or Belgian, watered by the river and its tributaries.

and Congo territories. We shall thus become acquainted with other inhabitants of the bush, the names of which have not yet been mentioned by me, because they exist rather in western than in eastern Africa.

The impression which these animals, new to me, made upon my first meeting them was rather strange. Kambombe and Msiambiri, who have accompanied me everywhere, and have alternately traversed with me the Ubemba plains and the Manyema hills, the Urua mountains and Stanley Forest, were much amused at the diversity of the species of animals,—they who had thought that the whole world was limited to what was known in their own country. The sight of each new species interested them enormously. " What's that over there ? Still another ' nyama ' ! "—" nyama " being the generic name for everything which is game in the Zambesi. If I killed the animal it was an occasion for endless comparisons on the part of my men, such as, " its head is like a hartebeest's," " its tail is like a bushbuck's," " its coat is like a koodoo's." I content myself with taking a note of the name given it by the Swahilis, or natives of the country.

Once when in the Manyema I saw some buffaloes' tracks which, owing to their size, seemed to be those of females. Leaving the column, I started off in pursuit of them in the midst of a very rugged country covered with vegetation as high as the waist, and in half an hour came in sight of some reddish animals which I took for hartebeests. The buffaloes' tracks being very fresh, indicating their nearness, I did not wish to abandon the chase : so I decided to leave the supposed hartebeests in peace. But the tracks led us straight to them, and I was beginning to ask myself whether I had not to do with buffaloes of another species when one of them turned round. I was then convinced that the animal was certainly not an antelope. I drew near within 150 yards without difficulty, and, not knowing whether these animals would allow me to shorten the distance, fired at one, which fell on the spot. Upon running up to finish it off I saw that the others had stopped near ; and I wounded a second mortally, which we found 100 yards away. It was a herd of Congo buffaloes, all the animals composing it being females. The female is reddish-brown ; the male darker, but not so black as the Cape buffalo. Smaller than this species, the Congo buffalo rarely exceeds 4 feet 10 inches ; its horns are short and crescent-shaped, resembling those of certain breeds of cattle.[1] Some Europeans who have shot them affirm that they charge exactly like the big East African buffalo. I have not been able to verify this statement, and, besides, have not hunted these animals long enough to form an accurate idea of their peculiarities. During my stay in the Congo I killed eight of them, and sometimes went into the thick jungle to hunt out others which I had wounded, and although several of them lowered their heads to butt, not one charged me.[2] It must be mentioned

[1] Perhaps this is the *bos euryceros*.
[2] The majority of the large antelopes also lower their heads to

that I approach wounded animals with such precaution that I often get within ten yards, seeing them distinctly, without their suspecting my presence. Apprenticeship with the buffalo of the south is so dangerous, and it exercises your faculties so well, that other animals of the same species, even when vicious, do not appear much to be feared.

In the Lower Congo, in the direction of Lukolela and in the hilly districts,—that is, at the extremity of the equatorial forest,[1]—buffaloes appeared to me to be more plentiful than at the eastern boundary of the Manyema.

The antelopes which I have shot in the Congo, both in the forest and in the Manyema, are the pookoo (*cobus vardoni*) and the letchwe (*cobus letche*), which I had already seen and reported near Lake Bangweolo, a smaller variety of hartebeest than the *lichtenstein*, and with horns wider apart, on account of which it has been given the name of *lunatus* (it is also called " tsessebe "); the large hartebeest or *kaama*, which I had not seen since being in South Africa; and a small brown antelope with straight horns which abounds in certain parts of the forest, and somewhat resembles a bush-buck but is darker. In the villages I saw a fair number of horns, mostly those of *tragelaphus*; thus I feel certain that there are in the equatorial forest inyalas, situtungas (*tragelaphus speeki*), and koodoos,

butt when they are so seriously wounded as to be unable to flee. It is then dangerous to draw too near to them. The bushbuck and the sable antelope, for example, defend themselves desperately.

[1] Especially in the part called " the canal."

or at least, an antelope occupying an intermediary place between the last-named and the inyala.[1]

In the flat regions and at the extremity of the forest the zebra exists, since you see natives wearing their upper front teeth in their necklaces, or passed through their lips. As antelopes and other ruminants only have front teeth in the lower jaw, and as they are quite different in shape, it is difficult to make a mistake.

The rhinoceros did not seem to me to inhabit the region; only the natives neighbouring the lakes know it; it can only be found, in my opinion, on the eastern shore of Tanganyika. The lion is found only in Katanga and in the vicinity of the Uelle—that is, in the regions of grassy plains.

Leopards are very plentiful in certain parts of the Manyema, and cause many accidents there. The natives of that country, instead of pursuing and exterminating the man-eaters as is done in the Zambesi, let them alone, so much so that these carnivora, seeing they are unpunished, continue their depredations. They lie in wait in the bush for the natives in broad daylight, and when the natives come to cut palm-trees spring out upon them. I am certain they are always the same animals, encouraged by success, which cause these troubles. Is it not strange that pacific people like those of the Zambesi exterminate these carnivora at all cost, while essentially warlike and turbulent populations, like those of the Manyema, quietly support such tyranny? It is quite a matter

[1] Perhaps the *strepsiceros imberbis*.

of custom. The leopard strikes such terror to their hearts, that if a man sees one it is quite sufficient to retard a whole expedition. I have had experience of this when travelling through the country.

In short, the equatorial forest contains relatively little game, which stops altogether on boundaries near open countries. The elephant, itself, which needs daily a considerable quantity of straw or grass, cannot inhabit forest; it walks about in it, but only to get out of it soon afterwards. The Congo territory is well stocked with them.

On the other hand, the forest is the home of an infinite variety of quadrumana; one may say, indeed, that the Congo is the native country of the monkey, —all the species of Africa, from the small marmoset to the gigantic gorilla, are represented. In certain regions, every imaginable variety of hair and colour, all the various species of monkeys you see in the monkey-houses of zoological gardens, are met with on a day's march through the forest. Some flee as soon as they see you; others, bolder and more confident in the tree-tops, quietly look down as you pass and scratch themselves; entire troops walking about on the ground climb to the topmost branches of the trees upon your approach, while others, which are already there, madly fling themselves into the air and slide down the lianas to the ground, so as the easier to escape.[1]

Out of twenty monkeys which the 303 brought

[1] Several times I saw wild-boars and wart-hogs in the forest, but was unable to fire at them, because of the density of the vegetation.

AN ELEPHANT TRACK IN THE EQUATORIAL FOREST, UPPER CONGO.

down from the tree-tops, only two were of the same species. I regret that I was unable to preserve their skins, for there must have been unknown varieties among them: the weather being always cloudy and rainy, the moisture and continual changing of quarters prevented me from attempting to preserve specimens.

I noticed that if we proceeded with the main body of the expedition the noise made by such a large number of men caused a perfect blank in front of us. We saw nothing; everything seemed dead. If, on the other hand, I was two or three miles ahead, proceeding noiselessly and only accompanied by my gun-bearers, the forest had quite a different aspect,—everywhere there was life and animation. Often have I noticed the same thing in the African bush.

Large monkeys are met with only towards the middle of the forest—that is, in the direction of the Lomami. In this region, and in the Itimbiri, the people were able to answer my questions about the gorilla by reporting to me a large monkey, the soko, which, according to the description of the natives, must be the chimpanzee.

My interpreter, in view of my rather limited knowledge of the Congo language (a kind of Bangala mixed with Swahili), considered that I should better understand the portrait of the soko by demonstration than through a description; and, after having conversed with and questioned ten or twelve natives seated around us, from whom he asked every now and then fresh information, this is how he answered my minute questions about this animal. The whole population of the village having assembled to look at us, he began :—

"Its height? . . . About his size!" And he points out a ten-year-old child, who, seeing the gesture, and doubtless imagining that he is pointed out as suitable for roasting for my dinner, immediately takes to his heels.

"Its nose? . . . Like that!" He points out a baby which has no nose yet worth speaking of, which is in its mother's arms. The woman flees in terror, pressing her child to her bosom.

"Its beard? . . . Like that!" pointing out that of an old man who wears a thin beard. The old fellow smiles good-naturedly.

"Its stomach? . . . Like that!" and he almost touches the paunch of an old woman of dropsical appearance, who has no fear, but continues looking at him angrily, as much as to say, "Well! and what then?"

"Its face? . . . White as 'bwana's'" (master's), and all the natives in their turn burst out laughing, delighted with this comparison, which concerns me alone. The dropsical old woman finds this very funny, and a hearty laugh shakes her paunch, creased in accordion fashion, whilst from her half-open, toothless mouth come convulsive "Ha! ha! hahs!" Every one is delighted, and retires to reflect on this comparative dissertation on the soko, while I eat some bananas, which they give to me to furnish one more point of resemblance between the monkey and myself.

In short, I was only able to obtain certain indications of the presence of the gorilla at Ubanghi and thence to the coast. I saw a photograph at Nyangwe, but it was probably that of a chimpanzee. In the Congo, as everywhere, it is difficult to get information from the natives about animals, only hunters and trappers being capable of collecting accurate information; people who do not make a business of pursuing animals simply repeat fables which they have heard

ON THE UPPER CONGO.

about them, at the same time exaggerating and adding improbable stories.

I do not pretend, therefore, to settle the question of the habitat of the gorilla. I confine myself to noting what I have heard without having been in a position to verify the statements.

The forest and the banks of the Congo are inhabited not only by monkeys but by many species of birds and innumerable parrots.   Hippopotami, lamantins, and aquatic birds are found there in large quantities.

Precious collections for museums are to be made there; and the hunter can easily judge from what I have told him incidentally of the resources offered him by the Congo, that magnificent country of the future.   It is not unlikely that I shall return there some day to make myself better acquainted with the inhabitants of its forests.

And now let us conclude my big-game shooting of 1896 and 1897.

ELEPHANTS IN BATTLE ARRAY.

CHAPTER XIII

THREE NOTABLE ELEPHANT HUNTS

Elephants in battle array—A hunt on the plain : " La Grande Journée "—
  Tuskless females — Five elephants wounded — Msiambiri and I are
  charged—Msiambiri caught by an angry elephant—Victory.
Sport in the Congo country—Females assisting and safeguarding a wounded
  male—A colossal elephant—Its death—The finest trophy of my collection.
Conclusion of elephant-hunting—Sir Samuel Baker's opinion.

WE were again in the Barotse in June 1896, imper-
ceptibly proceeding towards Lake Bangweolo, through
a country never before trodden by European foot,
which had probably never echoed a rifle-shot.
Every day fresh elephants' spoors were seen,
and on each occasion I went in pursuit. Had
I killed at this time all the elephants which I
followed, a special caravan would have been necessary
to carry my ivory. Unfortunately, it was the period
of uncertain winds; and, if I did not see all these
elephants, they, on the other hand, scented me
far too often for my liking.

16

The country in this part of the Barotse[1] may be summed up in three words—plains, forests, swamps. The plains are covered with stunted trees and short grass; the forests are very dense, but not great in extent; the swamps are large patches of soft mud covered with an apparently solid crust, sparsely grown over with grass, which has formed since the end of the rainy season, and gives way under your weight.

One day we are in the middle of one of these marshy plains examining fresh elephant - tracks. Twenty yards in front of us is the edge of the forest, similar to a black impenetrable wall. A few shafts of light enable us to distinguish gigantic gnarled tree-trunks and fantastic lianas. Invisible birds utter shrill cries, and vulturines[2] sing. We are preparing to follow the tracks into the forest when suddenly the birds become silent, as though out of respect, and a great rustling of leaves mingled with the noise of broken branches, at first at a distance and then drawing nearer, makes us stop short. We remain motionless as statues, our ears on the stretch. What can it be? If the noise had been dying away we should have thought of some elephant or other in flight; but, since it comes towards us, we are struck with the idea that it must be caused by a herd of buffaloes, extraordinary though it would be to see them in such a spot. . . . We have not quite got over

---

[1] North-west of the Aroangwa river.
[2] A kind of guinea-fowl (*Numida Ȩdouardi*). Its native name is Kanga-tole.

our surprise, when I witness a spectacle which I shall never forget.

Medium-sized trees sway backwards and forwards, lianas and foliage half open; and there appears at the edge of the forest first the back, then the head and body, of an elephant. By its side is another, then one more, and soon there are eleven of them marching straight upon us. Almost in a row—as they always are when they eat—they proceed quietly, some occupied in eating lianas and leaves, others grass and fruit. They do not scent us, as the wind blows from right to left between them and us. One or two of them gather up sand and dust with their trunks, blowing it all over their bodies and leaving reddish clouds behind them. Their large ears flap to and fro, and their trunks, moving incessantly, seem to mimic their impressions. I know we are not running any danger; but I do not ignore the fact that we have not a minute to lose if we wish to profit by this meeting. To hide being impossible, we must remain motionless.

While looking for the finest pair of tusks among the five males, which are bigger than the others by a cubit, I take my 8-bore, and Msiambiri gets ready my Express—that is, he cocks and holds it with its barrel high, ready to be handed to me.

For a long time past my men have been asking me to let them kill an elephant on their own account: so, on this particular day, I say to them, "Msiambiri will remain with me. You others can kill an elephant: only, wait until I've fired and you see your animal in profile." At the same time I ask Msiambiri in which direction we shall run afterwards. He points to the left. The elephants are by this time not more than sixteen yards away, and several of them must have already noticed our group of six men. "Don't move," I repeat. There is just a chance we shall escape if we keep still. My choice is fixed upon a magnificent male to the right.

After being much tempted to aim at the base of the trunk—that is, in front—I decide on the shoulder. While aiming to the left of the trunk, under the point of the ear, I look out of the corner of one eye at another male on my left upon which I decide as a fitting mark for my second shot. The elephants continue to advance in battle array. . . .

I raise my 8-bore, lean well forward ready to receive its violent recoil, and press the trigger. . . . All my attention is fixed momentarily on the elephant, which utters a ringing trumpet-blast. . . . The other one stops and then turns to the left. I fire my second shot right into its shoulder. . . . Throwing the 8-bore to the ground, I seize the Express and am selecting a third animal when Msiambiri cries, "Ti-t' awe!"—i.e., "Let us be off." Away we scamper in the direction agreed upon, at the same time that one of the elephants charges Tambarika in the very middle of the plain. Never have I seen a man run as he does! The elephant chases him for about 150 yards, and at one time almost touches him; but a slim, muscular man, possessed of stamina, can save his life on level ground. The animal's anger cools down, and it returns at a trot. As it passes within fifty yards of me I try a shot at its head with my Express through mere curiosity, without even knowing whether I shall hit it. . . . Much to my astonishment, it falls in a heap stone dead. Quite by chance the bullet entered the ear. As my men wounded it twice in the side and twice in the lungs, the animal belongs to them. It would most certainly have died from the latter injury.[1]

Let us return to the time I fired my first shot. All the elephants, like well-trained horses, stop dead. Some swing completely round on their hind-legs (a movement which they execute very swiftly) and make off towards the forest ; others, turning to the left, trot towards our right,—that is, to leeward,— those which had fled to the forest turning round and doing the same.

The moment the elephants swing round, Tambarika, Rodzani, Tchigallo, and Kambombe select a male to my right, and send a volley into his side. He immediately charges the smoke, at the very instant, indeed, I fire my second shot; and it is then that Msiambiri, seeing the animal charging us, warns me. But Tambarika, having fled on to the plain at the back of us, draws the elephant there after him ; and, while we look on at the race between man and animal, my other men escape to right and left.

As soon as the elephant falls, we set off in search of the others. Rodzani affirms having seen one of

---

[1] According to rules in force among native hunters, an elephant belongs to the one who first fired at it.

them lag behind; but we can see nothing on the plain. One hundred yards farther on there is a bend in the forest, and this we reach just in time to see an elephant enter. It seems to have a broken leg, for it limps along so slowly that, when we get near it, its cruppers are still in view. It is the male at which I fired first of all. As I afterwards found, his shoulder was broken. Maddened by pain and his feeble efforts, the animal roars with rage, and, blowing furiously with his trunk, tears at everything within reach.

He sees us soon, and, half turning his head, tries to face the enemy. His cries and groans become so terrible that they must be heard a mile away. His breast is hidden : so I try to get into the forest to see him, but find the density of the vegetation an unsurmountable obstacle. I fire obliquely, therefore, trying to reach the heart, but without succeeding. I then aim at the back-bone. Crying more loudly at each shot, the elephant slides on to its hind-quarters, and is finally put out of its misery by a bullet behind the ear.

Leaving a man with the body, I return immediately to the track of the herd, which has skirted the edge of the forest. The marks on the soft ground could not be plainer; they can be followed into the distance like a broad strip of ploughed land. More than a mile is covered without there being any sign of blood—with nothing to indicate that an elephant has left its companions. Then we see that one has dropped out of the herd, and entered the forest. We find blood on the foliage. As the wind is unfavourable and we are sure to be scented, we withdraw after a moment's reflection, and make a long detour to the rear. But all our precautions are wasted, for we discover that the elephant only went into the wood to die. Again, it is a male, but younger than the two others.

This was, I believe, the only occasion during my long sojourn in the woods, upon which we met with elephants purely by chance. These eleven colossal animals, suddenly emerging in line of battle from the immense forest, was one of the finest sights I have ever enjoyed. It is one of those spectacles which a hunter sees but once in his life, as it was one of the grandest and most imposing manifestations which nature could show him.

I have two more hunts during 1897 to relate: the first in Moassi's country, west of Lake Nyassa[1]; the second in the Urua, part of the Belgian Congo contiguous to Lake Tanganyika. On one occasion,—my biggest day with the elephants,— I nearly lost Msiambiri; on the other, I killed the largest elephant I have ever seen. A great many elephants were killed before and after these two hunts, but none amid such remarkable circumstances.

The day on which I nearly lost Msiambiri, I, myself, momentarily ran the greatest danger. This was how it happened. We came across a herd of elephants, composed of one large male, an old tuskless female larger than he (probably his mother), two younger

---

[1] One day's journey from the east bank of the Aroangwa river.

males, some females, and two or three small elephants of various sizes. After my catching a glimpse of them as they proceeded along,—that is, in single file,—they spread out into a line to feed. The large male, which had just before led the column, was now almost in the centre, the old tuskless female, who never left him, being at his side. As they slowly advanced, we ran parallel to them. At a certain moment the large male was on the right wing. . . . I took up a position behind an ant-hill, ten yards from which they had to pass. The wind was favourable, and the elephants were unsuspicious. Seeing that it was impossible to fire at the male, I decided, first of all, to shoot the old tuskless female, and to fire the second shot at her son. It was a risky business, because, the elephants having slightly deviated towards me, they were barely eight yards away when they were on a level with me, and, if I had been charged, I should have had no time to escape. I got ready my men, and ordered them to fire if the dangerous animal turned to charge us. After that, we should see. . . .

As the female advances, still protecting her son with her immense body, I take careful aim with my Express No. 1 at a spot between the eye and the ear. Msiambiri holds the 8-bore ready for me to use immediately afterwards. The shot is fired, and the animal, her legs giving way under her all at the same time, falls with a thud to the ground. In so doing she uncovers her companion who, five seconds later, receives a bullet from the 8-bore in the heart. Owing to the echo, the elephants are puzzled to know whence the shots come. They trot here, there, and everywhere, perfectly bewildered as to what to do or which direction to take, until the females lead the way, and make off, followed by their young. I take advantage of the disorder, first of all to fire almost point-blank (I believe at four yards' distance), with my second 8 - bore, at an elephant which passes within reach; then, again seizing the Express and overtaking the laggards, I hit two of the animals with my two barrels. After that I stop to breathe, while the whole of the elephants enter a dense thicket situated nearly three hundred yards away.

Boldly entering the thicket on their heels, we follow them for about ten minutes without coming across any sign of wounded animals. They lead us to a more open spot where are clumps of trees and glades, like so many wooded islets surrounded by bare ground. And a very fortunate thing for us it was open, because, if the wood had been as thick there as at its entrance, one of us would not have left it alive.

Almost the first thing we see in one of these glades is a fallen elephant—the large male. We can tell at a glance that he did not get there the same way we did, but by a parallel pathway which is sprinkled with blood from his mouth. He separated from his companions upon entering the forest, and, as the other wounded animals may have done the same, we think of returning on our steps to find their tracks. But before doing so, wishing to convince ourselves that we are not mistaken, we push on fifty yards farther to a place where the spoor is very distinct in the open daylight, deciding that if there is no blood we will return. No sooner have we arrived than, within terrifying proximity, there breaks upon our ears a cry of rage, a shrill trumpet-blast similar to the shriek of a *sirène*, and a black mass, which we have not even time to look at, so near is it to us, bursts like a locomotive from the thicket which we are skirting. Each of us leaps aside in search of safety. . . . Kambombe and Tchigallo, who were ahead, make off to the left; Tambarika and Rodzani scamper off the way we came; Msiambiri and I dash straight ahead through the hole made by the herd. . . . The ground trembles. . . . A sinister rustling of the leaves, the breaking of branches, the shriller and shriller trumpet-blasts tell us that the elephant is behind us and overtaking us. . . . There is no doubt about it. . . . We throw down our heavy rifles: so as to run the quicker.

It is impossible to describe the terror, mingled with rage, which fills me at this moment. During our mad race all my thoughts are summed up as follows :—" No rifle . . . many elephants killed with impunity, and this is the hour of reckoning ! . . . the game is up . . . a rapid vision of my native country." . . . That is all. . . . And now, clenching my fists, I run and jump in a supreme struggle for life. . . . Minutes slip by and seem to be hours. Some one, whom I recognise as Msiambiri, though without seeing -him, brushes past me. . . . Our feet pass

swiftly over the ground ; trees upon trees flash past.
. . . Behind us the shrill cries stop, but on our heels
are heavy footsteps which shake the ground ; a
powerful, spasmodic breathing is heard ; then, warm
air passes over my shoulders and neck. . . . Heavens !
it is its trunk ! . . . "Tchitamba ! tchitamba !" (trunk),
murmurs the wretched fellow at my side. On we
fly, maddened and blinded, bruising ourselves in
grazing trees, insensible either to thorns which tear
us or to branches which whip our faces. . . . It is
useless ! . . . I shall soon grow feeble and fall. . . .
Then I hear, as in a dream, the cry, " A mâla !" (" It
is all over "), uttered in despairing accents, and I see a
body rise in the air. . . . I am alone. . . . The noise
has ceased. . . . I continue running for a few seconds
unconsciously, but the awakening comes. . . . I stop,
and the terrible reality stares me in the face. . . .
Yes : I am saved ; but the other is dead !—and
through my fault. . . . Remorse and regret complete
my distraction. . . . I lean against a tree, faltering,
overcome. . . .

However, after a time, reflection and calm return.
I listen. There is little noise. My heart hesitates
between the danger which is there and the desire to
aid my servant. After a little struggle, I decide to
retrace my steps, unarmed.

Still trembling, I advance carefully, and soon get
a back view of the elephant, which has stopped in
the middle of the thicket. Its head is low and its
trunk hangs down ; it grunts slightly and begins to
move slowly. . . . I draw near at once ; but it stops

and turns half round with an indecisive air. Ah! is it again going to charge? No: it resumes its journey and makes off. . . .

I scrutinise the place where it stopped, looking for a corpse and fearing to discover one. I look at the tree-trunks with the fear of finding blood on them. Ah! at last I perceive poor Msiambiri stretched on the ground. As I draw near, he raises himself on his elbow and looks in the direction of his enemy. His face is that violet hue which is equivalent among the negroes to pallidness. His loin-cloth is stained with blood. I bend over him.

"Are you wounded, Msiambiri?"

"No. . . . Nothing is broken; but I have pains everywhere."

"What happened?"

"It seized me by the waist and threw me under its feet to crush me; but it threw me too hard. . . . I passed through its legs and fell here. I didn't move any more: so I escaped its eye. It searched on the ground, but only on the other side. The wind is in our favour. He has not scented me."

"Did it hurt when it seized you with its trunk?"

"Not at all. I thought it was going to break my head against a tree, or pin me to a trunk with its tusks, as happened to poor Katchepa; but it wanted to crush me with its feet. . . . Have you seen the dead elephant?"

"Which one? The big one over there in the glade, at the moment we were charged?"

"No: another. We ran quite close to it. You mean to say you didn't see it?"

"No: I must confess that I was thinking of something else. I thought that I could not run as fast as you could, and that I should be the one the elephant caught. . . ."

"You did frighten me just now when you were looking for me: you were as white as though you were going to die. But you're all covered with blood, like myself." [1]

"That's nothing, Msiambiri. I'm not yet accustomed to being trampled under foot by elephants. But don't let us lose any time: I will call our comrades."

And while Msiambiri is shaking the earth, sand, and dry leaves from his body, I give the recognised whistle. Soon a similar signal answers, and in five minutes two of my men are by our sides. I explain first of all, in answer to their questions, that our wounds are unimportant. "Come along quickly," Tambarika then says. "As we were coming we saw the elephant enter a thicket. Our companions are watching it. By going this way we shall not be scented. Here is a rifle. We shall have time to look for the others afterwards. Moreover, considering the place where they are, it would be too dangerous—we should be charged again."

Tambarika gives me my Express No. 2, and we return by the route which winds round the thicket.

---

[1] The scratches and cuts we received all over bled freely. My clothes and Msiambiri's loin-cloth were in tatters.

After going a short distance, we see in the centre a motionless, hardly visible, black mass, which my men point out as the elephant. But it is impossible to fire so far with precision. In trying to get a little nearer I make a noise, and the animal with ears raised, turns towards me, uttering a by no means engaging grunt. If I delay another minute, I say to myself, I shall be charged; and this time it will be fatal, as I can no longer run. . . . For want of a better spot, I aim right between the two eyes, at the base of the trunk. I fire both barrels at once and then jump aside. "Affa!"—"He is dead!"—cry my men with a sigh of relief, as the elephant falls down heavily in the midst of a great noise of breaking branches.[1]

When the rifles are collected we go to look for the elephant which Msiambiri saw, and find it about ten yards from the place we passed in our headlong career.

These three elephants must have remained in the thicket, being too seriously wounded to follow their comrades. Two of them died as we were arriving; the third had scented us and tried to avenge them.

Four elephants in one day is very good work, but I narrowly escaped paying very dear for this victory.

The photograph which will be found at the end of this chapter represents the skull of the female which charged us on the day in question. It bears the marks of the two bullets which despatched it.

---

[1] You can fire in this way at an elephant which is at rest, but during a charge the head is raised and the shot would be wasted.

MSIAMBIRI AND HIS ADVERSARY.

About the middle of 1897 I tried to reach the Congo, before taking the Manyema route, by way of Urua. The worry and great anxiety which my fate and that of my men gave me at the time left me little leisure for following my favourite sport. However, as the country was full of game, I had a few elephant-hunts during my stay in the Luapula valley.

One morning, upon going out in search of carriers, —we were then camped not far from the sources of the Luizi—I found the spoor of about ten elephants which had passed that way not more than a quarter of an hour before. At that time Msiambiri and Kambombe were the only two of my hunters remaining with me, Tambarika and his companions having returned home. As assistants I had engaged two Baluba natives; very fine fellows, although cannibals. As my many carriers were asking me for meat, I began to follow the ten elephants with the intention of killing the first I saw, but without going too far out of my way. But a hunter's promises are of small value! Hardly have I looked at the tracks when I discover that a male of large size is among the herd; in fact, the spoor are so large that I do not remember ever having seen similar. So I decide to possess it even if I have to go fifty miles to do so. Pursuing the herd, we enter a comparatively easy country, consisting of dense woods, small in area, surrounded by bare and hard ground,—veritable islets of vegetation in the midst of a plain as smooth as a lake. We overtake the elephants after three hours' travelling. Fourteen in number, they advance at a

moderate pace, and at the moment I perceive them—
we are issuing from a thicket on their heels—they
are crossing one of the open spaces in the direction of
another clump of trees. The large male is in the
middle, and it seems to me that there are only females
round him. One of the latter—a large, old animal
—is in the rear. I could easily overtake her and fire
if I wished ; but I covet the giant which exceeds all
his congeners in height by $2\frac{1}{2}$ feet, and is big in
proportion : such a monster as I have rarely seen.

The wind is in our favour. I decide to await a
more timely opportunity for firing : so I follow the
elephants at a distance into the thicket, which they
simply cross. The male, in stopping to eat, loses a little
ground, and I think that perhaps it will end by being
last. That is, in fact, what happens, for upon reaching
another open space I see it in the rear in company
with the old female, who now looks quite small by his
side. Running parallel to him, I arrive on a level
about ten yards away. The cruppers of an elephant
preceding him prevent me from seeing if he has
tusks. If only he has ! Stopping for a moment and
holding my breath, I fire two shots with the 8-bore
at intervals of one second ; then I make off as fast as
my legs will carry me in order not to be trampled on ;
for at the same moment the whole herd shows signs
of irritation, and the females begin trotting about in
all directions, retracing their steps and executing a
quadrille, the figures of which were none the less
interesting for not being regular. An old female
without tusks, driven wild by the reports and uttering

FEMALE ELEPHANTS ASSISTING A WOUNDED MALE TO REACH A PLACE OF SAFETY.

cries of rage, gallops several times round the group in her search for the enemy, exactly like an enormous sheep-dog when it is reassembling its flock. I keep at a distance, following the elephants' movements. Soon, calm seems to have returned to them, and they continue their journey in the direction of another thicket. The male, which one can still distinguish by his high back, is in the middle of the herd; but suddenly I see him slacken his pace, hesitate, then stop dead and remain behind, motionless in the middle of the plain. Just at the moment I am going to rush forward to give it the *coup de grâce* all the females turn back and surround him; and I distinctly see them pushing him along, making him walk in spite of himself, almost carrying him, as the unfortunate animal sets its heels well in the ground. At last, by force of efforts in the midst of grunting, a great flapping of ears, an entanglement of raised, lowered, or twisted trunks — the wounded animal, carried, pushed, and supported by the females, takes a few more steps and enters the thicket, which I reach close upon their heels.

I could easily have killed several females during this scene and that which had preceded it; but, not wishing to tarry in the country unnecessarily, I decided to content myself with the male. As to thinking of killing it as long as it was surrounded by its sorrowing companions—that was impossible. I should have run a very good chance of being charged.

After a few minutes' waiting in order to see whether the elephants remained in the thicket, I make a rapid circuit of it, and see the herd already in flight well out of range. At the speed they are going the wounded male cannot be accompanying them; besides, there is no blood on the track. It must, therefore, be in the thicket. I return there, and, advancing with great precaution in the gloom, distinguish immediately at a distance of ten yards, in the midst of dense vegetation, one of the animal's ears—nothing more. Nevertheless, I see that the animal is not lying in the direction in which its companions have gone : it has turned round and faces me : so it is impossible for me to advance on the spoor. It is probably on the watch, ready to sell its life as dearly as possible.

On account of the wind, I could not think of taking the animal in the rear. The track must, therefore, be abandoned, and the animal reached from one side. In order to do so, a passage had to be made through vegetation so thick that you could advance only by passing through it first of all your arms and rifle, then your head and body, and finally your legs. A charge amid such circumstances meant certain death : so I take care not to get too near. By taking a thousand precautions, I get within fifteen yards of the elephant in half an hour's time ; but the branches and foliage are so thick that its head, shoulder, and crupper are hidden—all I can see is its back and part of its stomach. I move to one side, therefore, so as to fire on the slant, aiming at the animal's side in order to reach the heart. The elephant not moving in response to the bullet from the 8-bore, I fire another, and yet a third. Kambombe informs me

THE COLOSSAL ELEPHANT.

from a tree of the elephant's movements, because the smoke would have prevented me seeing anything had he charged. Each time the smoke clears away I fire again. Thus I exhaust the whole of my stock (which usually consists of ten 8-bore cartridges), without the elephant having moved or seemed even to notice them. Taking my Express, I begin a fresh series, when at the first shot the elephant falls heavily, crushing everything round it, knocking down trees the tops of which almost fall on our heads, collapsing with a great noise in the midst of lianas, branches, and shattered trunks.

We draw near, and I look upon the largest elephant which I have ever killed. Its enormous tusks protruded from its mouth 6 feet 2 inches, and were $22\frac{1}{2}$ inches in circumference at the juncture of the flesh; their total length was $8\frac{1}{2}$ feet, and they were both of exactly the same weight—namely, $114\frac{1}{2}$ pounds. As to its size: it was 12 feet $2\frac{1}{2}$ inches from its withers to the ground, carefully measured. Once the ground was cleared, its height, lying on its side, reached 5 feet 11 inches—that is, a man of medium size could not look over the top.

I kept the skull, intending to bring it to Europe with the tusks. Not less than eleven additional carriers were required for this trophy: six to carry the skull without the lower jaw-bone, when properly cleaned and emptied; two for each tusk, and one for the lower jaw. Later, the difficulties of transport and the lack of carriers for indispensable articles forced me to abandon these cumbersome packages, and, much to my regret, the skull of my big elephant was left behind. But the tusks accomplished the journey. They form, to-day, two of the finest objects in my collection, and are the admiration of all who see them.

In the preceding chapters I have narrated to the reader the principal episodes in my elephant-hunting experiences. May he have taken some interest in

ELEPHANT SKULL.

them! Certainly elephant-hunting is the greatest and noblest sport in the world. The following is the opinion of the celebrated English sportsman, Sir Samuel Baker, one of the greatest authorities on this subject :—

It is the fashion for some people to assert that the elephant is an innocent and harmless creature—that, like the giraffe, it is almost a sin to destroy it. I can only say that during eight years' experience in Ceylon and nearly five years in Africa I have found that elephants are the most formidable animals with which a sportsman has to contend. The African species *is far more dangerous* than the Indian, as the forehead shot can never be trusted ; therefore the hunter must await the charge with a conviction that his bullet will not fail to kill.[1]

---

[1] See *Nile Tributaries of Abyssinia*, p. 360.   London : Macmillan and Co., Ltd. (1894).

THE MORNING OF OCTOBER 7, 1896.

CHAPTER XIV

RECORD DAYS WITH LIONS

Meeting a troop of lions—Fruitless pursuit—The forgotten stick—Death of
    the big male—Fatal shots.
Nocturnal roaring—Off to encounter wild beasts—Face to face—A wounded
    lion—The shot at the neck—Photographing and skinning—An alarm
    —Lionesses—Death of one of them—Search for and discovery of the
    first lion—Three lions in one morning.
Third episode—A mother's death—The cubs—Conclusion.

THE two adventures with lions which I shall here
relate happened at different dates; but I group
them together, as constituting the finest incidents,
after those which I have narrated in the preceding
chapters, in my hunting reminiscences. In every
way they are a worthy pendant to those which precede.

As these two encounters occurred in the daytime,

I was able to observe my adversaries much better than would have been the case at night in the unsteady, precipitated light of the electric projector.

On November 3, 1895, we set out at dawn in pursuit of buffaloes, which had come to drink while we were at a night-watch. By about ten o'clock in the morning, we have proceeded far into a mountainous country. Abandoning the chase, we decide to return to camp by taking a short cut across the plain.

The hour may be about noon, and the heat is overpowering. Each of us walks along in silence, picking his way over the uneven ground. Here and there can be seen a few clumps of tall grass, which the fire has not destroyed; one in particular is on my right, at the foot of a large tree. Two of my men lead (I cannot remember which); Kambombe follows me at fifteen yards' distance with the 303; and the others bring up the rear. We tramp along without thinking—unless it be of that glaring sun beating down upon the desolate landscape.

As I get on a level with the big tree, a sudden growl makes me start. An enormous lion—looking bigger than he really is, because he is standing on an ant-hill—appears, and shows his teeth. I stop, and, throwing my stick to the ground, stretch my arm out behind me, according to habit, to receive my rifle. But nobody is there, and when Kambombe at last comes up it is too late. Seeing me stop to look at him, the lion has disappeared in the grass, and the whole family (composed of five — the parents and three large cubs) are seen making off at a slow trot.

We dash off in pursuit; but, the unburnt grass becoming thicker, we lose sight of them. However, Msiambiri sees them from the top of a tree, and also distinguishes the horns of a koodoo behind the ant-hill where we disturbed them. The family has evidently been gorging, and will probably allow itself to be approached. We continue to follow, therefore, with large strides; and it is not long before I see them—but too far off to permit me to fire. Then one of them stops for a moment on an ant-hill to look at us. We increase our pace, and several times see the whole troop; the female walking in front with her cubs, the male in the rear. Every now and then he turns round to look askance at us. What a monster! And he is without a mane!

As I have already said, the heat is terrible. Now and then the lions, tired of walking, stop to rest in the shade. But they trot away again, and cross an almost bare plain without giving me an opportunity to fire, being more than 100 yards off. A small wood of "mitsagnas," which we cross on their heels, is next encountered, and the lioness disappears with her cubs on to a grassy plain where it is useless to go in search of them. It is so hot, we have not the strength to express regret.

Discouraged, we stop for a moment in the shade. I place the hammers of my rifle at half-cock, hand it to Kambombe, and hold out my hand for my stick. But Kambombe had forgotten to pick it up when I threw it down. He does not usually forget things; but this time, in the excitement caused by meeting the lions, he did. As I am very fond of this stick (a souvenir of former hunting days), I decide to retrace our steps, instead of going forward. We cross the plain, and again enter the small wood. Hallo! look out! Rodzani, who is walking in front, almost steps on the big lion! . . . The animal, which was lying down, lazily rises to his feet, moves to the right out of our path, and passes behind us. I seize my rifle, but, prevented from firing by the shrubs, I run ten yards farther on to a glade which he is bound to pass.

Oppressed by the heat, and also, as I found afterwards, by its heavy meal, it walks along with head so low that I can see only its undulating back and powerful shoulders. Although he knows I am there, he does not even look at me. I aim at his neck, and, when he passes straight in front of me at a distance of six yards, fire. . . . He falls with a thud—stone dead.

If chance had not ordained our return in search of the forgotten stick, this lion would have remained quietly lying down where it was, while we thought it with its family. Probably he would have let us pass a second time near to him without disturbing him, if we had not, as it were, involuntarily stepped upon him.

I send some men to the camp immediately to fetch the camera. Meantime, we visit the koodoo, almost the only remaining parts of which are the bones. We find, however, a piece of meat on the neck, which we grill in the shade, awaiting the men's return.

After measuring the lion we dragged it into the

shade, and covered it with leaves. It was very large, as the accompanying picture will show better than any description ; to comprehend its size, you have only to compare my helmet to its head.

About four o'clock the men return with the water for which we are waiting impatiently, for, having given them all we had before they set off to the camp, we are almost dying of thirst. The photographs are then taken ; after which we begin to skin the lion, which is already in a state of decomposition, so great is the heat. We return to the camp in the evening, very tired, but, nevertheless, satisfied with our day's work.

One year later, on October 7, 1896, again at the period of night-watches, lions roar the whole night about three-quarters of a mile away. But they do not come to drink : they keep us, for five or six hours, in a state of excitement which you can easily imagine when you know that on that particular night we were seated only on the ground under a large tree without the smallest ant-hill to protect us in the rear.

As we can still hear them in the neighbourhood at daybreak, I decide to guide myself to them by the sound. On our route is the broad, deep bed of a river completely dried up. It is full of dead leaves, and its banks are bordered by large trees, dense vegetation, and tall grass which the fire has not injured.

Before reaching this river we stop to listen a while. The roars seem to get nearer ; two lions,

DEAD MANELESS LION: THE INCIDENT OF THE FORGOTTEN STICK.

with powerful lungs, are exchanging impressions.
The third or fourth time we hear them we have no
longer any doubt about it : they are coming towards us,
to all appearances towards the river bed, with the
probable intention of crossing it to drink. We hold
a hasty consultation. Some suggest returning to
the pool, hiding ourselves, and awaiting them ; but,
not sure that they are going there, I prefer to meet
them by approaching the river.

Guided by the roars of the lions, which still
advance, we turn to the right, so as to be on their
path ; and select a place where a slight promontory
covered with tall grass enables us to inspect the
surroundings. The wind is favourable to us. The
river's edge is barely ten yards away. Still the noise
comes nearer, making us change our position once
more ; in fact, no sooner have we got alongside an ant-
hill, than the rustling of leaves tells us that the lions
are crossing. . . . We wait, all our attention fixed
on the large trees. . . . It is a terrible moment of
suspense ! . . . Will they be together, or isolated ?
Shall we fire immediately, or let them pass ? . . .

The 303 is ready cocked, the cartridges well in
their places ; the priming has been inspected. I
look with admiration at this marvellous weapon, this
powerful auxiliary made by the hand of man. . . .
Its polished barrels flash in the rising sun. . . . Will
death leap forth once more ? Anyway, the Express
is ready at my side ; and the Winchester also, as a
last resource. . . . Attention ! . . . Here they
come ! . . .

By chance they emerge from the river-bed, hidden by the ant-hill, and one of us in leaning forward to see them makes some dry grass crackle under his feet. This noise, which it is imprudent to make so near lions, makes them start, and one of them, puzzled by it, comes out to our right, barely ten yards away, but, alas! at a trot. Instead of aiming at the neck, I fire at the shoulder-blades. Upon receiving my shot, the animal, which has passed without seeing us, prepares to charge, raises its tail, and springs forward with open mouth and raised claws. There being no smoke, and as we remain perfectly still, we do not betray our presence. Then, turning to the right, it disappears.

I have already reloaded, and my eyes are on the look-out for its companion, which we have not yet seen. We have not long to wait—there it is! It also comes out on our right, a little farther away, about twenty yards. Doubtless puzzled by the rifle-shot and its companion's deviation, it advances at a walk, looking in front of it and stopping, presenting to my rifle the finest mark which I have ever had. Never has lion seemed to me to be so big. I aim at the neck, counting the throbs of my heart, and . . . fire. It seems to me to fall like a lump of lead . . . but it has disappeared in the tall grass, and I cannot give a decisive opinion. . . . We climb on to the ant-hill, but nothing is to be seen. . . . Finally Kambombe informs us from a tree that the lion is lying over there as though dead. After throwing a few pieces of wood at it to make sure, we approach,

LION LISTENING: FIVE MINUTES BEFORE DEATH.

and I am able to admire to my great joy as fine and almost as large a lion as the one which the vultures helped me to find the year before, but this time a lion with a magnificent mane. In the neck is a minute hole made by the small 303 bullet.

My men run to fetch the photographic camera, and when everything is ready I take a photograph of this magnificent animal. The men from the camp then assist Tchigallo, Tambarika, and Rodzani, in skinning it.

This work is only half finished, and I am sitting down looking on, when a noise, at first indefinite and then very recognisable, comes from the direction of the river-bed,—the low roars which lions make when they communicate with one another. There is a general panic on the part of the men from the camp. "The wounded one is returning!" they cry, and all swarm, one after the other, into a tree which bends beneath their united weight. My hunters seize their rifles. I run to the eminence of which I have spoken, and upon noiselessly arriving, see two tawny backs pass a few yards away on a level with the grass. . . . There is only just time to aim at the neck of one of the animals before they disappear in higher vegetation. A dull sound responds to the report of my rifle, while the grass, violently parted, reveals the other animal in flight.

They are lionesses seeking for their lord and master, almost on the same track ; and if we had not heard the noise they would have passed unobserved, a few yards from the group busy skinning the dead lion.

You will easily understand my joy at having added a magnificent lioness to my lion. She was advanced in age and very large.

Again the photographic camera performs its work, and the skinning immediately follows, my intention being to dry the two skins the same day. The men carry everything, and we are getting ready to return to camp behind them, for it will soon be eleven o'clock in the morning, when the idea occurs to me to follow, for a short distance, the track of the first wounded lion. A few drops of blood indicate its passage through the grass. I follow the traces through sheer curiosity, being in every way satisfied with the day's sport, and not regretting inordinately the loss of the animal. On the bank of the river, which it recrossed, we glance into the dark mass of dry leaves, but nothing is to be seen. We are about to turn round when something like regret comes over me, and I say to my men, "Wait for me. I'm going to the opposite bank to look over the plain." At the other side, in fact, is a plain upon which nothing has been spared by the fire; which is, consequently, as flat as a billiard-table; the eye can see over it a great distance.

I jump down, cross the river-bed where the dry leaves are spotted with blood, and, climbing the opposite bank, part the shrubs to look through. At first I see nothing; but a little later I see something tawny, like an antelope, lying down more than 200 yards away. An antelope lying down in the midst of the unprotected plain at eleven o'clock in the

KAMBOMBE AND MSIAMBIRI WITH LION FIVE MINUTES AFTER DEATH.

morning! Impossible! "Halloo! Come along: there is something over there!" I cry to my men, who come up and gaze at the object. Is it a harte-beest or a reedbuck? Let us go see! We are quite certain as to what it is when forty yards away : it is the lion, dead, and already swollen.

What put us off the track was the fact that we could not see its mane, which, it may be said in parenthesis, was a very fine one. My bullet passed through the lungs and touched the heart, splitting in two places. I knew that I had missed the shoulder-blades, since the lion continued to run. When it sprang forward I really did think it was badly wounded, but, seeing it disappear at a gallop, I should not have believed it so seriously wounded as it was.

Three lions in one morning! I was so happy that everybody in camp received a triple present. The work of photographing and skinning was repeated. What a pity I hurried on the two former occasions! If I had waited until noon I should have been able to photograph my three lions together, and myself with them. But I could not foresee that I should have such luck that day ; and animals decompose so quickly, especially felines, that you cannot be too expeditious in curing their skins. It is probable that I might return to the bush for twenty years more without having such a windfall. What is so unusual is not having met four lions, but having been able calmly to kill three, one after the other, as soon as they appeared.

I now reach my third hunt, undoubtedly less extraordinary than the preceding, but meriting narration because it was concluded by the capture of cubs.

Two months after the day on which the three lions were killed—namely, in December—the expedition was on the march. We reached water about three o'clock in the afternoon. At that hour I kill a wart-hog for dinner. The carriers arrive, the camp is pitched for the night, and I set off, as is my custom, to inspect the surroundings in search of game. Kambombe alone accompanies me. In descending the stream on the banks of which we have camped, I see many lion spoor, which set me thinking of a means of establishing a night-watch at that spot. But the spoor are yesterday's. We will see if there are any of to-day. I remain, therefore, on one side, while Kambombe crosses the stream and searches on the other. I proceed noiselessly over the damp soil, and skirt a plain covered with thick vegetation which overhangs the river by about a yard. Wishing to glance over the plain, I climb on to the slope and first of all expose my head, next my shoulders, and then my body as necessity requires in my examination of the surroundings. These seem to me deserted, but 100 yards away I distinguish something in the grass which may be either the trunk of a fallen tree or an animal. I raise myself a little higher. The object moves. I make a sign to Kambombe to come to me. But he himself cannot say what it is. We must get nearer. In order to do so we descend to the level of the river and noiselessly

follow its bank; then we again climb the slope. "It's
a lion!" I murmur to my companion. The head of
the animal is about eight yards away. . . . "Or a
leopard," suggests Kambombe. As a matter of fact,
the heads of these two animals, seen afar off and from
behind, resemble each other very much. The animal
bends down and raises itself. It seems to be absorbed
by something near it. Fearing to make a noise and
to disturb it by getting nearer, I decide to remain
where I am. So, aiming between the two round
ears, full at the neck, I fire. . . .

Let us see what has happened, for the animal,
leopard or lion, has disappeared. Again skirting the
river, we draw near cautiously. . . . Kambombe,
climbing into a tree, discovers that the animal is a
lioness, and informs me that she is stretched motionless on the ground, with shattered, bloody head. . . .
He also sees that she has cubs. . . . After taking a
few precautions to make sure that the lioness is really
dead, we show ourselves. Two cubs are by the
mother's side, and a third, which she crushed in her
fall, dies as we hurriedly remove it from underneath
the body.

The lioness is of average size. The young are
four or five days old, and are as big as the two fists
put together.

With a cub in each hand, Kambombe at once
makes off to the camp. I ask him to hurry and
return as soon as possible with men and his comrades
armed, while I remain hidden behind a tree to watch
over the lioness's body in the hope of seeing the male

arrive. The least sound makes me prick up my ears, for I expect his return at any moment. If he sees that his companion is dead, and that his cubs have disappeared, he will not be in the best of humours, and then any one who is in his way, beware! . . . But he does not return. . . . Soon the rustling of grass and a well-known whistle announce the approach of my men, who make this signal to know whether they can appear. Upon receiving my answer in the affirmative, they appear on the scene; the feet of the lioness are bound together, a pole is passed between them, and we set off to the camp.[1]

I was afterwards informed that my men had declared to Rodzani, who had advised them to make a stockade for the night, that this precaution was unnecessary; that they would sleep quite well as things were; and that, besides, there were no thorns, etc. But after Kambombe brought the cubs to the camp, when the many spoor of their parents were counted on the river bank, and when the body of the lioness was carried in, everybody changed his opinion with great rapidity. Heaps of thorns were found immediately, and a veritable fortification, inside which was enough firewood for two nights, was made.

It is into this stronghold we retire, and the whole night through, in the glare of the big fires, we enjoy a lions' concert such as we have never heard before. The unfortunate widower must have assembled the

---

[1] I regretted, but too late, not having remained in wait for the lion. He left his family doubtless to search for food, and would certainly have returned before night.

whole of the lions in the neighbourhood, judging from their roars within terrifying proximity at the side of the stockade, where the wind reveals the presence of our two new boarders. I have already mentioned the profound, startling impression which the roar of a lion makes upon man. There is nothing more terrifying in the darkness than that powerful voice, which echoes several miles away, and shakes the ground; when it is heard only one or two feet away it is enough to shake the nerves of the coolest. The females appear to be the most furious, doubtless heaping upon us in their language their worst invectives. The noise prevents any one from sleeping. Several times I try a few rifle-shots to make them at least go away; but the night is as black as ink and very cloudy, and I seek in vain for the box in which the electric projector is packed.

Towards morning a storm joins in the chorus. The heavens rumble, mingling their voice with that of the king of the felines, at first in hollow tones, then with loud claps. Dawn at last slowly announces its appearance in black weather; rain extinguishes our fires. The peals of thunder end by drowning the roars, and the lions withdraw at daybreak.

I went out, but without meeting any of the members of the family. We then left the district, carrying with us in a basket the cubs, which from the first night took kindly to the feeding-bottle. Later they became accustomed to sucking at a goat which had to be tied with its head to leeward because of the terrifying effect the odour of its nurslings had upon it. One goat was soon insufficient, and two became necessary. When three months old the cubs were already the size of a large bull-dog. They followed me about everywhere, walked ahead of me on foot-paths, trotted backwards and forwards as dogs do, turned round to see me coming, and waited for me. . . . But walking did not agree with them; they got very tired, their paws hurt them, and they hung out their tongues like tired dogs. Rest and at least a less agitated existence than ours would have been necessary for success in rearing them. One of them soon died, and I parted with the other near Lake Nyassa, so as not to see it do the same.

A few words more on the subject of the death of the lioness. I have learnt from experience that the shot at the neck is excellent, and preferable to any other if the animal is in profile. If it presents a full front, everything depends on the way in which the lion holds its head; if it is high, it is useless to fire; if it lowers it, as it often does to charge, you must fire either between the two eyes, or between the two shoulder-blades, which can be seen distinctly when the head is lowered. If the charge has begun, wait until the animal is very near. The shot at the neck (four fingers' breadth behind the ears and in the centre of the thickest part of the neck) I have tried very often and always with the same success. There is one advantage which I should like to point out to those who make this shot for the first time: if you hit, the lion will be killed; if you miss, an easy thing to do, because the neck is not very big at twenty

yards, it will escape scot-free. Should you see
the lion clearly in profile, the shot at the shoulder-
blades, right in the centre, is excellent. The projectile
shatters these two bones, and almost always touches
the spinal column, which passes in the middle, thus
paralysing its fore-quarters, and placing it *hors de
combat*. But if you deviate, though there are chances
of seriously wounding it, you risk a long and dangerous pursuit. It is not always possible to hit a lion
where you wish, as I know very well; and if you
shoot carelessly you must take the consequences. As
a general rule, dangerous animals must be annihilated
at the first shot, or at least disabled. To do that you
must fully decide what you are going to do, and, I
repeat, fire at them when comparatively near, so as
to be quite sure of your result. With the shoulder-
blades or spinal column broken, the animal can
neither use its fore-paws nor move. You can then
easily finish it off. On the other hand, if it is
merely wounded (even to the heart), a lion will sell
its life dearly.

The three episodes which I have just narrated
conclude these records of a sportsman. May the
reader have felt in perusing them a pleasure akin to
that which I experienced when gun in hand.

Later, when my forces have diminished, when I
have given up travelling, and have definitely placed
my rifle in the gun-rack, I shall be able at my fire-
side, my heart full of regret, to turn over the pages
of these souvenirs, and, looking through these impressions, photographs, and trophies, live once more the

life of the chase. Like an old soldier who recollects his battles, more than once shall I, in thought, find myself face to face with the big game of Africa, and begin again, in company with my brave black companions, combats of former times.

MY LION CUBS.

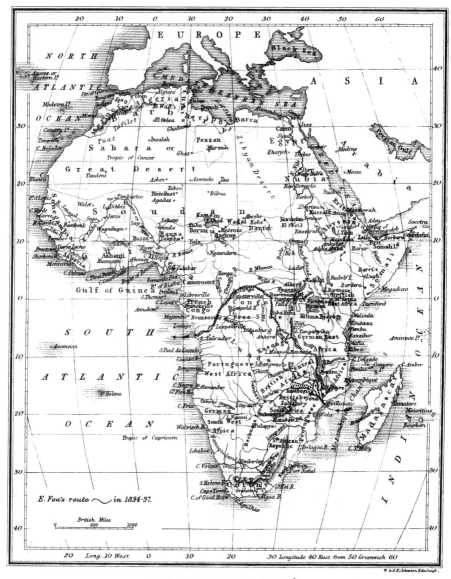

MAP ACCOMPANYING E. FOA'S
"AFTER BIG GAME IN CENTRAL AFRICA."

TABLE SHOWING SPORT FROM AUGUST 1894 TO NOVEMBER 1897 [1]

A.—WITH RIFLES.

LARGE ANIMALS.

Elephants	39
Rhinoceroses	14
Giraffes	1
Hippopotami	19
Lions	16
Cape buffaloes . . .	56
Congo buffaloes . . .	8
Panthers or leopards . .	5
Wolves	1
Jackals	1
Civet-cats	1
Otters	1
Lynx	1
Wart-hogs	31
Wild-boars	2
Elands	28
Zebras	11
Sable antelopes . . .	13
Roan antelopes . . .	5
Koodoos	17
Hartebeests (*kaama*) . .	2
,, (*lichtenstein*) . .	57
,, (*lunatus*) (Tsessebe)	3
Waterbucks	43
Nswalas	21
Reedbucks	22
Bushbucks	12
Inyalas	5
Situtungas	2
Pookoos	23
Letchwes	6
Duikers	4
Crocodiles	18
Total . . .	488

B.—WITH FOWLING-PIECE.

SMALL GAME AND VARIOUS.

29 guinea-fowls, 6 partridges, 1 hare, 233 various kinds of birds (shot in collaboration with my travelling companions), 91 wild - ducks or teals, 21 wild - geese, 58 aquatic birds (ibis, herons, pelicans, crab-eaters, egreto, flamingoes, marabouts, etc.), 37 various species of monkeys and lemuridæ, 1 fishing eagle, 2 nyangombas, 1 scaly ant-eater, 1 ant-eater, 1 python, 38 species of birds (parrots, ibis, wild-ducks, etc. etc. on the Congo).

Total 520

C.—I. SNARED, TRAPPED, NETTED, ETC.

2 oribis,[2] 8 bluebucks, 2 civet-cats, 11 agoutis, 165 Smith's macrocelides, 1 leopard, 2 hyenas, 1 oreotragus. Total . . 192

II. POISONED.

1 leopard, 3 hyenas. Total . 4

III. CAPTURED ALIVE.

2 lions, 2 zebras, 1 hartebeest, 2 reedbucks, 4 bluebucks, 2 civet-cats, 2 ichneumons, 3 monkeys, 2 wart-hogs, 7 waterbuck, 1 leopard, 1 ant-eater. Total . . 24

SUMMARY.

Large animals . . .	488
Small game	520
Various	220
Grand total . . .	1228

---

[1] See *Mes Grandes Chasses*, p. 320.

Table showing sport from 1891 to 1893 :—	
Large animals	319
Small game	271
Various	114
	704

[2] A small antelope of the duiker species.

APPENDIX

PART I

DURING the seven consecutive years which I have passed
in wild regions in search of large animals, I have had
occasion to notice more than one interesting peculiarity
in their habits. I consider as an indispensable supplement
to these records a few particulars about the animals which
have, to a great extent, formed their subject. I lay down
my rifle, therefore, to study, in their haunts as a naturalist
would, the three chief inhabitants of the African bush,—
the elephant, the rhinoceros, and the lion.

ELEPHANT (*Elephas africanus*)

ELEPHANT.—Age and signs of old age—Size—Circumference of the foot—
Reproduction—Young on the march or in danger—How they suck—
Maternal solicitude—The tusks, their weight and length—Tuskless
elephants—Tusks do not grow again—Use the animal makes of its
tusks—The trunk and its various uses—Supply of water in the animal's
stomach—Eye and ear—The food of elephants—Importance of the
wind—Marching orders: when travelling and when eating—Water,
mud, and sand baths—Intestinal worms—Sounds made by elephants—
Daily habits of these animals—Elephants' cemetery—Softness of their
bones—Dead ivory—Elephant countries—War made upon them everywhere—Their approaching extinction—Accidents caused by elephants—
The shot at the head and at the heart—Elephants' tracks—Method of
removing tusks—The elephant's only enemy—The true king of beasts—
A few words about its domestication.

I begin with the king of beasts, the one which study, experience, and common sense, whatever La Fontaine and even some naturalists may say to the contrary, points out as the true monarch,—namely, the elephant.[1]

It is very difficult to fix the age which an elephant can reach. It does not live more than 120 years in India; but in that country its life is shortened, it is thought, by captivity. We may presume, therefore, that 150 years constitutes extreme old age in the case of an African elephant. External evidences of advanced years are also difficult to determine. I have noticed that old elephants have very deep hollows at the temples, and that the jaw is prominent, in short, that the head is bony, as if the skin were simply stretched on the skull. The rest of the body, also, is thinner and more angular. Their size has, of course, reached its maximum.

I have written down in my notebook the sizes of almost all the elephants killed by me; and the comparative table which concludes this work gives the measurements of twenty of them for the information of my readers. The average which I have worked out is about 10 feet 7 inches for adult males with tusks weighing 44 pounds and above, and 9 feet 8 inches for females. I have killed females without tusks and a male much bigger than this; but that, I believe, is exceptional, except in some regions, still little frequented, where elephants can reach their full growth undisturbed.

The circumference of the fore-foot of the Indian elephant is almost exactly, it is said, half the height of the withers.

[1] In *Mes Grandes Chasses* (pp. 202, 291, 293, and 296) will be found a few words on the habits of this animal. I must correct two statements which experience has shown me to be inaccurate. The elephant does not always fall down when wounded to the heart. It bleeds from its trunk, shows signs of great prostration ; sometimes it remains on the spot and only falls down afterwards, but it can still go a hundred yards more. Seriously wounded in the lungs, it does not proceed more than 300 or 400 yards.

This rule cannot be applied to the African elephant. I have never found such a rule to apply ; nor has Sir Samuel Baker.[1] Generally, the circumference of the foot is shorter than half the withers, which would lead one to suppose that the African elephant's foot is relatively smaller than that of its Asiatic congener.

The sole of the fore-foot of the male and that of the female differ considerably, first of all in size and next in shape. It being slightly oval in the case of the male, and quite round in the case of the female, the hunter can distinguish the spoor of a small male from that of a large female. The hind-feet of both sexes are elongated ovals. The hair is also more developed in the male ; the lip, the interior of ʋⁱᵉ ears, the tuft at the end of the tail are thicker ; there is also between them, as in the case of all animals, difference in thickness of neck, chest, legs, etc.

If one lived for fifty years in an elephant country it would be impossible to get to know exactly how these animals reproduce. But I borrow from Mr. Sanderson, who, having been commissioned by the British Government during a period of thirteen years to capture elephants and to train them for work, is an incontestable authority, the following particulars, which, though they apply to Indian elephants, may also be applied to the African species :—[2]

" Females," he says, writing of the elephant in its wild state, *for it does not breed in captivity*,[3] " usually give birth to their first calf at sixteen years of age. The period of gestation in the elephant is said by experienced natives to be twenty-two months in the case of the male and eighteen for a female. Many wild female elephants are accompanied

---

[1] *Nile Tributaries of Abyssinia*, p. 199, small edition.

[2] *Thirteen Years amongst the Wild Beasts of India*, by G. P. Sanderson, pp. 59, 61-67.

[3] Cases are reported of females which have bred in captivity, but it is proved that they were with young at the time of their capture.

by two and sometimes by three calves of different ages. . . .
The tusks of the young elephant are visible almost from
birth. . . . A calf usually stands exactly 3 feet high at
the shoulder when born. Its weight is about 200 lbs. on
the second day after birth."

I have often seen females with their young, and noticed
that the young follow their mothers with the greatest ease on
long marches. Upon the approach of the slightest danger,
the young immediately take refuge between their mothers'
legs, generally under the chest, where, as we know, the
udders are situated. To suck, they throw their trunks
aside and use their lips, though the natives are persuaded
that they suck with " their noses," just as Buffon believed.
They use the trunks for drinking. The mother is full of
solicitude for her offspring: she supports her young, as I
have already narrated, when crossing a river; she also helps
it to climb hills by pushing it from behind with her coiled-
up trunk.

Tusks of males weigh on an average 33 pounds. Their
thickness and length differ according to the country in
which they are found. Thus, I have noticed that elephants
of the Upper Zambesi have little ivory, while those of the
Congo have much; that the tusks of the former are short
and thick, whereas those of the latter are long and slender.
They are generally the thickness of the fore-arm, 3 feet long,
and weigh on an average nine pounds in adult females;
the tusks of males average from 33 pounds to extraordinary
weights. I repeat that they are generally from 33 to
44 pounds, but I have killed elephants whose tusks
weighed 66, $83\frac{1}{2}$, $92\frac{1}{2}$, and even $114\frac{1}{2}$ pounds each. At
the Antwerp Exhibition among the Congo exhibits, was
a tusk weighing nearly 200 pounds! These weights are
quite exceptional. The ordinary length of tusks, varying
from 33 to 44 pounds, is about 4 feet 6 inches; but I have
seen them almost double that length. I believe that the
milieu in which elephants live—dry or wet country, plain

or forest—has a great influence on the quality and quantity of ivory, just as it has an influence on the size.

Side by side with elephants provided with tusks, which are in the majority, we meet with certain anomalies, tuskless elephants. These, in my opinion, are phenomena resulting from some caprice or other in dentition. I have never seen a male without tusks, and Mr. Selous reports one case only. On the other hand, I have met a fair number of females which had none; especially in southern Central Africa. From the region of the lakes to the Congo, these tuskless females appear to me to be rarer. They are distinguished from the other elephants by greater irascibility and larger size. The sourness of their temper seems to me inexplicable, unless the absence of tusks makes them suffer pain, which is difficult to admit. As to their great size, this must arise from the fact that native hunters fear these animals owing to their viciousness, and spare them because they are commercially useless. Not only is the absence of tusks not hereditary, but tuskless females are always, according to experienced natives, mothers of big males with ivory. I have seen several examples of this, and a case in point is mentioned in Chapter XIII.

Does a broken tusk grow again? It is generally believed that it does; but that is an error. I have seen several elephants with only one tusk, the other having been lost either during a fight between males, or owing to a clumsy rifle-shot.

The use which elephants make of their tusks is indicated by the name (*défenses*) which is given them in French. They constitute a redoubtable weapon with which males fight among themselves, indicate their superiority, or inspire fear in the herd. Females use them in the same way, and it is common to find elephants wounded or marked in several places by the tusks of their fellows. They also use them for digging up roots, for stripping bark from trees, and even for resting; in fact, they rest them against a transverse branch, or any other support, when they go to sleep. They have only four or five molars in each jaw.

I will add that about half the tusk only protrudes from the elephant's mouth. One-third is let into a powerful bony socket situated at the base of the trunk; a sixth is surrounded by the gums and lips; the rest is outside. Almost half its length, which tapers to a point like that of a horn, is hollow.

The trunk, although possessed of great strength, is the most delicate part of an elephant. Whenever there is danger, and the animal dashes on an enemy, it carefully folds and draws in its trunk, leaving its tusks alone prominent. Pictures can be seen in which an elephant is represented charging a hunter with its trunk raised in the air; but this is pure imagination on the part of the artist, and shows his complete ignorance of the habits of the pachyderm, which, even when running, half rolls up its trunk so as not to come into contact with obstacles. The opening, by means of which it scents and directs itself, is curled under the head and turned to the front. The trunk is then protected by the tusks. In places where the animal walks slowly and with suspicion, its trunk hangs down to the ground, and feels the way ahead. Its sense of smell is so keen that, if the wind is favourable, it can scent a man three or four miles away.

It uproots trees by leaning against them with its forehead, and not by using its trunk, which is used for taking hold of smaller objects. The trunk is a kind of hand which searches for fruit, smells, chooses, and carries food to the mouth; it delicately seizes a branch as thin as a pencil, stripping it of bark, and throwing away the wood; it seeks in the long grass for fallen fruit. The elephant uses it in the water as a pump. It fills it half full, closes it, curls it round, and squirts the water into its mouth; it transforms it also into a shower-bath for all parts of its body; or else, if there is no water, it collects earth and fresh sand to sprinkle over its back and ears, scorched by the sun. When fatigued by a long march in the sun it obtains water with its trunk from its own stomach,[1] with which to refresh its head and shoulders. Should an enemy's spear stick into its flesh, the elephant seizes it with its trunk, drags it out, and throws it aside. A powerful arm, a sensitive hand, and a delicate nose at one and the same time,—such is the marvellous organ with which nature has endowed this animal.

On the other hand, sight and hearing are imperfect senses. Its eye seems to be unable to discern the objects it sees. It may see a man distinctly, but, if unassisted by its sense of smell, it cannot distinguish him from an animal.[2] Very often, when the wind was in my favour, elephants have fixedly looked at me, flapping their immense ears as they did so, but without showing any signs of disquiet as I advanced towards them. Their trunks waved about in all directions, trying to scent me out; but, the wind bringing them no alarming message, they stood perfectly still. However, those animals which have already been wounded by a man sometimes flee simply upon seeing one a short distance away.

The hearing of the elephant is hardly better than that of man. I cannot compare it to anything poorer,[3] for what animal, even domestic, has not better hearing and smell than we have? I cannot speak about our ancestors in the caverns; but if their senses were as imperfect as ours, their lives must have been at the mercy of animals.

Having described their physical appearance, let me now say a few words about their habits. The large quantity

[1] Like the camel's, the elephant's stomach has a chamber which can be cut off from the proper digestive cavity. It is capable of holding ten gallons.

[2] Most wild animals are the same.

[3] The human voice is particularly disagreeable to them. Sometimes when they are wounded a cry or a call is enough to infuriate, and to make them decide to charge.

of food which they require forces them to travel long distances daily. They eat much grass, preferably green, or, lacking that, straw, reeds, leaves, bark, and especially thorny shrubs, which they like very much, and can smell at a distance. They also like the many kinds of fruit with which the African bush supplies them at various times of the year. Among these I have already mentioned the "matondos" in December and the "fulas" in May. Add to those the "mtudzi" in June, the fruit of the *hyphœnae* in September, "tchendjes," etc. They swallow them whole without masticating them. They like the young shoots of bamboos which grow in damp places, and they also eat the roots ("tsungwi"); they are fond of sorgho, Indian corn, and cucurbitaceæ, of which native plantations are composed; nay, even tobacco, with the result that they often, at night, make great ravages in cultivated places. An average of eight to eight hundredweight and a half of food is required by an elephant during the twenty-four hours, so that if there are twenty of them, it will be clearly seen, they cannot make long stays anywhere. As it is smell alone which guides them in the choice of their food, they feed either during the daytime or at night. Having scented at a distance the special kind of food which they require, they proceed straight to it. They do the same in the case of water. Consequently, an elephant track is a series of straight lines, marked over its whole extent by thorny shrubs, fruit trees, and pools of water,—in short, by everything which is necessary to their sustenance. For these various reasons, they march almost always against the wind; thus they know for certain that no danger is ahead. When feeding, elephants spread out in a line like sharpshooters, and trace parallel tracks, eating as they walk along.

They proceed in single file when travelling, and, as a pastime, take mouthfuls of grass or shrubs to right and left without stopping. Females with young ones are generally in front, or else a male; the other males are in the rear. Upon stopping, the males are very often in the middle, surrounded on all sides by females. When they spread out, on the other hand, there is no fixed rule; it is a case of every one for himself, and that is what causes the death of more than one elephant, for they are then an easy mark for the sportsman's rifle.

Reaching the edge of a pool or a river in the daytime, or during the hot nights, they begin drinking thirstily; then they enter the water and squirt themselves all over. Often they imprudently utter cries of delight, which warn the hunter of their presence. When there is any mud they cover themselves with it, let it dry, and then rub themselves against trees to remove the large ticks and other parasites which stick to their thick skins. Often, also, they swallow mud or earth,[1] with the object, doubtless, of purging themselves; or else it is to remove the short, large worms which are to be found in considerable quantities in their intestines.[2]

Elephants make various noises. I have already described that indicating anger; it is a shrill trumpet like a steam *sirène*. The animal makes it, I believe, with its trunk.[3] It utters deep, savage grunts with its throat when wounded and suffering; but low grunts, similar to those of a large pig, when it appears to wish to communicate with its companions,[4] or when it meditates a charge. In that case it first of all grunts in a low tone, then violently, and finally blows the " trumpet-blast" at the moment it dashes on the enemy. The low, deep noise which natives attribute to the

[1] Especially when it contains saline elements,—potash, rock-salt, nitrate of potash, etc.

[2] The same worms are found in the stomach of the zebra, and in the cervical chamber of the hartebeest. They are larvæ which must have been swallowed with water.

[3] It makes similar noises at night when bathing.

[4] I suppose that elephants must exchange sentiments by means of grunts; but I have never been able to get near enough to them to know exactly.

animal's stomach has already been mentioned in these pages; it is a noise which exactly resembles the roar of a boiler which is getting up steam. How it is produced I do not know, but it is probably made with the trunk.

Habits of elephants change according to the degree of security which the country in which they are offers them. In quiet regions, where hunters do not disturb them (and they instinctively come to know the quiet places), they rest during the hottest hours of the day in thickets impenetrable to the sun, generally resting against a tree or simply standing on their legs with their tusks on a branch. Thus, with bent head, you can see them sleeping. Every now and then they move their large ears to fan themselves or to listen. Their trunks hang down, or else rest on one of the tusks, with the openings turned in the direction of the wind; their eyes blink or are shut. The whole herd is there in various positions, motionless. About four o'clock they again set off to search for food until nightfall. Then there is another halt, generally at some place where there are trees, but this time open. Some lie down; others rest against an ant-hill, or sleep standing. As soon as they feel the freshness of morning they resume their journey or their feeding, until the sun forces them to seek shelter. They drink during their feeding hours.

On the other hand, in districts where they suspect danger, they drink, eat, or sleep when they can. But rest at night is generally done away with in favour of forced marches, repose during the day being prolonged so that they may start at nightfall, after having remained hidden the greater part of the day. Even when resting, the animal does not lie down, one elephant or several elephants being continually on the *qui vive*, and raising their trunks in the air in a disquieted manner to scent all suspicious smells. At the slightest alarm the whole herd, upon receiving an unknown signal, disappears with a swiftness and silence of which you would not think these enormous animals capable. As has been seen from the example which I have given of an old male assisted by females, elephants act together.

I have often been asked if I have met with those cemeteries where elephants are believed to collect to die. No: never have I seen a vestige of them, and I do not believe in their existence.[1] What has given birth to this idea is the fact that nowhere are elephants' bones to be found. But there is a very simple explanation for this. These bones are very spongy and soft; instead of being hollow and filled with marrow, like those of other animals, they are homogeneous and porous, composed of an infinity of hollow and longitudinal cells, in which the marrow flows in the form of liquid. As already stated, the ribs can be broken without the assistance of a hatchet, simply with the hands. It is probable, therefore, that the bones crumble away into dust, and are scattered to the four winds in three or four years' time. The skull, which is thicker and harder, lasts longer when the hyenas spare it. I have met with a few in the bush.

Bones of other animals, on the contrary, remain intact a long time. In *Mes Grandes Chasses* (p. 317) I mention one of my camps where I saw from my tent a passing lion. Going by the same place in 1896,—that is, four years afterwards,—I found the bones of animals which I had killed there, including those of the lion in question, some reed-bucks, water-bucks, zebras, etc. These four years of intemperate weather had not changed them in the least: hardly had it whitened them.

Only the tusks can resist the weather; but if a passer-by sees them he takes them. Dead ivory, which is seen in the market, has been found in that way; its dull appearance, the reduction in its weight, and its colour indicate that it has been long exposed to the inclemencies of the weather.

---

[1] I may even say that they do not exist. Formerly the blacks killed entire herds of elephants and perhaps the bones left by them have been mistaken for " cemeteries."

There are still many elephants in the Congo, in the region of the Nile, Lake Chad, and Lake Victoria Nyanza; but they are tracked everywhere, and, besides some being killed, many are wounded, which is worse than death to them. Native hunters are very clumsy with firearms. They always fire at the head, a shot which, as I shall explain shortly, is of great difficulty, needing preliminary study and precision which is not within the natives' reach. Often, therefore, they simply wound the elephant and make it furious, or else break its tusks. That is the reason one finds so many broken or spoiled tusks. In the Zambesi country I have never killed an elephant which had not several native bullets in its body, or did not bear traces of ancient or recent wounds. This fact is noted in the table at the end. Sometimes these wounds are full of matter and maggots, and must make the unfortunate victim of so much clumsiness suffer terribly. It is not astonishing that in this tortured physical condition, and already knowing the effect of firearms, an elephant immediately charges its aggressor.

In the region of the lakes, such as the districts of Moero, Bangweolo, and the Upper Luapula, where firearms are not found so often, natives hunt the elephant with the assagai. They also wound a great many without killing one; but these ravages are not to be compared with those which were made by the armies of hunters of the Zambesi. I say " which were made," for the reason that elephants deserted these regions several years ago, and that native hunters have had to find another calling.

In the Congo — that is, on the boundary of the great forest — natives construct traps. These consist of pits, into which elephants sometimes fall. Another method employed is to surround a herd by hastily making a stockade and killing every one of them. The pygmies shoot poisoned arrows at elephants, which make off to a great distance to die a miserable death, and serve as food for vultures. Finally, in the Darfour, north of Uganda, Arabs or Ethiopians, the "Agageers," hunt the elephant on horseback, and, after forcing it to the top of its speed, hamstring it. Owing to the great difficulty and danger of this form of hunting, they do not destroy many. In short, the whole of humanity is at war with the unfortunate elephant, myself included. But I am quite willing to lay down my arms if a general truce is proclaimed, a truce which it is quite time to conclude if we wish to find African elephants elsewhere than in museums. At the rate at which they are being killed at present, not one elephant will remain a hundred and fifty years hence in that part of the world.

But the elephant will not be annihilated without defending itself. One cannot attack such a gigantic animal with impunity, and accidents are many. Directly or indirectly, several accidents to native hunters have come to my knowledge between 1891 and 1897. As to Europeans, I found in the Upper Zambesi the grave of an Englishman who had been buried by a Portuguese mulatto at the foot of the very tree to which he had been pinned by the animal. On the trunk could still be seen, though the accident happened five or six years before, the deep marks made by its tusks. A worm-eaten wood cross, upon which were some words, partly obliterated, alone recalled the sad story. West of Lake Nyassa, near the Bua river, another Englishman was seized by an elephant, which broke his ribs, both arms, and both legs. Fortunately for the injured man, a European station was near at hand, at Kotakota, and there he was taken in a dying condition. In 1896, Mr. W———, another Englishman, when hunting at Lake Moero, was seized by an elephant, which knelt down twice to pierce him with its tusks, but missed its mark by extraordinary good luck, and only succeeded in ploughing up the earth at the sportsman's side. I myself have narrowly escaped being carried off or trampled upon several times, and, as will be remembered, one of my men only escaped a similar fate by the skin of his teeth. And this list only applies to a small corner of Central Africa. Comprise the whole of the Continent in your estimate, and you will obtain a fairly good idea of the annual mortality caused by elephants, and of the danger there is in facing so redoubtable an adversary.

I have said that the shot at the head is very difficult. The reason, of course, is that the brain of an elephant is very small. Protected on all sides by bony masses which are as much as nine inches thick, and some

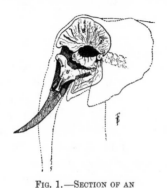 

Fig. 1.—Section of an
Elephant's Skull.

A, Brain cavity; BBB, Bony masses; C, Ear; D, Position of the eye.

Fig. 2.—Elephant at Rest.

A, Position of brain seen from one side; F, Direction of bullet when facing the animal.

of which, such as the frontal bone, are exceptionally hard, the brain can only be reached with certainty at a spot which is situated a little above the line joining the eye to the opening of the ear, a spot exactly four inches square. Taking into consideration the distance at which the hunter must stand, the shadow of the trees and vegetation, and the animal's movements, one can realise that this spot is most uncertain.

Facing the animal, *if its head is bent down* and its trunk

hangs to the ground, you can kill it by firing at the last fold of the trunk, right between the eyes, sometimes a little above. The bullet will then reach the brain, provided, of course, you have a powerful weapon.

But if it charges or looks at you, — that is, if its head is raised and the frontal bone is oblique, — it is useless to fire : you waste your time and risk your life. When an elephant has its head raised and its trunk is rolled up as though to charge, the hunter, by stooping down, can mortally wound it on the neck by aiming exactly on a level with the lower jaw at the hollow of the breast-bone. But one must only run these risks when quite sure of oneself, and when the nature of the ground does not prevent instant flight. The accompanying drawing shows exactly the place on an elephant's skull to be hit, and on its shoulder the position of the heart. I recommend sportsmen to try the shot at the heart.

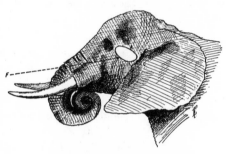

Fig. 3.—Elephant Charging.

A, Portion of brain seen from one side ; F, Direction of bullet when facing the animal.

Although it would seem to be easy to follow such large animals, an elephant-track is very difficult to recognise. You need much practice and patience before you succeed, and the majority of European elephant-hunters would be unable to follow a track if they had not natives with them. In my opinion one ought to do without them. Besides, is it not humiliating not to be able to decipher these marks on the ground when others read them fluently ?

In conclusion, I will explain how the tusks of a dead elephant are removed. There are two methods of going to work, according to the time at your disposal. When in a hurry, you remove the flesh from the bony sockets which hold the tusks and trim them with a small hatchet, the opening being made gently and with great care if you do not want to spoil the ivory. But if you have time you bury the head, or, a simpler method, cover it with wet earth; after a week's time the tusks, which already work loosely in their sockets, can be easily dragged out.

In the Upper Zambesi and in the Moassi country the natives call an adult male elephant "kunguru," a young male "katchende," and tuskless females "niungwa"; the generic name of the elephant being "nzoou" or "ndjovo." The elephant is said by them to have two enemies, carnivorous ants which creep into its trunk when it sleeps, and snakes which bite its stomach. There is hardly need to say how much these two assertions are due to the imagination. I should like to see the reception the first ants which wandered into an elephant's trunk would have; they would be cast out violently as though by an air-gun. As to snakes, their fangs have difficulty in penetrating the human skin, in which they often break,—let alone that of an elephant. The elephant has only one enemy—man. It fears none of the animals. In addition to intelligence relatively superior to theirs, it possesses strength, size, courage if need be, and, moreover, a sense of touch more delicate than that of any of them, even the monkey. It travels everywhere, swims like an amphibian, and crosses ravines and rivers, forests and thickets, without distinction. Everything gives way before it. It climbs and descends hills which one would think inaccessible to it; it crosses whole countries in a night, like an undisputed master in his vast domains; it is here, there, and everywhere, hiding like a mouse despite its great size, and noiselessly disappearing like an unseizable Proteus, much to the discomfort of the hunter; finally, if its life is spared, it is ready to become once more, as in former times when it fought by his side, the ally, the friend, the servant, and the protector of man. The elephant is the true king of animals. Compare this noble animal with the useless lion, that nocturnal prowler at the mercy of a pack of wolves.

Elsewhere, in speaking of colonisation, I deal with the domestication of the elephant as applied to the economic development of African colonies. I will briefly state here what I think of the subject from the point of view of material difficulties.

Those who think it possible to capture the elephant amid present circumstances—that is, when war to the bitter end is being made upon it on all sides—are very much mistaken. *Never will its domestication be possible so long as hunting it is not forbidden.* Even several years will be needed before it resumes its confidence and habits. One will then be able to watch, follow, and capture a herd, because it will remain in a well-defined region, and will have resumed its natural inclination to remain in a large country which offers it, according to the seasons, grass, water, swamps, trees, and shelters of which it is fond. At the present time a herd is here to-day, will be fifty miles away to-morrow, and the day afterwards will be somewhere else. Probably you will never see it again. You will meet other herds which will appear and disappear in their turn, owing to the need of moving about, which is engendered by disquietude, a sense of insecurity, the noise of firearms, and the scent of men who prowl about in their vicinity. Need of food has made the elephant a nomadic animal; fear makes it unseizable.

Although their intentions may be the best in the world, those who think to capture elephants under these conditions are labouring under a great mistake. They may capture one amid special circumstances; but what is one elephant? If they want to create establishments like those in India, and to try to remedy in a notable way the lack of means of transport, elephants must be captured by hundreds. How many years must elapse before African colonisation will profit by this experiment ? Meantime hunting will continue, and when establishments are founded there will be no more elephants to put in them.

The only thing to be done, in my opinion, is for European nations, in agreement with the Congo Free State, to prohibit elephant-hunting under pain of heavy penalty. The step is a radical one, and would momentarily injure trade; but a hundred years sooner or later we shall exhaust the supply of ivory, so we might as well try to conserve it now. Once hunting, as well as the exportation and sale of ivory, was forbidden, the authorities in each colony could proceed to confiscate the ivory found in the hands of natives. Ivory having no further value either to the native or to the European, hunting would stop of itself. Severe punishments might be inflicted upon those who slaughtered elephants for amusement or to obtain meat. When these results were achieved, means of capturing elephants [1] could be devised. With these guarantees there would be no difficulty in finding the necessary capital for the formation of large companies for the capture and training of elephants, companies which would sell to the colonists and Government animals trained for transport purposes.

I am persuaded that by applying in Africa the methods which succeed in India, by employing even the cornacs and elephants of the country, the result would be successful. As to the possibility of domesticating the African elephant, can one doubt it for a moment ? History tells us that in ancient times there were at Carthage hundreds of elephants trained for war and transport purposes, and what was done in Africa formerly cannot one do nowadays ? A few years' training under the management of a Hindoo staff would suffice to make expert cornacs in Africa.

[1] They are opposed in India to the capture of young elephants, the maintenance of which is very expensive ; they prefer capturing adult animals.

But as things are at present nothing can be done. It is as useless to try to capture elephants with rifle-shots as it is to catch flies with vinegar.

RHINOCEROS (*Rhinoceros bicornis*)

RHINOCEROS.—Its gradual disappearance—Its last places of refuge—Supposed age—Signs by which one can recognise it—Size of adults—Measurement of horns—Horns of the young—Use of the horns—Torn ears—Degree of acuteness of senses—Favourite places and plants—Habits—Method of sleeping—Accidents caused by rhinoceros.

I said just now that the African elephant is bound to disappear in a century or so if we continue to shoot it. The rhinoceros is much nearer extinction ; it has one foot in the grave ! Its congener, the *Simus*, has already disappeared ; the bicorn will do the same by virtue of that law of nature which reduces the size of men and animals as time proceeds, causing insensibly to disappear from our planet giants which existed in large numbers during the tertiary, glacial, and quaternary periods.

Apart from its destruction by man, the causes of the gradual disappearance of the rhinoceros seem to me to be its slowness in breeding and its fierce habits, which do not accord with the encroachment of human populations, for no sooner is a country inhabited than it leaves it. Certainly a large number of rhinoceros were very uselessly sacrificed formerly. Hundreds were killed in a few months, at various intervals, between 1824 and 1879 by expeditions in South Africa, and from 1880 to 1890 in Eastern Africa. Everywhere the natives wage war upon it with the simple object of procuring food, and there is nothing that some will not do to get this kind of flesh. Many thousands of elephants and rhinoceros must have been killed all over the continent. Thus the places where it is still found can be counted almost on the fingers of one hand. These are the eastern boundary of the province of Angola, on the Zambesi; the south as far as Victoria Falls, and the north as far as Barotse; German East Africa and British East Africa, the north of Victoria Nyanza, and the Upper Nile; in short, the heart of Africa has become their last resort.

I cannot say that the rhinoceros personifies beauty, grace, or elegance; but such as it is, and although I do not believe it is capable of serving any purpose whatever from the point of view of colonisation, it is an interesting animal. Moreover, it is not particularly harmful. It charges the hunter when it scents him, but that is because he has followed it into its distant retreats. Never does it lay waste cultivated lands in the same way as do the elephant, hippopotamus, and wart-hog; on the contrary, it flees places inhabited by natives.

Its disappearance would do no harm to anybody; but it is always sad to see powerful animals annihilated by man.

In the preceding chapters I have mentioned some of the habits of the rhinoceros. Here I am going to make a few supplementary remarks about this strange animal, which lives with difficulty in temperate countries, and the habits of which are so little known.

The age it can reach will probably never be determined; but, judging from the teeth, as in the case of the horse, I think it must live a very long time.

The molars are intact, or worn, as the case may be, though the size and appearance of the animals' bodies do not change. The horns also stop growing at a certain time, and, as the animal continues to use them when feeding, they end by becoming shortened and injured. And with age comes thinness; its sides become hollow; its viciousness increases. Age can be determined, therefore, by these three indications: condition of the molars, exterior dilapidation, bad condition and smallness of horns owing to usage. To fix an approximate age, I should think that the animal hardly ever exceeds one hundred years.

The average size of an adult male is 5 feet 6 inches; an adult female is generally a little larger. Its total length, from the tip of its nose to the root of its tail, is, on an average, 11 feet 3 inches. As to the horns, they reach very different dimensions in animals in the full force of their maturity; but those of the male are always much longer and thicker than those of the female. The first horn (that which is above the nose) may measure, on an average, 1 foot 6 inches; the second one is sometimes as long, although more often it is only from 6 to 10 inches.

I have rarely seen female rhinoceros with their young, and I cannot express an opinion on the question of breeding. The only thing I know is that the young inherit the ugliness of their parents, and that they do not begin to have horns on their noses until they have finished sucking. The young run very well, following their parents in their rapid gallop without difficulty.

The horn on the nose is used both as a weapon of defence and as a pickaxe. When charging, the rhinoceros always has its head very low, consequently its horn is almost horizontal; at the moment of striking it raises its head violently and generally strikes upwards. The animal uses its horn for unearthing roots, which compose a great part of its food, seizing and dragging them up afterwards with its slightly prehensile upper lip. The second horn serves it little or not at all, being situated too far back to touch the ground or to strike with ease.

I do not know whether rhinoceros often fight among themselves, or how they act if they do; but I have often killed animals which had torn ears, as though they had bitten each other. This hypothesis is hardly admissible, since the animals have neither canine nor front teeth. But one must not think, either, that these marks are made by other animals; because, though the rhinoceros when young may run some danger, no animal attacks it when it is an adult. I confine myself, therefore, to mentioning what I have noticed without attempting an explanation.

The rhinoceros' sense of smell is extremely keen, almost as much so as that of the elephant. As with the latter, also, its eye and ear are imperfect. The animal trots and gallops with extraordinary swiftness, but its usual gait is a slow walk, always with lowered head.

It is fond of dark impenetrable thickets, and, during the dry season, when the grass is burnt, it passes the whole day there. When the grass is very long, it is common to meet it on the plains in the shadow of large trees. At nightfall it sets off in search of food, and generally reaches water, as I have stated in Chapter X., either about ten o'clock in the evening or before daybreak in the morning, save exceptions. Strictly speaking, it does not travel ; but it is, nevertheless, a great walker. When it has chosen a district it does not generally leave it; there it has two or three favourite spots, often a long distance apart, where it goes in the morning to rest, after having covered sometimes thirteen miles during the night in marches and counter-marches. It often remains outside the whole day in cloudy and rainy weather, and, as it is very suspicious, the presence of men in its vicinity is sufficient to make it totally change its habits.

Rhinoceros are generally alone or in pairs. They are fond of roots, cacti of all sorts, and certain other plants ; they do not eat much straw. They take great pleasure after drinking in wallowing in mud, with which they cover themselves from head to foot.

Insectivorous birds rid them of many of their parasites while they are walking about in the daytime. During the hot hours of the day the pachyderm lies down on its side like a horse, and goes to sleep with its nose to the wind. When its sleep is heavy, you often see a white froth around its mouth. At that moment you can, by exercising infinite precautions, and on condition that the wind is in your favour, draw near and kill it point-blank. But it is a dangerous experiment.

The rhinoceros ranks after the elephant as the largest animal, and its approach at night or in the daytime is always very impressive. The number of people who have been forced to climb into trees, in positions sometimes comical, by a charging rhinoceros is considerable. Although accidents are less frequent than with the elephant, they do often occur with an animal so irascible.

LION (*Felis leo*)

The LION.—Only one species—Difference between the wild animal and the menagerie specimen—Measurements and weight of an adult—Colour of the skin—Legends about the lion—Their mistrustfulness—Various ways of dealing with a lion—Signs of anger—The charge—Attempts to intimidate—Hours at which they roar—Nocturnal fights—The lion's enemies—Its lairs—Lioness's period of gestation—Skin of the cubs—Troops of lions.

I will here complete in a few words what the preceding chapters have said on the habits of the lion. Once more let me repeat that there is in my opinion, and in that of all hunters of any experience, *only one species of lion*. The lion's coat changes colour or thickness according to its environment. That of the plateaus of Atlas and Kilimandjaro, at an altitude of 13,000 feet, must naturally have a thicker coat than that which inhabits the sandy plains of the equatorial regions; the mane which catches in thorny thickets is not so thick as that of the animal which lives on grassy plains; but, yellow or brown, with or without mane, it is the same animal. At the Cape, at Tanganyika, and in the country of the Somalis, you will find adult lions of absolutely the same species, magnificent animals, of which you can obtain but a poor idea from the specimens in menageries.

Take a small, pale, debilitated Parisian—a mean little fellow born in a lodging destitute of air and light—and compare him with the robust country boy with a herculean frame developed by physical exercise in the open air, and you will be able to form an idea of the relation which exists between the menagerie lion and the animal in a state of nature. The former was captured very young, if it was not born in captivity. Owing to its sedentary existence in a cage, and the regularity of its meals which require no effort, its weakened muscles are hidden under a thick coating of fat. Its mane develops to an abnormal extent, either because it does not catch in anything as it would in the animal's native haunts, or perhaps on account of the climate.[1] To make it look bigger, its cage is placed on a platform, and when it is two feet six inches high it is a colossus.

The lion, in its savage state, has had to struggle for its food from the tenderest age by always attacking animals stronger than itself, so that it has developed without hindrance. At its adult age its muscles stand out like whipcords. Its mane, when it has one, seems rather thin, having daily left a few of its long hairs on thorny bushes, or on the trunks of trees against which it has rubbed itself. As to its measurements, I have stated in Chapter IX. that an animal with 3-feet withers (recollect that the head is higher than the body) would measure more than 6 feet in length (not including the tail), 1 foot 4 inches at the chest, and that it would weigh about 500 pounds. Leaving legs out of consideration, one may say, therefore, that a lion's body is almost as large as that of a medium-sized horse. One can easily understand that such an adversary can overpower a buffalo which has 5-feet withers.

The colour of lions always varies according to their environments. The maneless lion is generally tawny. The

---

[1] The hair of zebras in this country is different from that found on the animal in Africa.

lion with a mane varies from light-brown to dark chestnut; its mane is either reddish-yellow or mixed with dark hairs, or even sometimes completely dark-brown, the last-named being rarer and much valued by collectors.

In a district with a radius of a few miles I have seen, at night-time and at the same drinking-place, lions appearing to belong to the same family some of which had manes and others none.

In sandy places, where everything is yellow or reddish, as in certain regions of the Somalis, antelopes and lions are similar in colour. Nature thus enables them to hide themselves completely. This colour also mingles with that of the grass and dry leaves in flat countries. Dark-brown blends well with wooded and sheltered regions. The end of the tail, a point on the inner part of the legs, and the back of the ears, are always black.

Many are the stories in circulation about the lion, which naturalists, some of the most competent even, have helped to spread, stories which are continually reproduced and taught to young people, despite the writings of the last twenty years of those who have studied the animal in its haunts. People still speak of the yellow or brown lion of the Cape, Senegal, Barbary, etc.; they still tell us that it is the king of beasts because of its magnanimity, strength, terrible effect of its tail, and its aptitude for carrying large animals to great distances; they still declare that it is unable to run quickly, that its eyes are phosphorescent, that when taken prisoner it is so cowardly it will allow itself to be bound, etc. So, when any one meets a hunter who has had some experience of the lion, the first thing he does is to ask him questions bearing on the above statements. I quite appreciate the difficulties which naturalists encounter in their work of teaching us about the anatomy, the natural characteristics, and the life of animals; but, as M. Milne-Edwards, an eminent member of the Institute and Curator of the Paris Museum, has said, "what interests us are the habits of these animals, of which we are so ignorant, and which we cannot study like the hunter." I have studied the lion near at hand, and, as seen in the preceding chapters, have tracked it and waited for it with indefatigable patience. The reader will do me this justice, that only a passion such as mine could determine a man to follow such a profession. The opinions which I express as follows have been gained during seven years' hunting in Africa.

By exerting all its strength, a lion can drag animals of the size of a buffalo fifty yards over flat ground. It is incapable of lifting, without the thing lifted touching the ground, an animal bigger than a goat, and it cannot, with or without a load, spring over a wall or a stockade. It can run more quickly than the fastest horse, and, as Mr. Selous has said, a mount beyond comparison is necessary to escape from a pursuing lion. Besides, as we know, it pursues and kills waterbucks and elands. As to its tail, I do not know that it can do anything else with it than flick its sides; it has better weapons at its disposal. And its eyes are like all eyes: they are light-green or have a reddish appearance when exposed to the light at a certain angle, but in the darkness you can no more see the eyes of a feline than it can see you. On the face of it, it would be unnatural if this animal, an invisible hunter of the night, put its quarry to flight by showing two glaring eyes. Amid such conditions, it would simply die of hunger. Nor do I believe in its courage. It fears man and always gives way before him. Sometimes it growls when withdrawing, but it makes off in the end. It rarely attacks man unless it is accustomed to eating human flesh, and I have lived for years surrounded by lions without anything happening to me. Often there has not even been a stockade to separate me from them; a few half-extinguished camp-fires kept them at a distance. The only accidents which have occurred to my knowledge have been in villages or in their vicinity, and all have been caused by man-eaters. Lions were attracted around my camp by meat.

When you meet them in the daytime they generally make off at walking pace in a very dignified and impressive way, every now and then turning round. As soon as they think they are out of sight they gallop away as quickly as possible.

The fact of the matter is that you never know how a lion which you meet is going to behave. It may run away or it may make for you. In the latter case, it is because its young are near, or because your approach has interrupted a meal, or simply because you have put it in a bad humour by waking it up, or for any of a thousand other causes unknown to you.

First signs of anger are shown as follows: its tail rapidly twists from side to side, the bottom slightly rising; and, the black tassel at the end beating the air, it lowers its head more than usual and growls, at intervals showing its teeth. Then its voice becomes louder, it roars, shows its teeth, and lowers its ears, the movements of the tail increasing all the time. At the time of charging—that is, at the height of its anger—the tail rises in the air until it is almost vertical, the black tassel continues to move, the ears are flattened completely, and the animal comes towards you at a slow trot, then at a gallop, and finally springs forward with open mouth and extended claws. Sometimes it shows these various symptoms without charging, restrained by prudence; but it never charges without showing them. When the tail rises the hunter can bring his rifle to his shoulder and await his opportunity. In hunting, a man who is on his guard is worth four. A charge is extremely dangerous, almost always fatal when unexpected, either because of dense vegetation or other causes; but if you see the animal getting ready, flight is useless. Stand your ground: the only thing to do is to keep cool and trust in your weapon. If you have not confidence in yourself it is prudent to avoid measuring your strength against these animals.

A lion will often try to intimidate you. It will take a few steps towards you, growling and showing its teeth, and then will stop; if it sees that you do not move it will very probably retire. But when it makes this feint it will look you full in the face, and you will see neither its tail raised nor its head lowered.

I have already described the intense impression made by a roaring lion when you hear it near at hand for the first time; I have also described its method of capturing animals. Let me add that it generally roars at night-time or very early in the morning, sometimes until eight or nine o'clock; but that is exceptional. It only becomes so noisy when satiated. One night I heard a struggle between a lion and a buffalo quite near to my camp. The bellowing of rage, the heavy breathing of the buffalo, the stamping of hoofs, and the blows with its horns against trees made a striking contrast to the silence of its terrible adversary. The struggle, most of the phases of which we divined by the noise, must have been formidable. Finally the buffalo bellowed plaintively and there was perfect silence. The lion announced its triumph in the dead of night and the conclusion of his feast by formidable roars, and upon hearing the cracking of bones we knew that it had given place to the hyenas. Both the buffalo and the lion were enormous. What magnificent combats there are daily in the African bush! As I have said, the lion has a deadly enemy in the African wolf. Similarly, everything which resembles a snake, near or far off, inspires in it a very decided terror. One day two natives, who had taken refuge in a tree, got rid of a rather troublesome lion by throwing at it a wavy and climbing liana called *peça*, which more or less resembles a snake. Thorns are disagreeable to it, and it carefully avoids them. Several times have I found wounds caused by them in its paws, and these prevent it hunting.

During the day the lion takes refuge in the long grass and in the scrub; rarely does it go into the woods. It utilises caves in mountainous districts as lairs. In the grass it hears the approach of a man at a very long distance, and gets out of his way, as the leopard does, without him knowing it. This is the explanation why you rarely see felines by daylight.

I have seldom seen lionesses with more than two or three cubs. I believe their period of gestation is three months and a half, and that they suckle for six months. Up to the age of three months the cubs are covered with curly hair, marked longitudinally, like tigers, with brown stripes. I have seen the skin of a young lioness which was killed in the Somali country by one of my friends upon which these were still very distinct, but that was an exceptional case.

Do lions go about in pairs or in families? It is difficult to fix a rule. I have seen four, five, and as many as eleven lions in a troop; but the average is four.

Imposing and magnificent in its bearing, possessed of a physiognomy expressive of pride, the lion is one of the noblest animals which inhabit the African bush, and one of the most redoubtable adversaries with which man can meet.

PART II

WITH the object of aiding hunters and travellers who wish
to collect, I conclude with some information on the method
of measuring animals accurately, on the way to prepare
their skins for collections or museums, and on the
subject of preservation laws and licences in various African
colonies.

As the most authoritative works on hunting published in
France and in England do not give the measurements of
elephants, I have attempted to fill this gap by carefully
measuring those I have killed every time I have had
leisure and means. These measurements I have classified
in a comparative table. The same has been done in the
case of lions and rhinoceros. I regret having been unable
to do the same in the case of all animals without exception;
but circumstances do not always permit of carrying out
one's wishes. Incomplete though they may be, these tables
will give an idea of the size and proportions of the three
chief inhabitants of the African jungle. I have also
assembled data of the measurements of antelopes' horns
for comparison in case of need, and have given the native
names by which animals are known in the parts of Africa
visited by me.

Method of measuring animals—Measurements to be taken—Skinning animals
—Preparation of skins—Drying—Preparation of bones for mounting—

LARGE AND SMALL MAMMALS

In order to measure an animal, you lay it on its side, the legs stretched out one on the top of the other before the rigidity of death makes this difficult. By means of two assagais, two pieces of wood, or else two rifles which you place perpendicularly, one against the sole of the fore-foot and the other against the withers, you measure the animal's height. Then you take the total length from the tip of the nose to the beginning or the end of the tail, passing along the forehead between the two ears and along the backbone. Then you note the circumference of the neck, and that of the chest, which you take exactly behind the fore-legs and over the withers.

In the case of elephants, you may take the circumference of the fore-foot around the nails, and in case of lions that of the fore-leg, this measurement indicating the degree of strength.

After noting down the measurements you proceed to skin the animal. In order to do this, you stretch the animal on its back, and have it kept in that position by your assistants, the legs well apart. Then you yourself make the first incision, which must set out from under the chin or from the corner of the lip, pass along the throat, and down the middle of the breast and stomach. The sexual parts are left adhering to the skin on the right-hand side, as well as the rectum, and you continue the cut the whole length of the tail. From this central incision are made transverse ones which set the limbs free, cuts which can be compared to the branches of a tree shooting off from the trunk. Beginning at the chest, you make one of these cuts up the centre of the right leg, the other up the centre of the left as far as the pastern or wrist, which you sever and leave adhering to the skin. The same operation is performed in the case of the hind-legs. If you have experienced assistants you can leave them to do the remainder, which consists in removing the skin from the body, always respecting the cartilages of the ears and the interior of the eyelids and mouth. The best thing to do is to cut these parts summarily, leaving the mass of flesh adhering, and finish the work after the whole skin is removed. The pasterns, wrists, or paws are opened; everything useless is removed; and ways are made for the preservative liquids to penetrate to the extremities. The leg-bones and skull, which must be preserved with the skin, are placed on one side.

The skin of the head of horned animals is removed by cutting the skin right round the base of the horns. If these horns are straight that is quite sufficient; but if they are branched you must join the two holes made around them by a lateral cut, and make a third perpendicular cut towards the neck. The third cut must be proportionate to the breadth of the horns, which you pass through this opening by turning the skin round so that the cut is in the same direction as the broadest part of the horns. But in the case of a buffalo, for example, you will have to open the entire side of the head by making a cut from one horn to the ear, and from the ear to the neck. In the case of animals with manes, such as a koodoo, zebra, and sable antelope, it is better to cut the mane in two longitudinally in such a manner that the seam can be easily hidden when mounted. With specimens intended for mounting you must be very careful over the last-named point.

The skin having been well cleaned and entirely rid of flesh and fat, you remove the clots of blood on the hair by washing it, and with an awl and strong thread immediately sew up the holes which have been made by bullets, assagais, or through the clumsiness of the men who have cut up the animal. The skin is then stretched in the sun, with the hair underneath against the ground (which has been swept), by means of wooden pegs or hooks, through which pass cords attached to stakes driven into the ground.

In Europe you are recommended to tan the skin with a mixture of alum and salt, and to place it in the shade. That is impracticable in Africa, for if you are not quick in drying it, flies and insects of all kinds get into it, and before it is dry it is spoiled and full of larvæ. On the other hand, you have a chance of preserving the skin by placing it in the full light of the sun, where flies do not venture. As to ingredients, arsenical soap and sublimate are more efficacious than alum. The use of salt must be avoided, first of all because of its scarcity, and next because the moisture in the air makes skins which contain salt sweat. When the skin is well pegged down you pass a first coat of arsenical soap or paste over it, using the preparation freely at the head, feet, and other fleshy parts. This has generally to be done several times.

If these parts are not dry in the evening you cover the skin with a sailcloth to protect it from the night damp, and leave it in the sun one day more, or else you roll it up, leaving only the head and feet, if they are not dry, still exposed. Upon the flesh side being perfectly dry you turn the skin over, and, after carefully brushing it, you pass over the hair, with a brush or piece of rag, a solution of alcohol and sublimate in the proportion of 1 per cent (ten grammes to the litre). The alcohol evaporates and the sublimate remains on the hair, keeping away the myriads of insects which are the enemies of animal matter, and against which the naturalist must continually wage war.

Bones and skulls intended for mounting with skins you simply boil for one hour. By this means the flesh is removed, after which you wash them, put some of the alcohol and sublimate solution upon them to remove smell, and place them in the sun.

As soon as they are dry you note down in a special notebook the following particulars : number of skin, bones and skull, species of animal, size and measurements, place and date of capture, date of despatch, native name, various observations, habits, etc.

After the skin is completely dry you roll it carefully with naphthaline, pepper, powdered tobacco, camphor, or any other similar substance, and wrap it in sacking with the thigh-bones and skull, which must be ticketed with the same numbers as the skin. A label, reproducing all the indications in the notebook, is attached to the package.

When you only wish to preserve the animal's head and neck, you cut the skin around the withers and shoulders, proceeding to cure in the same way as you cure the whole skin. Only, as the skin of the head is very thick and cannot be rolled once it is dry, you must take care when drying it to keep it in a convenient shape for packing on your return journey. Heads of antelopes and other animals mounted on oak shields make a pretty collection ; but it is ephemeral, for worms get into it in two or three years, and the hair comes off in places. The specimens begin to have a mangy appearance, and, moreover, as often happens, if they are not well stuffed (to give to each animal its true expression is a veritable art), the general effect is pitiful and grotesque. You can only preserve entire animals, or parts of animals, for a great length of time, by putting them under glass cases, as they do in museums. The most practical collections, and those which last almost indefinitely, consist of animals' skulls properly cleaned, or horns with the frontal bone only attached to them, according to the space at your disposal. If you wish to possess a fine collection of that kind you must take care not to boil the bones after the manner above recommended for specimens intended for mounting. I learned to my cost that this was a mistake, because the fat impregnates the bone, and it is difficult or impossible to bleach it afterwards without spoiling it. This is the method of proceeding with skulls which you intend to bleach and preserve. If you are pressed for time and on the march, simply remove the greater part of the flesh with a knife, clean out the brain with a stick, leave it to dry *in the shade and in a cool place* (the sun would melt the grease), and pass over it a little sublimate, so as to keep off insects ; not that they would injure the bone, but because they would get into other delicate specimens which the traveller might have with him. On the other hand, if you have plenty of time, place the skull in running water until the flesh has become soft enough to be removed with the hand or a piece of stick, without using a knife, and until the bone has become quite white, and leave it for a week during the daytime in the sun and at night in the dew. All that will be required to have perfectly white specimens will be a simple cleaning upon your arrival in Europe.

At least once a month you must examine your specimens, opening them out and casting your eye over them, but not shaking them. Upon detecting the least smell at the feet or head you must use more preservatives. I have often used turpentine and sublimate for the hairy side of skins. Corrosive sublimate or bichloride of mercury being, like arsenic, a violent poison, you must avoid, as far as possible, placing your natural history specimens with eatables.

Finally, you must not in Africa keep your specimens too long, especially during the rainy season ; you must send them to Europe whenever you have the opportunity.

BIRDS

The preparation of birds is very delicate work which you cannot entrust to natives. Tchigallo became an excellent preparator, and I did not fear to entrust him with a lion without further troubling myself; but Bertrand and I were obliged to look after the birds. On the average, it takes an experienced hand twenty minutes to skin a bird the size of a sparrow.

I begin the operation by cutting the skin, not in the middle of the breast, but at the side under the left wing, which advantageously hides the cut when the bird is stuffed. Birds' skins generally come off very easily by using the fingers or the handle of a scalpel. You must be very careful in removing the bird's body through the incision; as soon as you come across the thigh or the wing you must cut it with a pair of scissors at the joint, on a level with the body, doing the same with the neck and the coccyx, which must be cut at their base. Rapidly remove the trunk in such a manner as to prevent the liquid or blood staining the feathers, and dry the skin by sprinkling it with ashes or any other substance capable of absorbing moisture. Seizing the legs left inside the skin, you pull them towards you, remove all flesh (which is supplanted by an equal volume of tow or cotton-wool, prepared with arsenical soap), and push them back definitely into their places. The neck, which is cut off at the base of the skull, is dealt with in a similar manner; the brain is taken out by means of a small piece of wood, the tongue and its cartilages are removed; the skin is pushed back over the beak, and the eyes are taken out. The neck is filled up by a piece of wood of the same length, surrounded with tow, the skin being pressed down over this artificial neck after it has been well coated with arsenical soap. Tow prepared with arsenical soap takes the place of whatever else has been removed. When the head is bigger than the neck and cannot pass through, as in the case of wild-ducks, you make a cut at the neck. The neck and legs well in their places and in their natural position, the skin is well covered with soap, stuffed, and loosely sewn up. After this has been done the bird's stomach is opened in order to discover its sex;

information which is written on a label together with details as to the colour of its eyes, coruncles, thighs, and claws. The feathers are then smoothed down, the bird is placed in a natural position, it is wrapped in tissue paper, and placed to dry.

NECESSARY INSTRUMENTS

For large-sized mammals you cannot have anything better than a few knives with short blades and without points—the shape of kitchen knives. In addition, you must have two large scalpels, some small ones, and, for birds, two pairs of tweezers (one pair of large size), a hone, and a large brush for putting the arsenical soap on the skins.

PRESERVATION LAWS AND LICENCES

During the past few years measures have been taken in certain colonies and countries within the sphere of European influence in Africa to prevent total destruction of animals, either by ordering close seasons or by prohibiting sport altogether. On the other hand, in other colonies, including most French possessions, no such measures are enforced.

The following is a *résumé* of some of these regulations :—

I. *British East Africa.*

A licence of £1 a year for shooting antelopes; £25 a year for shooting rhinoceros, elephants, and giraffes. The elephant is rare in this colony. Recently there was talk of prohibiting its destruction, but I do not know whether anything came of it.

II. *German East Africa.*

Elephant and rhinoceros hunting, as well as the destruction of the giraffe and the crested crane (!), is in principle forbidden. As there are very few elephants, or none at all, this law is not of great importance. You can, however, obtain special permission from the authorities to shoot elephants and rhinoceros under the following conditions, which are calculated to make the bravest hunter start back in astonishment:—licence, 500 rupees;[1] for the first elephant killed 250 rupees, for every subsequent one 200 rupees; for the first rhinoceros 250 rupees, and for every subsequent animal 50 rupees; deposit for introducing foreign natives into the country, 10 rupees per man. You are forbidden to take natives out of the country; there is a tax of 10 per cent on the value of your rifles, and a further payment of 10 per cent on exported ivory. Such was the information given to me at Ujiji, on Lake Tanganyika, in July 1897,—enough, in my opinion, to stop all sport.

III. *Portuguese East Africa.*

Licence of 100,000 reis (£20) a year for elephant hunting. Tax on guns and ammunition fixed by the local authorities, and 10 per cent on exported ivory. There are hardly any elephants in the colony.

IV. *British Central Africa—Nyassaland.*

Licence of £1 for shooting antelopes; £25 a year for rhinoceros, elephant, and giraffe hunting. The two last-named animals not inhabiting the colony, you pay £25 for the chance of meeting one of the rare rhinoceros still to be found there. Zebra hunting is prohibited. There are certain preserved hunting regions. Shooting the last remaining hippopotami and crocodiles is free. A tax of 10 per cent on value of rifles and ammunition. Gun licence, £10 a year. Tax of 2s. 6d. for introducing fire-arms and ammunition into the colony. You cannot introduce large bore-rifles (8, 10, and 12-bore) unless provided with £25 licence to shoot elephants. Tax of 5 per cent

---

[1] The rupee may be valued at 1s. 3d.

on exported ivory, which must be above 15 lbs., exportation of tusks under this weight being forbidden.[1]

V. *Transvaal.*

The laws in the Transvaal are better defined, although there is very little game. You can still find a few animals on the confines of the colony, but they are daily being driven farther afield by man's encroachment.—

> No. 1. Small birds—January 15 to August 15, 10s. a year.
>
> No. 2. Ostrich—February 1 to July 15, £10 a year.
>
> No. 3. Small antelopes—February 1 to September 15, £1 : 10s. a year.
>
> No. 4. Large antelopes and zebra—February 1 to September 15, £3 a year.
>
> No. 5. Eland, buffalo, rhinoceros, and giraffe—February 1 to September 15, £10 a year.

Elephant and hippopotamus hunting is forbidden; a regulation which for a very good reason will be observed. Nos. 2 and 5 are licences which will not enrich those who obtain them; it is a long time since an ostrich, or a giraffe, or a rhinoceros, was seen in the Transvaal. Rifles : entry tax, £1 a barrel; 5 per cent on ammunition.

VI. *British South Africa—Cape Colony.*

The shooting of elephants, hippopotami, buffaloes, elands, koodoos, hartebeest, oryx, reedbucks, zebras, gnus, or antelopes of all kinds is forbidden. Special licences will be granted by the Governor of the Colony upon naming the species, number, and variety of animals you wish to shoot. In certain parts of Cape Colony are a few herds of elephants which the Government protects. (Licences range from £10

---

[1] This measure is excellent, because it compels sportsmen to spare very young animals and females.

to £100, according to whether you wish to shoot a spring-buck or an elephant.) It may be added that, in spite of everything, very few animals remain in the Colony.

The shooting of the secretary-bird is forbidden. Shooting other animals, such as koorhans, bustards, guinea-fowls, pheasants, partridges, and hares is authorised at fixed times, continually varying, upon taking out a licence of £5 a year.

Bechuanaland.—Close season from September 1 to March 1. Same regulations as above.

Entry tax of £1 per barrel on arms in these two colonies.

VII. *Portuguese West Africa.*

Same regulations as in Portuguese East Africa.

VIII. *Congo Free State.*

Licence to carry a rifle and kill animals other than the elephant, 20 francs per annum. Licence for elephant hunting, 500 francs a year; 10 per cent on exported ivory; 5 per cent on arms and ammunition.

IX. *French Congo.*

No regulation concerning hunting.

Conventional Basin.—Entrance tax of 10 per cent on arms and ammunition.

Non-Conventional Basin.—Arms, 20 francs each; cartridges forbidden. What is the good of one without the other? 7 per cent on exported ivory.

X. *Cameroon.*

There does not exist to my knowledge any regulation about hunting. Entrance tax of 10 per cent on arms and ammunition; 5 per cent on exported ivory.

XI. *Niger.*

The former Niger Company, which is at present in a

state of transformation into a British colony, forbids the entrance of arms and ammunitions, and even Europeans. Moreover, hardly any ivory is exported from this region.

XII. *Dahomey—The Ivory Coast—Senegal.*

No regulation about hunting. Five per cent *ad valorem* exportation duty.

TABLES OF MEASUREMENTS

I.—ELEPHANTS

Year.	Sex.	Height of Withers. (Ft. In.)		Circumference of Forefoot. (Ft. In.)		Number of Bullets Fired.	Number of Native Bullets found in Skin or Body.	Weight of Tusks.		Observations.
		Ft.	In.	Ft.	In.			Right. (Lbs. Oz.)	Left. (Lbs. Oz.)	
1892	Male	10	6½	4	4	3	11	50 9	50 13	Three scars caused by bullets on tusks of other males.
1893	,,	9	11	4	3	3	1	48 6	48 4	
,,	Female	10	1	3	11	2	3	8 14	8 13	One open wound.
,,	,,	9	7	3	7	1	30	6 1	6 1	
,,	,,	8	4	3	3½	2	19	5 8	5 8	
1894	,,	9	8	4		1	11	11	11 3	Ear, length, 3 ft. 5½ in.; breadth, 2 ft. 4 in.
1895	,,	9	6	3	7	1	1	10 11	2 4	Left tusk broken.
,,	,,	11	1	3	5	2	4			Without tusks.
,,	,,	10	7	4	2	1	…	6 11	6 11	One scar.
,,	,,	9	8	4	1	2	6	6 11	6 11	
,,	,,	10	1	4	1½	7	4	9 14	9 14	Ear, 3 ft. 7½ in.; 2 ft. 4½ in.
1896	Male	9	8	4	3	2	17	46 8	46	Two scars.
,,	Female	10	4	4	1	1	5	5 8	5 9	
,,	Male	8	11	4	4	2	8	26 14	28	Root of right tusk pierced by a bullet.
,,	Female	10	7	4		2	7	7 11	7 11	
,,	Male	10	4	4	5	3	…	83 13	82 14	Ear, 4 ft. 1½ in.; 2 ft. 8 in.
1897	,,	10	3	4	1	2	1	70 6	69 13	Two scars.
,,	,,	10	9	4		6	2	65 6	65 3	Ear, 4 ft. ½ in.; 2 ft. 6½ in.
,,	,,	10	7	4	6½	5	…	90 3	92 6	
,,	Female	10	7	4	5	4	5	…	…	Without tusks. Ear, 3 ft. 11½ in.; 2 ft. 5½ in.
,,	Male	12	2½	5	2	11	5	114 6	114 6	Ear, 4 ft. 8 in.; 3 ft. 1 in.

AVERAGES OF ABOVE MEASUREMENTS

Male elephant: size, 10 ft. 6¼ in.; circumference of foot, 4 ft. 5 in.; ear, length, 4 ft. 3 in.; breadth, 2 ft. 9 in.
Female elephant: size, 9 ft. 8¼ in.; circumference of foot, 3 ft. 11 in.; ear, length, 3 ft. 10½ in.; breadth, 2 ft. 4½ in.

Appendix

II.—Rhinoceros

| Year. | Sex. | Height of Withers. | Circumference of Foot. | Horns. | | Total Length from Nose to Tail. |
				Front.	Back.	
		Ft. In.	Ft. In.	Ft. In.	Ft. In.	Ft. In.
1892	Male	5 6½	...	1 7	1 4	...
1895	Female	5 5½	...	1 4½	8½	...
,,	,,	5 3½	2 1	1 8½	1 2½	11 2
,,	Male	5 1½	2 0½	2 2¾	1 5	11 1½
,,	Female	5 7½	2	2 4	1 3	...
,,	Male	5 5	1 11	1 11	1 3½	11 3½
,,	Female	5 3½	...	2 2	1 3	...
1896	Male	5 9	2 3	2 6	1 7½	...
,,	,,	5 8	1 10	1 7½	11	...
,,	Female	5 7½	1 10½	1 11	1 0½	11 5½
,,	Male	5 6½	...	1 7½	7½	...
1897	,,	5 4½	2 0½	1 10¾	9½	11 7½

Averages of above Measurements

Male rhinoceros : height of withers, 5 ft. 6 in. ; circumference of foot, 2 ft. ; horns, front, 1 ft. 11 in., back, 1 ft. 1 in. ; total length from nose to tail, 11 ft. 3½ in.

Female rhinoceros : height of withers, 5 ft. 5½ in. ; circumference of foot, 2 ft. ; horns, front, 1 ft. 11 in., back, 1 ft. 1 in. ; total length from nose to tail, 11 ft. 3½ in.

III.—Lions

Year.	Sex.	Length from tip of Nose to tip of Tail.	Length of Skull.	Circumference of Foreleg.	Height of Withers.	Mane.
		Ft. In.	Ft. In.	Ft. In.	Ft. In.	
1892	Lion	8 11½	1 2	1 4	2 11½	Short, tawny
,,	,,	9 1	1 3½	...	2 10	No mane
1894	Lioness	9 1¼	1 0½	...	2 11	...
1895	Lion	9 6	1 3¾	...	3 5	Tawny
,,	Lioness	9 2½	1 1½	...	2 8	...
,,	Lion	8 5½	1 2	1 5	3 6½	No mane
,,	,,	10 3½	1 4½	1 7	3 1	Tawny
1896	,,	9 7½	...	1 4	3 6½	Semi-black
,,	,,	11 8¾	1 5	1 9	3 4½	Black
,,	Lioness	8 10½	...	...	2 11½	...
1897	,,	8 7	1 1½	...	2 10¾	...

Averages of above Measurements

Male lion : length from tip of nose to tip of tail, 9 ft. 8½ in. ; length of skull, 1 ft. 3 in. ; circumference of foreleg, 1 ft. 5½ in. ; height of withers, 3 ft. 2¾ in.

Female lion : length from tip of nose to tip of tail, 8 ft. 11 in. ; length of skull, 1 ft. 2 in. ; height of withers, 2 ft. 10½ in.

N.B.—These averages only refer to about half the animals killed.

VOCABULARY FOR THE USE OF THE HUNTER

NAMES OF LARGE ANIMALS MENTIONED IN THIS WORK IN ENGLISH, DUTCH, AND IN VARIOUS NATIVE LANGUAGES OF AFRICA

Name of Animal.	AUSTRAL AFRICA.		CENTRAL AND EAST AFRICA.		Arabic.
	Dutch.	Mashonas, Matabeles.	Zambesi, Atchekundas, Magandjas, Lake Nyassa.	Swahili, Zanzibar, the Great Lakes, Upper Congo.	
Elephant	Oliphant	Inkubu	Nzau, Ndjovo	Tembo	Fil
Rhinoceros	Rhinaster	Upeygan	Pembere	Kifaru	Karkaddan
Hippopotamus	Zee-Kue	Infubu	Nvuo	Kiboko	Frass el mâ
Buffalo	Buffel	Nari	Niati	Mbogo	Djamous
Lion	Lieuw	Isiluan	P'andoro¹ Mkango	Simba	Essed
Leopard or Panther	Teegre	Nkuai	Niarug'we	Tchui	Nimmer
Wolf or Wild-dog	Vilde Honde	—	P'umpi	Mbua-muitu	Dib
Hyena	Teegre voolf	Piri	Fissi	Fissi	Dâb
Wart-hog	Vlaakte Vaark	Kolubi	Ndjiri	Ngurue, ndume } Ngurue	Khanzïr
Bush Pig	—	—²	Kumba		
Giraffe	Cameel	Ngabe	—	Tuiga	Zeraf
Zebra	Quagga	Pitse	Bidzi	Pundomilia	Hmar el owouch

	(Dutch / Afrikaans)	Mohu	Nchefu[1]	Mpofu	Rzâl[1]
Eland . . .	Ehland	Mohu	Nchefu, nt'uka	Mpofu	Rzâl el Kbar (large gazelles)
Koodoo . .	Kudu	Noro	Ngoma	Puru	
Sable Antelope .	Zwaart-vit-pens	Umtigele	Palap'ala	—	⎫
Roan ,, .	Bastard Ehland	Etaka	Palap'ala	—	
Hartebeest . .	Hartebeest ⎰	Kaama	Ngondo, Gondonga ⎱	Kongoni	
Tsessebe . .	Bastard Hartebeest	Inkulanondo	—		—
Blue Wildebeest or Brindled Gnu .	Hartebeest	Incolomo	Nyumbu	Nyumbu	—
Waterbuck . .	Kring-ghat	Inkone Kue	⎰ Niakodzue, Tchiuzu ⎱ Tententsidia	Kuru	
Impala or Nswala .	Rooibok	Litumoga	Nswala	Swala	
Reedbuck . .	Reitbok	Impala	Mp'öio	Porke	
Bushbuck . .	Boshbok	Inziji	Mbawala	Mbawara	Rzâl (gazelles), generic name given to all small antelopes.
Inyala . .	—	Imbabala	Boo	Parahara	
Sitatunga . .	Waterskaap	Inyala	—		
Pookoo . .	—	Sitatunga	—	Sunu	
Letchwe . .	Letche	Pookoo	Kassegne	Cherua (?)	
Oribi . .	Oribi	Lekue	Nyassa, guapi, Insa, Rumza	Icha	
Duiker . .	Duikerbok	Oribi	—	,,	—
Bluebuck . .	Blauwbok	Impuzi	⎰ Mbarare, ⎱ Tchinkoma	,,	—
Klipspringer .	Klipbok	Egogo		—	
Crocodile . .	—	—	Ngona, Niakoko	Maamba	Timsah
Game . .	—	Nyama	Nyama	Nyama	El Ham

[1] An apostrophe indicates an *h* aspirated.

[2] A dash indicates animals which appear to me to be unknown in the region.

AVERAGE MEASUREMENTS OF HORNS OF ADULT ANTELOPES AND BUFFALOES [1]

Name	Sex	From Point to Base		Following the Curves		Circumference	Distance between the Points		Distance between Exterior Curves	
		Ft.	In.	Ft.	In.	Inches	Ft.	In.	Ft.	In.
Eland * [2] (*oreas canna*)	♂	2	2			10	Variable			
,,	♀	2	6			8	Variable			
Sable antelope* (*hippotragus Niger*)	♂			2	2	8				
,,	♀			1	10	6½				
Roan antelope* (,, *leucophæus*)	♂			1	8	7½				
,,	♀			1	4	5½				
Wildebeest (blue)* (*connochætes taurinus*)	♂			1	4		1	1½		
,, (black) (,, *gnu*)	♀			1	6			10		
Hartebeest* (*bubalis kaama*)	♂			1	2	7½				
,, * (,, *lichtenstein*)	,,			1	1	6½	Variable			
Tsessebe* (,, *lunatus*)	,,			1	9	6				
Koodoo (*strepsiceros kudu*)	,,	2	11	3	9	10	2	6		
Inyala (*tragelaphus angasi*)	,,	1	6	1	10	7½		6		
Situtunga (,, *spekei*)	,,	1	6	1	11	8		8		
Bushbuck (,, *sylviaticus*)	,,	1				4		4		
Waterbuck (*kobus ellipsiprymnus*)	,,			2	1	8		2		
Pookoo (,, *vardoni*)	,,			1	1	6		7½		
Letchwe (,, *letche*)	,,			1	9	7½				
Nswala (*æpyceros melampus*)	,,			1	8	5½		10		
Reedbuck (*cervicapra arundinacea*)	,,			1		5		9		
Klipspringer (*oreotragus saltator*)	,,		3			2		2½		
Duiker (*cephalophus ocularis*)	,,		3½			2		2¾		
Bluebuck (,, *pygmæus*)	,,		2½			1¾		2¼		
Oribi (*nanotragus scoparius*)	,,		3½			2¼		3¼		
Buffalo* (*bos caffer*), breadth of forehead	,,	1	8				2	8	3	4
,,	♀						2	8	3	2

OBSERVATIONS : Hartebeest—The horns of the female are as large, but slenderer, than those of the male.

[1] This table is given as a guide to the sportsman as to what constitutes or not a trophy worthy of figuring in his collection. Horns reaching or exceeding these measurements may be kept; those under should be rejected. I am not speaking of "record" measurements, only fair average ones.

[2] Females of animals not marked with an asterisk have no horns.

INDEX

THE END